Praise for *Capital and Its Discontents*

"Enveloped by a crisis that seems to have no end, heirs to ideas that seem unable to carry us through the present—the combination is disorienting. For that, it is right to scour the intellectual malcontents to gain from their recovery of ideas from the past and their sense of how to understand the present. Ideas are the soul of social activism. Without them action dissipates into futility; the ideas help us focus our energy toward building the kind of alternative world that our hopes encourage. Sasha Lilley's *Capital and Its Discontents* is a superb introduction to some of the best traditions, given to us through some of the sharpest thinkers of the Global North."
—Vijay Prashad, author of *The Darker Nations: A People's History of the Third World*.

"Few journalists can match Sasha Lilley's knowledge of political economy, nor her keen instinct for the important questions. Read these interviews—with some of the left's most clearheaded thinkers—for a far deeper understanding of contemporary capitalism and its problems, and, perhaps more surprisingly, a bracing and contagious optimism."
—Liza Featherstone, author of *Selling Women Short: The Landmark Battle for Workers' Rights at Wal-Mart*

"These conversations illuminate the current world situation in ways that are very useful for those hoping to orient themselves and find a way forward to effective individual and collective action. Highly recommended."
—Kim Stanley Robinson, *New York Times* bestselling author of the *Mars Trilogy* and *The Years of Rice and Salt*

"In this fine set of interviews, an A-list of radical thinkers demonstrate why their skills are indispensable to understanding today's multiple economic and ecological crises."
—Raj Patel, author of *The Value of Nothing* and *Stuffed and Starved*

"This finely tuned assemblage of radical voices, both familiar and fresh, will be an indispensible *vade mecum* for opponents of capital and empire in the new century. Lucid analysis, a penetrating but sympathetic interlocutor, and signposts pointing beyond the horizon of the neoliberal order—altogether a superb addition to PM's Spectre series."
—Iain Boal, coauthor of Retort's *Afflicted Powers: Capital and Spectacle in a New Age of War*

"Sasha Lilley, one of KPFA's all-time finest broadcasters, turns to print, producing a splendid volume of interviews on a wide range of economic and political subjects. In *Capital and Its Discontents*, Lilley glides past worn-out stereotypes and exhausted explanations to get right to the heart of today's most pressing issues. She does this with a light touch but a sure hand and brings out the best from each contributor—economists, sociologists, political activists—producing a compelling collection."
—Cal Winslow, coeditor of *Rebel Rank and File: Labor Militancy and Revolt from Below During the Long 1970s*

"*Capital and Its Discontents* presents the thought of many of the most astute analysts of contemporary political, economic and cultural developments in accessible interview form. Sasha Lilley's wide-ranging and probing questions prompt her interviewees to address the intersecting crises of our time and to outline frameworks for understanding and responding to them. This collection of interviews introduces the reader to much of the best thinking about social issues on the U.S. left today."
—Barbara Epstein, History of Consciousness, University of California, Santa Cruz

"At a time of economic crisis but great political opportunity, *Capital and Its Discontents* provides a much-needed roadmap for turning radical ideas into action. The hegemony of neoliberal ideology can be paralyzing at times, even on the left. The contributors to this book do a rousing job of reminding us that another world *is* possible—if we all pitch in and make it happen."
—Steve Early, author of *Embedded with Organized Labor: Journalistic Reflections on the Class War at Home*

"Reading this wonderful book feels like having a face-to-face discussion with each author. These brilliant radical thinkers from many parts of the world generously and lucidly share their knowledge and insights on capitalism, empire, and resistance."
—Roxanne Dunbar-Ortiz, historian and author of *Red Dirt* and *Outlaw Woman*

"Sasha Lilley is the very best interviewer I have ever encountered. I don't think that I have heard as good a set of questions as she poses in these stellar interviews, and the depth of the answers she elicits will help develop the confidence to get these ideas out even more widely. Taken together, these interviews allow the left to think collectively, and that's the real starting point for building an effective alternative politics, the kind of vision one has for a different kind of society and intermediate steps to get there."
—Leo Panitch, editor, *The Socialist Register*

"This is an extremely important book. It is the most detailed, comprehensive, and best study yet published on the most recent capitalist crisis and its discontents. Sasha Lilley sets each interview in its context, writing with style, scholarship, and wit about ideas and philosophies."
—Andrej Grubačić, radical sociologist and social critic, coauthor of *Wobblies and Zapatistas: Conversations on Anarchism, Marxism, and Radical History*

Editor: Sasha Lilley

Spectre is a series of indispensable works of, and about, radical political economy. Spectre lays bare the dark underbelly of politics and economics, publishing outstanding and contrarian perspectives on the maelstrom of capital—and emancipatory alternatives—in crisis. The companion Spectre Classics imprint unearths essential works of radical history, political economy, theory and practice, to illuminate the present with brilliant, yet unjustly neglected, ideas from the past.

Spectre

Greg Albo, Sam Gindin, and Leo Panitch, *In and Out of Crisis: The Global Financial Meltdown and Left Alternatives*

David McNally, *Global Slump: The Economics and Politics of Crisis and Resistance*

Sasha Lilley, *Capital and Its Discontents: Conversations with Radical Thinkers in a Time of Tumult*

Spectre Classics

E. P. Thompson, *William Morris: Romantic to Revolutionary*

Capital and Its Discontents: Conversations with Radical Thinkers in a Time of Tumult

Sasha Lilley

Capital and Its Discontents: Conversations with Radical Thinkers in a Time of Tumult
Sasha Lilley
© PM Press 2011

ISBN: 978-1-60486-334-5
Library of Congress Control Number: 2010927769

Cover by John Yates / Stealworks
Interior design by briandesign

10 9 8 7 6 5 4 3 2 1

PM Press
PO Box 23912
Oakland, CA 94623
www.pmpress.org

Printed in the USA on recycled paper.

Published in Canada by Fernwood Publishing
32 Oceanvista Lane, Black Point, Nova Scotia, B0J 1B0
and 748 Broadway Avenue, Winnipeg, MB R3G 0X3
www.fernwoodpublishing.ca

Library and Archives Canada Cataloguing in Publication
Lilley, Sasha, 1970–
Capital and its discontents: conversations with radical thinkers in a time of tumult / Sasha Lilley.
Includes bibliographical references and index.
ISBN 978-1-55266-394-3

1. Capitalism. 2. Globalization—Economic aspects. 3. Imperialism.
I. Title.

HB522.L54 2010   330.12'2   C2010-904887-3

Published in the EU by The Merlin Press Ltd.
6 Crane Street Chambers, Crane Street, Pontypool NP4 6ND, Wales
www.merlinpress.co.uk
ISBN: 978-085036-677-8

To my mother
Kathleen Lilley

Contents

Introduction
Sasha Lilley

THE PAST SEVERAL YEARS HAVE WITNESSED THE SPECTACULAR UNRAVELING OF CAP-
italism—or so it has appeared. Venerated investment banks have vanished
overnight, titans of industry have permanently shuttered their doors, and rich
nations have lurched perilously close to default. The ideology of the free
market, once seemingly unassailable, lies in tatters. While the death knell of
capitalism may not yet be tolling, the crisis is undoubtedly of a different order
of magnitude than anything seen in decades.

Crises can be openings: moments when the stanchions are kicked out from
under the status quo, when the pieties of the recent past fall away, and a revital-
ized sense of collective power takes shape. But crises aren't always—or only—
opportunities for radicals, mechanically ushering legions of the downtrodden to
the barricades. In times of crisis, the far right often harnesses the insecurities of
the precarious, as well as the monied, in the service of xenophobia and austerity.
Paradoxically, crises of capitalism are opportunities for capital. Notwithstanding
any frontal challenges to the old order, those capitalists who survive the shake-
out and destruction of competitors can find fertile ground for a new round of
expansion. Such demolition and regeneration are often aided by force of arms:
contrary to the pacifist slogan, war *is* the answer, razing old capital and clearing
the way for the new. Even the crisis of nature is fortuitous for capital, spawning
green commodities and product lines as coral reefs, rainforests, freshwater lakes
and rivers perish, and myriad species disappear forever. Capitalism begets crisis
and then crisis begets opportunities for profit. And so it goes. Or so it has gone.

For better or worse—often for worse—the left has a long history of diag-
nosing the death throes of capitalism and the final conflict heralding radical
change.[1] As the old witticism has it, Marxists have predicted ten out of the last
two economic crises, a perpetual chronicle of a crisis foretold. Yet in the midst
of what arguably is the fourth global crisis of the capitalist system,[2] radicals—
whether in North America or South Korea—find themselves adrift and tenta-
tive. We should be thankful for the departure of the old mechanistic view of
the world, at least from most quarters. But what has taken its place? Anxiety
about day-to-day survival has deepened the abiding anti-utopianism of our
age. An enduring fatalism about the possibility of radical social transformation, the scar tissue of dashed hopes and sanguinary defeats, has us firmly in its

grip. With the exception of a few pockets of militancy (and at times adventurism) the idea of organizing for a postcapitalist future commonly seems delusional: one thinks here of the now oft-quoted saying that it has become easier to imagine the end of the world than the end of capitalism.[3] Another crisis, one of both vision and organization, is painfully in evidence.

It doesn't have to be so. We are living through an era of considerable flux. Ideas alone won't solve the crisis of the left, and revolutions cannot be summoned by fervent wishes. But ideas matter, as the often-tragic history of the left has proved. They are born out of action and shape the deeds of the future. They help us understand the world we unwittingly have helped to construct, grasp the many vulnerabilities of the current order, and weigh, and devise, avenues for fracture and revolt.

While emancipatory politics have been effectively in retreat over the past three decades, vital ideas have flourished in isolate places. They grapple with the remarkable durability of capitalism, the serpentine contours of neoliberalism, and the multifarious reasons for the ebbing of the left.[4] The premise of this volume is that, in a moment of crisis for capitalism, a renewed radical project in the Global North would be fortified by these critical ideas.[5] The thinkers collected here do not necessarily agree with each other, but they provide—with no pretense to being complete—much of what I believe the left regularly misunderstands to its detriment. A good deal of this work could be classified as political economy broadly defined, although rejecting iron laws of history of all stripes. And much, but not all, is rooted in critical and contrarian lineages of the Marxist tradition. Yet many of these thinkers are not known to radical activists. Current ideas about neoliberalism, globalization, and capitalism have more likely been shaped by an outraged political liberalism, variously yearning for a more humane version of capitalism rooted in postwar regulation, a nineteenth-century ideal of small artisans and shopkeepers, or in some cases even further back to a pre-industrial pastoralism.

This is not, however, a book of prescriptions. No glorious blueprint for the left resides within its pages. Rather it brings together crucial perspectives for understanding capitalism and the world we inhabit. While the assessment of capitalism and its opponents may seem bleak, the conclusion of the book is not. The way forward is to be found by arming ourselves with unsparing analysis of the predicament we find ourselves in, while having the fortitude to once again think ambitiously about broad emancipatory change.

The ideas contained in this book range widely. Yet if there is one rich vein that flows throughout, it is the theme of commodification. The process of creating commodities from nature and labor is essential to capitalism's drive for profit. In the neoliberal era, capitalist commodification has reached into new realms, straddling great distances and seizing upon the most intimate aspects of our being, including our genetic code. In the Global South and North, it has entailed the wholesale dispossession of people from land and livelihoods, leaving them dependent on the market for survival. It has meant the enclosure of nature and the commons—both in the city and the countryside—and the perpetual creation of ever-new objects for sale and disposal. If one prescription were to be proffered, it would be this: that the answer to the crises of nature and capital lies in public abundance replacing private wealth.

The book is separated into three parts, looking respectively at empire, neoliberalism, and crisis, the inner workings of capitalism, and its various antagonists. Most of the chapters originated over the last several years as interviews for *Against the Grain* and the conversations were expanded for this volume.[6] In the first section, Ellen Meiksins Wood considers the evolution of empire, from empires of property and commerce to the empire of capital today. David Harvey traces the rise of neoliberalism, in thought and deed, and probes the barriers capital must overcome to remain vital. Leo Panitch and Doug Henwood look at the myths of globalization that afflict much of the left, while Panitch, Sam Gindin, and Greg Albo analyze capital in crisis and the prospects for radical renewal. And David McNally examines the current crisis through a global lens.

John Bellamy Foster considers, in the second part of this volume, Marx's writings on ecology, and the complex legacies of the Enlightenment and socialist conceptions of nature. Jason W. Moore appraises the socio-ecological crisis and rejects a Malthusian understanding of environmental destruction and ecological footprints. Gillian Hart explores the agrarian question in South Africa and how the history of dispossession from land crucially shapes capitalist development and the forms political resistance takes, both rural and urban. And Ursula Huws analyzes the processes of commodification under capitalism and the ways that the system transforms work, consumption, and collective action.

In the book's final section, which turns to capitalism's discontents, Vivek Chibber considers the history of the developmental state in the Global South and the legacy of alliances that were forged between the state and labor. Mike Davis reflects on the importance of anti-Stalinist critic Isaac Deutscher. Looking back at the anti-war movement of the Sixties, Tariq Ali analyzes the turn to the right by many *soixante-huitards* and lessons for anti-imperialism today. John Sanbonmatsu explores the phenomenal rise of postmodernism and its consequences for the fates of the left. Noam Chomsky argues for a society based on the self-organization of workers, while Andrej Grubačić offers a potential means to get there, based on a nonsectarian melding of radical traditions.

★ ★ ★

I.

It is telling that at a moment when the need to transcend the system seldom has been so apparent, many of the ideas and analyses greeting the crisis from the left in the Global North have been so restrained and self-limiting. A good deal of this originates—and understandably so—from blunted ambitions in the wake of numerous defeats. Yet much could also be traced to confusion about the nature of capitalism in crisis and the economic system that has taken hold in the past three decades: neoliberalism.

At the start of the financial meltdown, various left luminaries heralded what they perceived as the return to Keynesian state intervention, following the nightmare years of neoliberalism.[7] The bailout of the banks and massive involvement by governments to shore up the system apparently indicated the return of the state and the retreat of the market. They seemed to forget that a hallmark of the neoliberal project was perennial intervention by the state to protect financial interests, whether in the Global South or North.

Eulogies for neoliberalism have now faded. The expectation that, following Karl Polanyi's notion of the "double movement," an era of the unfettered rule of the market would be replaced by a kinder, gentler variant of capitalism have not panned out.[8] Indeed, the hopes that elites would realize the need to protect society and nature from ruin have been dashed against the sharp rocks of austerity. Yet the call remains for a return to the type of regulatory system of the Keynesian postwar welfare state, which ostensibly held the depredations of capital at bay. The rationale runs along these lines: in the 1940s, '50s, and '60s, corporations were kept in their place by a state that imposed checks on banking and manufacturing. Starting in the late 1970s, the state retreated and let the market run wild. If we could only go back to the heyday of American capitalism, all would be well.

But is a return feasible and, if it were, would all be well? The present crisis and the limitations of such alternatives may be best grasped by examining the roots of neoliberalism in the crisis of capitalism in the 1970s, afflicting the system's vaunted postwar "Golden Age." The era that many on the left look back to with longing, combined a welfare state (to a greater extent in Europe and Canada and a lesser extent in the U.S.) and a Keynesian commitment to full employment in the Global North and varying degrees of state planning in the Global South. It was shored up by the international financial stability of Bretton Woods, which regulated the international monetary system with the U.S. dollar at its center. During its zenith, it delivered relative economic prosperity in the Global North and moderate development in the Global South.

Yet by the late 1960s the welfare state system was running out of steam. As the 1970s arrived, it sputtered out. The costs of the Vietnam War and domestic spending put significant strain on the U.S. dollar. Until that point, the dollar was guaranteed convertible to a set quantity of gold, and other major currencies were pegged to it, providing great solidity to the global financial system. Nixon elected to delink the dollar from the gold standard, bringing Bretton Woods, and the monetary stability it afforded, effectively to an end. By the early 1970s profits for capitalists who had prospered in the preceding decades were being squeezed, following a peak in profitability in the mid-1960s. Under conditions of high employment, workers became increasingly combative without the fear of permanent joblessness. And many of these workers were disinclined to accept the compromises of their trade union leaders. In the U.S., manu- facturing and service workers—often people of color and women—became ever more militant, initiating wildcat strikes not sanctioned by their bureau- cratized unions. Three million American workers struck in one year alone— 1970—in a decade and a half of widespread rank and file militancy.[9] In Europe, hot autumns of industrial action and winters of discontent roiled the govern- ing Social Democratic parties intent on freezing wages and imposing austerity. Workers demanded not just higher wages, but greater control over production and working conditions. At the same time the profits of U.S. manufacturers were eroding from competition from German and Japanese industry. Having recovered from their decimation during World War II, these rivals were often more technically sophisticated than their North American counterparts.[10]

In Africa, Asia, and Latin America, the strategy of state-led Import Substitution Industrialization—the counterpart of sorts to the Keynesian state in the Global North—came unraveled by the 1970s. Developmental states in the Global South pointedly had subsidized local capitalists in order to spur on new industries and reduce their dependence on imports from the industrially developed world. Yet while these capitalists were happy to take public resources, they were disinclined to use them for their intended purposes. The result, as Chibber points out in this volume, were enormous trade imbalances for coun- tries in the Global South with a few notable exceptions.[11] The fiscal crises that resulted from lopsided trade, along with profligate spending by elites, left the populations of these countries particularly vulnerable to battering from the new neoliberal order—what was later dubbed the Washington Consensus.

What followed has left its smoldering mark around the world. Ruling classes went on the offensive to restructure class power and a new social order was marshaled to restore the flagging system's profitability.[12] Pinochet's Chile and New York City in the midst of a fiscal crisis—where the investment bankers dictated what would be cut and who would be paid—were proving grounds for the fledgling order. Paul Volcker, the Chairman of the U.S. Federal Reserve, raised interest rates to 20 percent in order to force up unemployment and put an end to the militancy of American workers, declaring, "the American standard of living must decline."[13] The following year Reagan fired the striking PATCO air traffic controllers en masse, as a signal to the relatively well-paid workers that militancy of any kind would not be tolerated. In the UK, Thatcher took on the most powerful unions—culminating with the attack on the miners—and privatized nationalized industries including steel, gas, electricity, railways, airlines, and telecommunications. Other countries in the economically developed world followed suit to varying degrees (including in the 1990s the countries of the former Eastern Bloc—where following the implementation of neoliberal shock therapy in Russia, Kazakhstan, and elsewhere, life expectancy plummeted dramatically).[14]

In the Global South, the burgeoning ideology of neoliberalism was buttressed by the presumption that state planning spawned colossal inefficiencies—ignoring that such inefficiencies were born from an arrangement where private capital called the shots. States that had racked up huge debts were bailed out on the condition that they would remake their economies in neoliberalism's image. The International Monetary Fund and the World Bank, dominated by the United States, and often in alliance with Southern elites, prescribed a regimen of privatization of state enterprises, the decimation of public services, and throwing open markets to international capital. In the decades preceding neoliberalism's advent, the labor movements of those countries had effectively forfeited their autonomy and power in their "developmental coalition" with the state and national capital. As a consequence, trade unions found themselves markedly weakened and often unable to mount effective resistance to the unfolding neoliberal order.[15]

Privatization and unrelenting attacks on workers and their right to organize was accompanied by the restructuring of production and the labor process. Workers faced the erosion of their power over the production process through speed up, contracting out, casualization, the scaling back of wages, and downsizing, alongside the introduction of new technologies. That restructuring involved the geographic relocation of much of manufacturing to China and East Asia and *maquiladoras* on the U.S.-Mexico border, as well as the shift of manufacturing to lower wage or non-union regions within the countries of the Global North. The intensification of exploitation of workers in both North and South was the result of this wonderfully successful drive on the part of capital.

Neoliberalism also entailed the dispossession and incorporation of massive numbers of new workers into the waged labor force. While commentators forecast the end of the working class, in the past decades vast numbers of men and women around the world have been proletarianized. In East Asia alone, the ranks of the working class have increased ninefold since 1990, from 100 million to 900 million.[16] The expansion of the global pool of labor has eroded labor's bargaining power, making it much harder for workers to demand higher wages without capital going elsewhere. The face of the new working class worldwide is unmistakably female: in 2009 women surpassed men as the majority of workers in the U.S.—where wages have been stagnant for the past thirty years requiring two earners to maintain the prior standards of living—while a great many of the new proletarians in the Global South are women, typically from rural backgrounds.[17]

Many of these workers have found themselves seeking waged work (in both the country and the city; often as migrants in foreign countries or internal migrants in their own) because of the collapse of smallholder agriculture or due to the enclosure of common lands and resources that their livelihoods had depended on. While enclosure has been the hallmark of capitalism since its inception, the process of privatizing the commons has been accelerated under neoliberalism, including the enclosure of resources that had previously been privatized, then nationalized—whether as a result of postcolonial regimes, social democratic states in the Global North, or the countries of the former Soviet Bloc—and now have been privatized anew.

Neoliberalism has also meant the continued and accelerated commodification and plunder of nature. Corporations and governments (often via displaced and dispossessed smallholders) have intensified the logging of the rainforests for timber, cattle grazing, commodity crops, and biofuels; the fishing of the oceans; and strip mining and extracting of minerals and oil and gas deposits to power intensified and extensive manufacturing.[18] The result has been the mass extinction of species and the wholesale destruction of marine and terrestrial ecosystems, to say nothing of the people who are dependent upon them. The ravaging of nature is nothing new, either under capitalism or class society more broadly, but with neoliberalism the breadth and depth of that destruction have been magnified.[19]

By its nature, the neoliberal way of organizing capitalism is tremendously unstable. This system has required the enormous financialization of the global economy, necessitating the creation of all sorts of byzantine derivatives as a hedge against international transactions where the value of currencies is no longer fixed, following the demise of Bretton Woods. The United States has played an imperial role in the center of the system, intervening via the International Monetary Fund to bail out countries when the volatility of global finance proves too much, as in Mexico in 1982. This system, which allowed for vast restructuring and integration of production globally, reaped great rewards.[20] The immense profitability of neoliberalism, however, petered out in the late 1990s, and financial crises in East Asia, Russia, and Argentina followed.[21] In the past decade, as growth slowed down and wages remained stagnant, governments and individuals continued to borrow to keep themselves afloat. The U.S. state stepped in after each smaller crisis and burst bubble to protect U.S. financial interests, prevent the system from crashing, and keep the U.S. public as the world's consumers of last resort. When the U.S. housing bubble burst, the system was brought to its knees.

Neoliberalism in practice, therefore, has turned out to be a very different beast than the ideology of neoliberalism. One would be sorely mistaken, hence, to take neoliberalism at its word as "getting the state out of the market" (reducing the state to a size where it could be dragged to a bathtub and drowned in it, in Grover Norquist's indelible words).[22] Unfortunately, this is what much of the left has done: the conventional wisdom, on the right as well as the left, is that neoliberalism ushered in the rise of the market, unfettered by the state. Consequently, the state is seen as the polar opposite, and therefore the antagonist, of the market—when in reality the state facilitates the market in countless ways.[23]

The Keynesian welfare state was not any less a profitable order for ruling elites, nor was it one where the state restrained capital.[24] But the way that system was able to remain profitable was ultimately constrained by the latitude it provided for worker militancy and class struggle under conditions of high employment. A change was in order. For these reasons, it would be very difficult to go back now.

*   *   *

Panitch has suggested in this volume that what we have witnessed may be the fourth global crisis of capitalism. The first two crises—in the 1870s and 1930s—led to protectionist barriers impeding the expansion of capital internationally. The third crisis in the 1970s, by contrast, resulted in a new global expansion of capital. The question remains as to whether this crisis will lead to a retrenchment of what has been awkwardly termed "globalization." Capitalism's ability to emerge out of crises with a new momentous phase of accumulation and growth, as Moore reminds us, has historically been based on access to cheap labor and cheap food—the latter helping bring down the cost of the former—as well as cheap energy and cheap raw materials to commodify. These are generated by new technological innovations and new enclosures. Moore is dubious that such prerequisites exist now that would allow for a new phase of capitalist development coming out of the crisis.[25]

Huws suggests otherwise. She avers in chapter 9 that while capitalism periodically runs up against limits, what it can bring into the money economy appears boundless. Commodification and enclosure are at the center of capitalism and magnified in its neoliberal form. By its very nature, capitalism must unceasingly bring forth ever-new commodities to survive. The dynamism of capitalism is based in part on its ability to generate new commodities and desires from those activities outside of the market. In the twentieth century, capitalism has been partially fueled by products that have their origins in domestic, and usually female, labor. In this process, use-values outside of the money economy are often first turned into mass services before they end up as even more lucrative commodities. (For example, food preparation in the home is brought into the market as a service industry—restaurants and catering—and reaches its commodity zenith in the form of the packaged meal.) And often these new commodities give rise to new services, and subsequent new commodities, offshoots in a never-ending cycle interrupted only by periodic crashes. As long as the system survives, this process is once more set into motion.[26]

Huws argues persuasively that the process of creating new commodities from activities formerly outside of the market—turning use-values into exchange-values—is an unbounded relentless process, a never-ending enclosure, as it were, with no end in sight.[27] The constant movement towards ever-new commodities has been coupled, under neoliberalism, with the commodification of things previously brought into the public sector, use-values such as public education, daycare, and healthcare. The privatization of the public sector has provided a significant impetus to capitalism and continues to do so during this period of crisis, as have industries where governments are the customers, such as the military.[28] And as old capital is destroyed and workers are thrown out of their jobs, many companies are reaping record profits by squeezing the workers who are left.[29]

These processes of commodification, enclosure, and dispossession leave deep yet uneven marks on the manifold forms in which capitalism expands or contracts, including in crisis. They intersect with cleavages of race and gender and produce them anew. The explosive economic growth of China and the industrial success of countries such as Taiwan and South Korea have been underpinned by very distinct agrarian histories of forced dispossession and land redistribution in contrast to a country like South Africa under colonialism, apartheid, and now neoliberalism. These differences, as Hart demonstrates, have profound consequences for the conditions of capital accumulation, including the social wage—the de facto costs to a worker for housing, food, and other necessities of life—and the conditions under which workers are able to weather moments of sharp crisis.[30] They also influence the ways in which resistance against capital may, or may not, take shape—such as whether struggles over land are successfully linked with labor.[31]

As we have witnessed, in the wake of the crisis, capital responded not with a lasting shift to Keynesianism, large bailouts and stimulus spending notwithstanding, but by ratcheting up neoliberal belt-tightening. There do not appear to be any genuine efforts by elites for a "double movement" away from the ravages of the market, perhaps because they do not sufficiently fear a backlash from the dispossessed. With the obvious exception of China, which is working from a different blueprint of capitalism, austerity is now the order of the day.

Austerity has its dangers. As Harvey reminds us in his contribution to this book, capitalism tends to resolve its crises in ways that lead to new forms of crisis. In a climate of cutbacks (and now reined-in credit) layered on top of many-decades-long wage repression, capitalism is flirting with chronic lack of demand for goods from consumers too broke to spend, to say nothing of the potential for backlash from below.

What of other traditional avenues out of crisis? While war is supposed to be the midwife of revolution, it can also be the doula of capitalist renewal—decimating old accumulated capital and restoring capitalism to health. Yet although the U.S. state has been engaged in brutal trillion-dollar wars around the world, with occupying armies on multiple fronts, these conflicts have preceded the crisis. And the type of warfare it has been waging does not have those broad-based salutary effects for profits—that is, besides the very lucrative arms business and contracts for limited reconstruction—such as rebuilding cities in toto, replacing destroyed machinery, and stepping over one's decimated competitors. The U.S. has been heavily involved, of course, in razing cities and destroying the lives and livelihoods of people in Iraq and Afghanistan. But these are cities and villages overseas in foreign lands, which can be mainly left in ruin irrespective of the horrific damage done.

War, in this case, does not appear to be the means for capital to move beyond crisis. A war on the working class and the poor will have to suffice. And judging from profit rates—some of the highest returns recorded to date for U.S. capital—it appears to be an eminently successful strategy.[32] But the volatility of an entrenched neoliberalism, based on financialization and the accelerated exploitation of workers and nature, haunts capitalism and provides pitfalls and openings for the rest of us.

★   ★   ★

II.

As capital pursues an advantageous way out of the crisis, what of any other routes through and beyond it? What of the discontents who stand to suffer most from capital's solution to the crisis of its own making?

The ideology buttressing free-market capitalism crumbled—an early casualty of the crisis. Capital's brief moment of soul-searching and existential angst displayed on the pages of the business press is now a distant memory.

But capitalism has been shaken to the quick, and few are those who expect a return to the status quo ante.

The austerity imposed as a result of the crisis has spurred combativeness of all sorts. It brought down Iceland's government; generated civil unrest and recurring general strikes in Greece and France, as well as country-wide strikes in India, Spain, and Portugal; and led to pan-European trade union actions, mass student walkouts and protests in the UK, and significant labor militancy in China. Factory occupations have taken place in South Korea, Turkey, Venezuela, China, France, Spain, Ireland, Scotland, England, Northern Ireland, Egypt, Indonesia, Ukraine, Canada, Argentina, the former Yugoslavia, and the United States.[33] French workers pioneered the strategy of boss-napping, while in the U.S. activist groups returned evicted residents to their foreclosed houses.[34] While such actions may yet build into formidable challenges to the system, so far many of these responses have taken place on a limited and reactive basis.

Yet while some mobilize for radical demands, others rally to the cause of reaction. For the recognition of capitalism's bankruptcy does not ineluctably translate into anticapitalist politics, particularly in the parts of the world where over the past three decades radical and working class movements have been vanquished, fallen apart, or quietly receded.

The obstacles to conceiving a new emancipatory politics are formidable. There are many reasons for this. Capitalist neoliberalism has undermined the basis for organizing in myriad ways. Neoliberalism has meant a gloves-off form of class war, borne out by the assault on militant unions, relentless restructuring of employment, speed up, wage slashing, and intentional unemployment as a means of disciplining workers and breaking organized labor. In the United States, trade union density is at its lowest level in nearly a hundred years, while in Japan and the countries of the European Union membership has been falling since a spike in the 1970s.[35] Similarly, over the neoliberal period, unionization rates have declined in Latin America, Asia, and Oceania, while rates for sub-Saharan Africa remain low with a few notable exceptions.[36] Perhaps as significantly, the increasing precariousness of employment has put a damper on workplace militancy, as workers are hesitant to take actions when they may easily be put out on their ears.

Yet neoliberalism has operated in other ways, which are subtler, but no less destructive. The enormous growth of finance over the past three decades and the integration of the working class into financial circuits, through pensions, mortgage, and credit card debt, have bound people into the system, a point emphasized in this book by McNally and Albo, et al.[37] This has been significant for the recent trajectory of capitalism, as more and more people kept the system afloat by borrowing money on credit and mortgages when their stagnant wages were not enough to get by. But just as consequential, it has caught workers up in the system, giving them a stake in its survival. The hope of individual advancement within the system, or simply hanging on, has become in many cases a substitute for collective social change. Privatization and the soaring cost of higher education have contributed to more debt and entanglement in the financial system. In the U.S., students—often a constituency of the left—must take part- or full-time jobs to pay their tuition and expenses while they are studying. Upon graduation, they are burdened with such high levels of debt that they typically choose jobs that will allow them to pay their financial obligations, rather than opting for avenues that would be more conducive to political engagement and activism.

Speculation generated housing bubbles in Ireland, Spain, India, the UK, and elsewhere. In the United States, the vast wave of foreclosures has been the emblem of the economic crisis for suburban and urban middle and working class people alike. The predatory nature of mortgage brokers in the U.S. targeting often female-headed Latino and African American households has been well documented. So have the ways that working class people supplemented their falling incomes by taking out mortgages and other forms of debt. But less explored have been the political consequences of homeownership for working class and poor people, which took off in earnest in the U.S. in the 1970s—not coincidentally during a period of working class militancy. Mortgage holders may be hesitant to rock the boat through job actions and strikes because of the need for a steady income, while homeownership more subtly changes people's perceptions about their stake in the survival of a financial system into which they are tied.[38]

The idea that working class homeownership might serve as an effective way to foster conservatism and the maintenance of the status quo is not a new one. Following the bloody Homestead Strike of 1892, Carnegie Steel offered workers not higher wages but loans to buy their own houses.[39] Other large enterprises of the time did the same. A representative of one such company summed up the philosophy behind this: "Get them to invest their savings in their homes and own them. Then they won't leave and they won't strike. It ties them down so they have a stake in our prosperity."[40] Yet while the working class had been integrated into the circuits of finance before the neoliberal era, under it their assimilation was greatly accelerated.[41] A key tenet of neoliberalism in the UK—and one of the ways that consent was further manufactured for it—was the privatization of public housing under Thatcher, where tenants were sold their state-owned council houses at a discounted rate. The "Right to Buy" plank of the Conservative Party's agenda was fueled both by the desire to cut working class people adrift from the social supports and public services of the welfare state and to transform them socially.[42] Similarly, in the U.S., where homeownership was already widespread amongst white suburbanites, the desire to open up a new market by extending mortgages to the urban poor was coupled with a social ideology of creating upstanding and obedient citizens. While George W. Bush is associated with the notion of an ownership society where state provisions like Social Security are replaced by "individual responsibility" and the market, it was Bill Clinton who gave a big boost to homeownership in the mid-1990s, through both deregulation and a campaign to promote owning one's own house to working class and poor renters.[43] It was twinned under Clinton with the gutting of welfare as a means of slashing public expenditures.[44]

The privatization of social housing fed into the distended real estate bubble in places such as Miami, where low-income public housing was bulldozed and not replaced.[45] Poor residents, whether as renters or owners, have been frequently forced from their domiciles through the use of eminent domain and more crude forms of land grabbing in the Global South and North. Cities around the world have been reconfigured into playgrounds for the wealthy, transforming social spaces that have historically been centers for collective action. (And as private washing machines replace public laundry services, as cars replace public transport, the social spaces where people encounter each other and have a sense of themselves beyond their individual identities and perhaps find political common ground shrink.)[46] The evisceration of rent control likewise further undermined the economics that allowed people to participate as radical activists or engaged intellectuals without needing full time employment to make ends meet. Similarly, until it was dismantled, welfare had allowed unemployed activists, particularly in Europe, to involve themselves in radical action, strike support, and the nurturing of communities of struggle. Under post-crash austerity, more such cuts are being meted out, further diminishing the resources people can draw upon to mobilize.

Privatization has been twinned with the propagated ideology of self-help and individual responsibility, with the undercurrent that other people—particularly people of color—are a burden on the system and the taxes one pays towards it. The political scapegoating and criminalization of immigrants and people of color in many countries, and the attendant fear mongering, has resulted in the incarceration of millions and further fragmented and separated the working class. The working class has long been divided, with workers of color persistently excluded from better paying jobs. The unemployment that results from periodic crises of capitalism force down wages for all workers, but workers of color tend to be hit disproportionately. Yet the blame for this disparity is often laid at their feet, as the result of personal or cultural dysfunction.

Long work hours, particularly in North America, East Asia, and much of the Global South, have eroded the time that workers have for other pursuits. In addition to extended workdays, sometimes divided between several jobs, the rise of telecommuting has further blurred the division separating work and one's own time. Working class people increasingly lack the time to engage in political action or to spend reading and talking to others. While workers in the past have successfully organized while toiling way beyond the eight-hour day, other constraints on contemporary workers diminish the time they have for contemplation and social interaction.[47]

A working class that is debt-ridden, deeply incorporated into the circuits of finance, increasingly atomized, forced out of public spaces that have been enclosed, divided by racism, and lacking the social supports and time to engage with each other is at a distinct disadvantage in facing the assaults of capital or organizing in its own interest. Its members often lack the wherewithal to, as E. P. Thompson phrased it, "identify points of antagonistic interest ... commence to struggle around these issues and in the process of struggling ... discover themselves as [a] class."[48]

This is not to suggest that resistance has been absent during the neoliberal period. Far from it. The biggest strikes in U.S. history took place in 2006 when immigrants took to the streets in unprecedented numbers on May Day. In the largest public demonstrations the world has ever seen, millions rallied in opposition to the impending invasion of Iraq. But these actions have flared up momentarily without turning into sustained movements that build over time. The perennial challenge during this era is how to organize beyond these fleeting eruptions of outrage.

★   ★   ★

Neoliberalism's ascendancy has undoubtedly impeded resistance in many forms. Yet unfortunately the left itself cannot be held entirely blameless for its rapid rise, which emerged both in reaction to the militant social movements of the 1960s and '70s and, in complex ways, was fostered by social dynamics that intersected with these movements. The latter was most strikingly seen by the defection of many Sixties radicals to the neoliberal cause, often in Social Democratic parties. This was in no way unprecedented. Tariq Ali points out in this volume that throughout history the pendulum has swung from radical advance to reaction, with erstwhile revolutionaries switching their allegiances from the former to the latter. If the cause of radicalism does not emerge victorious, counterrevolution comes swinging back.[49]

At the same time, the New Left seemed to embody elements of the emerging new socioeconomic order, which may have facilitated neoliberalism's rise—a "subterranean elective affinity," to use Nancy Fraser's suggestive term, for the celebration of the free market unfettered.[50] Provocatively, Harvey posits in this book that the New Left simultaneously combined a radical call for social and environmental justice and a libertarian call for personal freedom from the constraints of schools, social mores, bureaucracy, and the state. In answering the question of how, in liberal democracies, consent was garnered for the emergence of neoliberalism, he argues that the libertarian impulse was ultimately channeled into the individual freedom of consumer choice under neoliberalism.[51] People could express their individuality against the conformist pressures of society through consumer choices and niche lifestyles of various kinds offered up by the market.[52] In the same way that the alliances between trade unions and the developmental state in the Global South corroded the former's ability to resist neoliberalism, the left in the Global North was ill-prepared to resist the rise of neoliberalism and in some ways gave tacit support to the project.

It certainly would be comforting to believe the spirit of the Sixties was simply co-opted by neoliberalism. The counterculture certainly proved fertile ground for the creation and sale of new commodities and forms of consumption. Radicals and subversives were able to "commodify their dissent," to paraphrase The Baffler, with the accoutrements of bohemianism, which differed little from the consumer culture that they were raging against. Thomas Frank has illustrated that industry in the U.S., particularly advertising, was aware of this kinship, and not simply as something to appropriate: "Like the young insurgents, people in more advanced reaches of the American corporate world deplored conformity, distrusted routine, and encouraged resistance to established power. They welcomed the youth-led cultural revolution not because they were secretly planning to subvert it or even because they believed it would allow them to tap a gigantic youth market (although this was, of course, a factor), but because they perceived in it a comrade in their own struggles to revitalize American business and the consumer order generally."[53] "Far from opposing the larger cultural revolution of [the Sixties], the business revolution paralleled—and in some cases actually anticipated—the impulses and new values associated with the counterculture. Art Kleiner, who worked as an editor of the Whole Earth Catalog before taking up business history, is explicit about the connection between management theory and the counterculture. He depicts the 1960s as a long struggle to recover what he calls 'vernacular' human relationships amid the hyper-rationalism of the technocracy, an effort that 'could only have existed against the backdrop of the counterculture.'"[54]

The dovetailing of the New Left and neoliberalism can be seen with arguably the most enduring success of the era—the women's movement. It transformed for the better, albeit incompletely, the lives of women and men across a wide swath of society. Yet as feminist theorist Fraser posits, it provided fuel for the emergence of neoliberalism in the 1970s.[55] This was not simply through the cooptation by free-marketeers of the second-wave feminist critique of the paternalistic, male-centric bureaucratic welfare state during a moment when the Keynesian state was under attack. It was connected on a deeper level. Neoliberalism depended on drawing women into wage work, often low-wage service jobs, as falling salaries meant that the "family wage" of a single (male) wage earner could no longer support a family. As Fraser indicates, feminism left behind the social justice dimension of its earlier agenda to focus on women getting a leg up in the job market, breaking the glass ceiling, and finding emancipation through entry into the market. Undoubtedly this gave women a new sort of power, as members of the waged working and middle classes with the ability to act collectively in the workplace—as white- and blue-collar workers, women had a potential strength that differed from the atomized unwaged work of the home.[56] But such priorities were no longer framed within an anti-capitalist agenda or struggle, and overlapped easily with the drive to tap into a pool of labor hitherto outside of the market.[57]

Not coincidentally, at a moment when the political pendulum was beginning to swing back to the right, a set of ideas took hold within the intellectual left in the late 1970s. Postmodernism, greatly influenced by the New Left, tended toward an antipathy to class politics and the working class at a time of phenomenal rank-and-file militancy.[58] It ended up dominating the intellectual landscape, in and out of the academy, for subsequent decades. Sanbonmatsu argues in this volume that postmodernism rose not on its own merits, but as a result of the neoliberalization of the Western university system and partially reflected the strivings of academics to distinguish their ideas as products or "knowledge commodities" for career advancement across a changing academic terrain.[59] While positioned on the leftward end of the spectrum, postmodernism evinced an affinity for the flux, flows, fragmentation, and hybridity of globalized capital. Celebrations of an immaterial world of networks and border crossing shared much in common with breathless neoliberal paeans to a brave new world of information technology and "placelessness."[60] That notion of a new weightless, placeless globe was seriously disconnected from the globalized capitalism it described, as proven in stark material terms when it all came crashing down with the stock market bubble in the late 1990s. Postmodernism seemed to embody both the political defeat of the radical left in the face of neoliberalism and the libertarian pole of consumer choice of the New Left that Harvey describes.

Large-scale membership based organizations, including trade unions, waned at the same time postmodernism was on the rise.[61] They were replaced in many cases by nonprofit organizations, funded not by the donations of members, but rather the largesse of foundations or rich individuals, interested in quarterly deliverables, not dismantling the capitalist system. As others have commented, the rise of the nonprofit industrial complex has had a deleterious effect on the shape, demands, and direction of the left.[62] (Even the World Social Forum, hailed by many as one of the bright lights of the left, is largely comprised not of movement-based organizations but nonprofits from the Global North and governments from the Global South.) Consonantly, the form protest has taken, as Sanbonmatsu notes, has largely been as expressions of outrage—a tendency dating back to the New Left—which often foreclose attempts to reach out to and convince those beyond activist circles.

*   *   *

John Maynard Keynes, during an earlier era of *laissez-faire* hegemony, mused on the difficulty of judging what makes a person more conservative—knowing nothing but the present, or nothing but the past. Both could be said true of the dominant aspects of the left today. The neoliberal period of the past three decades, with its all-encompassing ideology of self-advancement through the alchemy of the market, appears to have impeded severely the subversive imagination. As noted previously, it is ironic that the most radical alternative to the current order that many leftists can envisage is a return to the Keynesian welfare state system.[63] Others believe that utopia is emerging already through the cracks within capitalism, to be found in farmers markets, bicycle kitchens, urban homesteading, and other small-scale projects.[64]

Abandoning pessimism and nostalgia and looking forward are not easy—particularly given the multitudinous defeats and self-inflicted wounds of the left. Yet we are living through a moment when capitalism has melted down on a breathtakingly grand scale and the crisis of nature is writ large. One might hope that the monumental crises around us would encourage more ambitious thinking in place of the piecemeal and timid nature of even those projects labeled utopian, to aspire beyond a tamed version of capitalism or a dubious Golden Age that shimmers behind us.

It should come as no surprise that pervasive fatalism gives rise to such diminished expectations. They need to be challenged nonetheless. The piecemeal idea of change is not an answer to defeat, but rather the fetishization of it.[65] There is nothing wrong with people experimenting with living differently, of carbon-free mobility, growing food in cities, and challenging restrictive societal mores of various kinds. Creating a culture of resistance to capitalism—if that is in fact what is being created—should be lauded and encouraged. But as a political orientation, often with strong moralistic overtones about individual consumption, such projects should not be an end in themselves, as they often are. The further a larger utopian vision of social transformation recedes, the more detailed and moralistic the blueprint many activists have for daily life in the present becomes. As anarchist historian Grubačić points out, when the Industrial Workers of the World called for building the new in the shell of the old, they saw it is part of a broad-based revolutionary transformation, not a matter of individual consumption choices.[66]

Taken as a whole, such incrementalism makes for a pretty dreary notion of utopia: little businesses, small-scale farms, and local currencies in a small-is-beautiful version of capitalism. It might be best characterized as a middle class idyll, which doesn't challenge the social relations between (small) capital and labor. Size isn't the problem; capitalism is. (It should perhaps give us pause that the vision of big capital encroaching on wholesome small businesses and "local" communities is one shared with the far right.) Small farms are not any better for the earth or for their workers, than larger ones; the question is what takes place on them.[67] Community banks are not more virtuous than rapacious corporate banks. The former were more likely to make bad loans than their large counterparts and, as Henwood points out, feed into the same financial circuits as the latter. Similarly, small businesses in North America tend to be non-unionized, pay less, and provide their workers with fewer benefits, if any.[68] It is hard to see where the radical potential lies.

In the Global South, a number of social movements that champion farmers against big capital and the state have been much romanticized by activists in the North for the same reasons. One example is the Karnataka Rajya Raitha Sangha, or KRRS, an initiator of Peoples' Global Action and a member of Via Campesina. The organization, which claims a membership of ten million, has been lauded for its opposition to genetically modified crops—most notably with the "Monsanto, Quit India" campaign celebrated by Vandana Shiva. Yet KRRS is an organization of rich farmers, who exploit the poor peasants and landless workers they employ. One of their demands is that they should get subsidies for chemical fertilizers.[69] KRRS are not atypical of the rich farmers' movements embraced by activists in the Global North as representing a model of environmental and social justice, an admixture of class myopia and Orientalism. There are a plethora of movements in the Global South eminently worthy of radical support—from the Western Cape Anti-Eviction Campaign in South Africa to the independent trade union confederation in Mexico, the Frente Auténtico del Trabajo, to movements of rural workers and poor peasants around the world. A desire to extend solidarity to movements in the Global South should not, however, blinker the left from the complexities of class struggle and other significant divisions.

The turn towards the local or the regional, accompanying this piecemeal notion of radicalism, is beset with blind spots. It ignores why some places are rich and some are poor in the first place, and the role that capitalism plays in creating geographic unevenness. This is the parochialism of the affluent and bountiful. It includes wealthy provinces no longer wanting to subsidize their poorer neighbors (such as Slovenia and Croatia, whose secession sparked the bloody war dividing Yugoslavia, and the desires of the Northern League in Italy or the natural-gas-rich Santa Cruz region in Bolivia to break away) and the more benign movements for eating food grown within a hundred-mile radius of where you are—which perhaps not surprisingly originate in agriculturally rich locales like Northern California and Sussex, rather than North Dakota and Caithness. It unquestionably makes great sense to rationalize a trade and agriculture system that needlessly ships food from one side of the world to the other. But this is merely one example of the dysfunctional aspects of a capitalism that is predicated on the exploitation of nature and human beings—the world both within us and around us. And seeing "the local" both as victim and alternative to global capitalism, as Hart emphasizes, misses the fact that "the global," or global capitalism, is constituted by local places. Capitalist social forces indeed exist where we all live, whether they are organized on a large or small scale.

Russell Jacoby has written of the Cold War liberals—Isaiah Berlin, Karl Popper, Hannah Arendt—who promulgated the idea that collective utopian ambitions on a grand scale automatically lead to the gulag.[70] They argued that any attempt to fundamentally reorder society for the social good is ill fated— that, in the words of Kant, "out of the crooked timber of humanity no straight thing was ever made." Throughout history, utopian thought at its most radical aspires to a society based on leisure, equality, comradeship, peace, and— its "red thread"—the abolition of private property and the redistribution of wealth. The anti-utopian view in its contemporary form, as Fredric Jameson has pointed out, is grounded on the assumption "that the system (now grasped as the free market) is part of human nature; that any attempt to change it will be accompanied by violence; and that efforts to maintain the changes (against human nature) will require dictatorship."[71]

That liberal view has become pervasive within part of the left, as well as within postmodernist thought where many of these ideas have been expanded: that utopian grand projects are doomed to end up soaked in blood. Better to leave society to small-scale incremental changes, than risk the danger that arises from utopian yearnings toward broad transformation.

That some utopian experiments have ended violently is not necessarily a testament to their desire to reorder society. Rather, as in the case of the Paris Commune of 1871 and the German Revolution of 1919, radical aspirations were crushed by the countervailing forces of reaction. But there is no question that any hopes for reviving such thoroughgoing radicalism require coming to grips with the failures of the radical left in the twentieth century: the perversion of emancipatory hopes in the Soviet Union and other similar attempts at communism, and the inability of other experiments, such as the anarchists in the Spanish Revolution, to hold onto power and transform society.[72] Was the impulse to reorder society for the good their downfall? It would be hard to argue that they were: bureaucratism, stratification, and repression, especially of the cadre of the revolution, motivated their stifling. It would be difficult to suggest that the Soviet Union and other examples of "actually existing socialism" in any way ultimately constituted a free association of producers, of "an association in which the free development of each is the condition for the free development of all," in the words of *The Communist Manifesto*. Such liberatory yearnings have not been met in any enduring form. That does not mean that very difficult questions do not need to be answered about why these terrible failures took place. But blame should not simply be left at the feet of the utopian.[73]

The fear of totalizing ambitions—that grand utopian aspirations will lead to the extermination camp and the gulag—leaves the totalizing horror and daily violence of capitalism unchallenged in any fundamental way. Incrementalism, whether through the market or piecemeal solutions in particular localities, will not suffice to halt the destruction of our ecosystems. Nor is it sufficient to end the suffering that poor and working class people contend with the world over as a result of capitalism, both in and out of its neoliberal form.

A call to bring back utopian ambitions does not mean that simply wishing for a broadly transformative revolution will conjure one up or transcend the reasons for the left's defeats. Those defeats, as I have argued, cannot be attributed simply to the intensity of the backlash against radical organizing. And rejecting piecemeal politics does not signify opposing anything that is not immediately revolutionary. Short-term struggles are important in themselves and crucial for building consciousness and a sense of collective power for larger struggles.[74] Nor am I suggesting that urgency about the socio-ecological crisis should impel us to replace careful thinking and strategizing with panicked action for action's sake. That is, unfortunately, yet another legacy of the left with which any emancipatory project needs to come to terms.

An appeal to utopian ambitions similarly does not mean glossing over the painful past of the left. Quite the opposite. An anticapitalist worthy of the name must confront these and other questions: How to avoid the horrors and tragedies of the past? How to address the ecological crisis and the plundering of nature—found equally under "actually existing socialism" as in the capitalist countries (pioneering ideas by Aleksandr Bogdanov and others about conservation and ecology in the early Soviet period notwithstanding)?[75] And how to get from neoliberal capitalism to an emancipatory socialism—how to get from here to there?

The left has an often-disastrous history of organizing itself and trying to organize others. The Stalinism that gripped generations of the left in the Global North and South did incalculable damage to the shape that radical politics took in the twentieth century. That legacy is still with us. Mike Davis reflects in this book on that history in considering the life of Isaac Deutscher, who in many ways, represented a bridge between one of the critical, emancipatory lineages of the Old Left—with Rosa Luxemburg, Victor Serge, C. L. R. James, and others—and the New Left; although with hindsight one can say, not critical enough. Like E. P. Thompson, Deutscher both recognized the importance of social forces and class consciousness, and remains an exemplar of resolute anti-sectarianism, with scant few contemporaries.

The Old Left's heritage of sectarianism was unfortunately passed on. It was spectacularly built upon by the New Left, where in the U.S. and elsewhere radicals inadvertently assisted the state in the destruction of their movements through fierce infighting, the Leninist party, and the politics of voluntarism—that revolution might come through taking the most militant posture. The pox of sectarianism has tragically withered many opportunities for radicalism.[76]

Thinking that one is saved from that history by not organizing, or simply acting spontaneously, however, is fatally flawed. Sloughing off the blight of sectarianism requires changing the culture of the left itself, which is a prerequisite for a transformative anticapitalist project that has any chance of succeeding. An essential place to start would be to address the sordid history between socialists and anarchists, in which the latter—along with communists of various leftwards stripes—have been at the receiving end of violence at the hands of the Soviet state and Communist Parties. Much could be gained by laying down the hatchet between Marxists and anarchists, as the ideas of both benefit from proximity to each other. Anarchism would be enriched by the understanding of capitalism as social system provided by the rich tradition of Marxist political economy. And Marxism would benefit from anarchism's wariness of the state as an end in itself, and its emphasis of creating a culture of struggle that embodies the values of comradeship and solidarity. Anti-sectarianism does not mean jettisoning one's political and ideological differences, but it does mean debating them in a comradely fashion and finding points of unity on which to organize collectively.

These two traditions intersect and overlap in fruitful ways in the visions of council communism and anarcho-syndicalism, of which Chomsky is the most notable proponent and elaborates upon in the penultimate chapter of this book.

A return to the unitary spirit of nineteenth-century socialism, prior to the disintegration of the First International would well serve a renewed anticapitalist left in the early twenty-first century. Chancellor Otto von Bismarck, on hearing of the split between Marxists and anarchists in the First International, declared that "crowned heads, wealth and privilege may well tremble should ever again the Black and Red unite." Perhaps after decades of defeats and divisions, it is time to heed those words. Raymond Williams warned, at a moment when capitalism was assuming its current shape, against "the received alternatives of triumphalism and pessimism."[77] Long before the present crisis, radical triumphalism had fallen by the wayside, leaving a murky legacy for the left. If we move between and beyond the twin dangers of which Williams warned—unfettered by the fatalism of the age and the blinders of neoliberalism, while clear sighted about the defeats and hubris of the past—where might we land? What might an anticapitalist vision entail?

Any sustainable anticapitalist project worthy of the name must situate public abundance—in place of private wealth—at its center. Mike Davis points one way forward in balancing his own deep pessimism about global warming with the potentialities of a large collective project of social-ecological transformation. He looks to cities, which under capitalism are the largest source of carbon emissions, arguing that under socialism the city could be a key vehicle for ecological sustainability.[78] "Left to the dismal politics of the present, of course, cities of poverty will almost certainly be the coffins of hope," writes Davis, but a reconfigured radical city could also provide the best means to reduce carbon emissions through population density, economies of scale, preservation of green space, and most importantly, by replacing private ownership and private commodities with public affluence.[79] He evokes visions for city organization from the garden cities of the Guild Socialists and the early Soviet attempts in the 1920s to restructure daily life through experiments in communal living and urban planning, to the radical public housing of the Karl Marx-Hof on the Ringstrasse des Proletariats, where militants barricaded themselves during Red Vienna's February Uprising in 1934. It goes without saying that such a reconfiguration would not, or should not, end at the outskirts of the city.

Doing away with commodification and the commodity form would similarly be paramount, a question wrestled with by cultural radicals, from William Morris more than a century ago to Rodchenko and the artists of the Constructivist movement who sought to transform it with their notion of object-as-comrade.[80] Going further, Huws has argued suggestively that the left needs to move beyond its fixation with manufactured objects, challenging the notion of merely replacing commodities produced under the logic of capital with different ones produced under socialism.

Such a vision would need to answer fundamental questions: about transcending the division of labor between intellectual and physical work; resolving the separation between the city and the countryside and reintegrating the two as a means of living equitably and sustainably; reorganizing our relationship with nature and ourselves as part of nature; and radically transforming work and leisure, well beyond the abolition of wage labor. Morris gives us a sense of those possibilities when he writes, "when all are working harmoniously together and there is no one to rob the worker of his time, that is to say, his life; in those coming days there will be no compulsion on us to go on producing things we do not want, no compulsion on us to labor for nothing; we shall be able calmly and thoughtfully to consider what we shall do with our wealth of labour-power."[81]

A fatalistic incrementalism precludes such a vision, but we should not opt to do the same. It appears increasingly obvious that the ecological systems on which life depends cannot endure the ravages of capitalism indefinitely. To be sure, we need to guard against seeing the crises we are living through as automatically auspicious moments for radicals—after the deluge, us. Crises unleash many things, a great deal of them not the least bit amenable to the left, much less to an overarching radical vision of social transformation. Capital is in the process of resolving the crisis by imposing ever more neoliberal austerity, which ensures that the type of capitalism ahead will be a particularly unstable one. The triumphalism of capitalism, however, has crumbled away and pessimism may be lifting. The future is unwritten. One can only hope that a route out of the darkness will be navigated, where the discontents are finally able to seize control of their collective destinies.

Part I
Empire, Neoliberalism, Crisis

CHAPTER ONE

Ellen Meiksins Wood:
Empire in the Age of Capital

While empire long precedes capitalism, contemporary imperialism is inseparable from capitalism. What, then, are the distinguishing features of capitalism as an economic system, as you see it?

EMW: I think the essential characteristic is that all of the major economic actors are market dependent, dependent on the market to maintain and reproduce their conditions of life. This also means that the relationship between classes is mediated by the market, so that unlike precapitalist systems in which exploiting classes were able to extract surplus labor from exploited classes by means of superior coercive power, direct noneconomic coercion, in capitalism the compulsions are economic imperatives. So in a mature capitalist economy, the capitalist doesn't need to have superior political, legal or military power over workers, the way a precapitalist landlord had to have power over peasants who had nonmarket access to land. Wage laborers have to sell their labor power to a capitalist simply in order to gain access to the means of their own life, their own labor, and so on. And of course the capitalist depends on the market for access to labor and to realize the profits the workers produce. Of course there's a huge difference between propertyless workers and the owners of capital, which means a huge imbalance of class power. But capitalists are no less dependent on the market to maintain themselves and their capital. The whole capitalist system is operated by market imperatives, the compulsions of competition, profit-maximization, and capital accumulation.

Why don't commerce or trade in goods constitute capitalism, as some might assume?

EMW: I make a distinction between market opportunities and market imperatives. And I think it's only in capitalism that you have a system in which people are obliged, are compelled, to enter the market simply to guarantee their own existence and their own self-reproduction. There have been markets throughout history in which people have brought their surpluses to sell, but there's never been a system before capitalism in which producers and appropriators both were absolutely dependent on the market for their most basic conditions of life and therefore compelled to follow the dictates of the market in order to sustain themselves.

You write that the exploitation that is a necessary part of capitalism is hidden in certain ways, unlike the coercion that characterized feudal societies where naked power was more apparent. How is exploitation under capitalism opaque?

EMW: The contrast that you just indicated, between capitalism and feudalism, is a useful one. If you think about what the relationship is between a feudal lord and a dependent peasant, it's a very transparent relationship, which is even legally recognized as a relationship of inequality.

In capitalism, the capitalist and the laborer begin, on the face of it, as equals. They're legally equal, and on top of that, the capitalist actually pays the workers instead of transparently extracting surpluses from them. In the case of feudalism, the peasant is obliged to do labor services or to transfer surpluses directly to the lord; whereas in capitalism, the relationship appears on the face of it to be the opposite, because the capitalist actually pays the worker up front before realizing profits from the worker's labor in the market. So it takes some complicated calculation to figure out how it is that the worker's surpluses are transferred to the capitalist and how it is that the capitalist derives a profit from the worker's labor.

What are the main features of capitalist imperialism?

EMW: The main feature of capitalist imperialism is that it operates as much as possible via economic imperatives, instead of by direct colonial rule. I think that if you had talked about American imperialism before the invasion of Iraq, you would likely meet the objection that the United States doesn't really possess colonies. But I actually think it remains true that it's not a colonial power in the sense that we've traditionally understood it. I think the United States would still prefer to stay out of colonial entanglements and operate its domination through economic imperatives.

I think that the United States is actually the first, and so far the only, truly capitalist empire, which has exercised its domination largely by these economic imperatives, by making subordinate powers subject to economic compulsions emanating from the United States and from American capital.

So in the case of the U.S. occupation of Iraq, would you say then that it is an exception to this rule?

EMW: I think the mess that they made of it in Iraq, and the complete lack of planning for after the war, probably testifies to the fact that they hadn't really intended it to be this way. They hadn't intended to be an occupying power. What I think they hoped would happen was that they could decapitate the regime and just install some more compliant leadership and then allow

American capital to insert itself comfortably into the Iraq economy and into the production of oil. The very fact that they made such a hash of it seems to me to confirm the point, rather than the reverse.

What is it about capitalism today that allows empire to exist and to flourish and to expand without the need for military colonialization?
EMW: When we were talking about the relationship between capital and labor, I talked about the ways in which capital can exercise its domination over labor, because workers are market dependent and obliged to enter the market, to sell their labor power, simply in order to gain access to the means of life and self-reproduction. In a way, an analogous thing has happened on the global plane, in which more and more parts of the world have been subjected to these market imperatives by making them dependent on entering the market. Capitalists have to pay workers up front before they realize profits from the workers' work through the market just to gain access to the means of maintaining themselves. You only need to think about the conditions imposed by the IMF on developing economies, which are designed to make them more dependent on global markets and foreign capital. Or, for example, think about agricultural producers who have been forced into single cash crop production and increasingly forced to orient themselves towards the external market and export. The more they've been oriented in that way, the more susceptible they've became to the imposition of this kind of domination from the advanced capitalist countries.

Why wouldn't smaller, poorer countries just try to stay independent of a global economy in which the winners are clearly the richer countries?
EMW: This is obviously the toughest question for anybody in these countries to answer. The extent to which economies can withdraw themselves from the global capitalist economy is obviously a matter of huge contention and, frankly, I can't answer it myself. It's really difficult now to imagine a world in which people could be independent and completely autonomous of the global market. But I think that what has happened is that increasingly, through the IMF and so on, these countries have more and more subjected themselves and allowed themselves to be drawn even more into this form of domination, more dependent on foreign capital and finance.

Take Brazil for example. The Brazilians in recent years have liked to talk about their independence or decoupling from the global economy, but in reality, even under the Workers' Party, they've made themselves more dependent on international capital, and some economists far more expert than I am have raised questions about whether this has been wise or even necessary. You might think that an economy as big and potentially autonomous as this could have detached itself much more than it has been prepared to do. Whatever the press is now telling us about the Brazilian recovery from the current crisis, there's ample evidence that they've suffered more from the recession than they needed to do or than they would have done had they not been following IMF principles and made themselves increasingly dependent on the global economy. But I really don't feel qualified to comment on this with any confidence.

You distinguish empires of capital—capitalist imperialism—from at least two other kinds of imperialisms that have existed and to some extent flourished in the past for a time: empires of commerce and empires of property. You regard the Roman Empire and the Spanish Empire in Latin America as conforming to the latter. What defined these empires?

EMW: I selected these two forms of empire and distinguished them from the empire of capital because a focus on property and on commerce are something that we associate with capitalism. I wanted to show that it was possible, and historically did happen, that empires could be property-oriented or could be commercially oriented without being capitalist and without responding to the same capitalist imperatives.

The Roman Empire is probably the first really to be grounded in the acquisition of private property. The reason I called the Roman Empire an empire of property is because, first of all, it was responding to the interests of private propertied classes in ways quite different, for example, from empires like the Chinese, where private property was well developed but where the imperial state was a primary mode of appropriation for officeholders and the main source of great wealth. In the Roman Empire we're talking about property in land as the principal source of power and the empire was constructed on that foundation. The republic that created this empire was basically an oligarchy of propertied classes and it was their interests that were being expressed in imperial expansion. And, in fact, although they created an imperial state, the imperial state never became the primary source of wealth for the ruling classes. Property was always the objective, the sole reliable source of wealth, while the imperial state served as an instrument of appropriation indirectly by protecting and expanding private property. The Roman Empire was basically one big land-grabbing operation.

All the ruling classes enriched themselves big time. They also, to some extent, used imperial land to pacify their own peasant armies, whom they had basically been expropriating at home. But they also effectively created local propertied classes in their colonial territories, even in places where aristocracies of property hadn't existed before. So the empire was in a sense more a coalition of local landed aristocracies than an imperial state.

What empires of commerce, which are based on commerce and trading routes, stand out to you historically?
EMW: Probably the most commercialized empire that ever existed before capitalism was the early modern Dutch Empire. But you can also identify the Arab-Muslim Empire in these terms and, for example, the Venetian and other Italian commercial city-states. The principal reason that I call them noncapitalist is that their commercial success depended on their extra-economic powers, political, military, and so on. I have this complicated argument—and this is obviously very contentious and controversial—about how the Dutch economy, as commercialized as it was, was not driven by capitalist imperatives. It was above all a commercial power, but its commercial successes depended not really on competitive production. Although it did introduce quite a few innovations in production, its main successes had to do, for example, with its naval power, its navigational skills, its extra-economic command of trade routes and its imposition of de facto trade monopolies in various places.

So trade, which would involve buying low and selling high, is not a hallmark of capitalism, which involves a certain kind of competitive production to continually make products faster and better at less cost.
EMW: Right. One way of looking at it is to say that precapitalist commerce depends on fragmented markets. In other words, you buy in one market and sell in another and that's why long-distance trade was the most wealth-creating form of commerce. Whereas an economy driven by truly capitalist imperatives is in effect an integrated market, ideally, in which all producers are subjected to the same competitive imperatives and have to adopt productive strategies to meet those imperatives.

In the case of the Dutch, for example, it's certainly a case of dependence on commerce, in the sense that even Dutch farmers were obliged to enter the market for some of their basic inputs like grain. But the way they achieved their success was to command, for example, the Baltic grain trade and to import cheap grain from relatively low-cost producing areas, while the Dutch farmers themselves were able to move onto semi-luxury goods like dairy products and meat and so on. It was never a question of their competing with cheap low-cost producers. They actually benefited from low-cost production elsewhere. They were able to keep their output prices high and keep their costs low simply by their command of this vast trading system.

Let's turn to the British Empire, which you regard as the first emerging instance of capitalist imperialism. How did capitalism emerge in England? What happened to production and agriculture there?

EMW: It wasn't some single revolutionary moment that brought about capitalism, but what emerged in the English countryside was a distinctive network of agrarian relations in which tenants increasingly held their property on economic leases, not rents fixed by custom, for instance, but rents that varied according to the movements of economic forces. And you had landlords who became increasingly dependent for their wealth on the competitive productiveness of their tenant, rather than on their own superior force, their own coercive power to extract more surpluses. So you had a system in which both appropriators and producers had an interest in increasing the labor productivity, at first by innovative land use and then by technical means, and embarked on this project of what they called "improvement" to increase the productivity of agriculture.

Improvement, the idea of improving uncultivated or poorly cultivated land, was used to justify seizing the land of others, whether in England or Ireland or elsewhere. How did the philosopher John Locke, perhaps the most influential proponent of the concept of improvement, shape Western ideology about the value of property?

EMW: European imperialism was often justified by claiming that unoccupied land was available for appropriation—the so-called *res nullius* principle. This wasn't an uncommon defense of colonial appropriation. But what happens with capitalism, which is absolutely distinctive, and what you get with the capitalist ideology to which Locke contributed so much, is that it isn't simply a question of unoccupied land being available for appropriation. The argument now was that anything which was not being fruitfully and productively used, by the standards of English commercial agriculture, was itself subject to justifiable appropriation. So that applied, for example, to indigenous lands in the Americas where the indigenous people did not improve their land by the standards of English commercial agriculture and did not increase the exchange value of what they produced.

And that's critical: the notion of exchange value is the really essential point. Locke is very explicit about this. He indulges in these calculations about how much of the land's value derives from nature and how much from human labor, and in an improved economy, the value created by labor is maybe 99 percent or something like that. But it soon becomes clear that the essential point isn't labor—the expenditure of effort—but the creation of exchange value; and the point then is that, no matter how much effort may have been expended by the indigenous peoples in America, they weren't actually doing what needs to be done to establish their rights of property, because, in the absence of a well developed commercial economy, they weren't creating value.

And so the production of exchange value becomes effectively the basis of property both domestically and abroad. Now this doesn't mean that once somebody seizes a piece of land and renders it productive, somebody else can come along and claim it on the grounds that they're going to be even more productive. Locke says that we establish a right to property when we mix our labor with something. But you have to follow the argument a bit further than that, because it isn't just a question of our mixing our labor with something that gives us a right to property. What establishes property is adding to its commercial value by rendering it more productive.

That created a whole new justification for empire, although I have to say that Locke wasn't the first one to think of it. There's a fascinating document, which I refer to in my book, by one of the architects of British imperialism in Ireland, a lawyer named Sir John Davies, who decades earlier than Locke justified seizing Irish land by arguing that the Irish themselves were not really using the land because they weren't improving the land. Not that they weren't cultivating it, because they obviously were, so it wasn't just a question of unoccupied or uncultivated land being open to appropriation. But they simply weren't improving it, they weren't increasing its exchange value sufficiently, so the English were entitled to claim it. And it became the objective of English imperialism in Ireland to transform Irish property relations in such a way that they could try to reproduce the effects of English agrarian capitalism—until of course Ireland itself threatened to become a competitor and then they started obstructing Irish development. But that's another story.

How do you regard the British Empire in India in light of your contentions about territorial empire and the imperatives of British early capitalism?
EMW: The British were never able to transport their social property relations to their empire in the way that they tried to do in Ireland. In the case of India you had a prosperous highly developed economy operating on its own principles, which were not about to be transformed in a direction that would have suited the British. But the British did hope to be able to just derive great advantages from it as a commercial resource. And for a while they were capable of doing that, especially through the East India Company. But increasingly the state rather than the East India Company got drawn into the process, because to defend their commercial preëminence in India they were being increasingly drawn into military adventures to keep order and this meant being increasingly drawn into a territorial kind of empire. Partly this was because the East India Company itself wasn't operating on what might be called capitalist prin-

ciples. The East India Company had become a revenue-extracting instrument. People like Edmund Burke in England, who was quite critical of the way the empire was being conducted and of the East India Company, said that they simply weren't operating on commercial principles.

So the state, ironically, was drawn into dominating the empire, not just to get its share of the revenues, but in order to get it to operate on commercial principles that would suit the British. And this produced a territorial imperative. The empire increasingly became what you might call a military dictatorship. And I would argue that in the long run this represented a contradiction.

There's a lot of debate about the extent to which India was profitable for the British and I can't possibly settle the question of whether it was profitable or more of a drag on British resources. But I do think that there was a fundamental contradiction between, on the one hand, the attempt just to derive commercial advantage from it, and, on the other hand, the increasingly territorial and military nature of the empire. So I could easily be persuaded that in the long run it really wasn't as profitable as they would have liked it to be, even as profitable as it may have been for some individuals engaged in the empire. I think in the long run, a very persuasive argument could be made, and in fact has been made, that in the long run it was more of a drag than a benefit, precisely because of the cost of this kind of territorial empire. And that's why I say that the American empire is the first truly capitalist empire, because the British were not able to pull it off. They weren't able to govern their empire by economic means, whereas the Americans have come closer to doing that than anyone else has ever done.

In capitalist markets, where labor is exchanged in the market without any overt coercion, people are supposed to be free and equal. What impact did the identification of capitalism with freedom and equality have on the rationale for subordinating certain people as slaves?
EMW: The first point obviously is that even though capitalism is conventionally defined in terms of wage labor, that didn't prevent it from making use of slave labor at certain moments in its history. There's a lot to be said about how capitalism has exploited slavery and, conversely, how slavery was shaped by capitalist imperatives, which didn't exist in earlier forms of slavery.

I think that it's possible to argue that the extreme racism that was associated with slavery in the United States, an extreme kind of racism that didn't exist in the same way in ancient slave societies, has to do partly with the fact that the ideology of capitalism, which argues that all human beings are contractual equals, found it difficult to deal with a situation in which people were transparently not legally equal. And so one justification for this anomaly was simply to write a whole section of people out of the human race. It was possible to say all humans are equal, but these people in effect were not human—or, in milder forms of so-called cultural racism, that they were perennial children, who could never rise to the level of adult responsibilities and rights.

As you just mentioned, one of capitalism's central characteristics is the prevalence of wage labor where non-economic forms of coercion are not necessary. How, then, should we understand systems of coercion under capitalism, such as apartheid in South Africa?

EMW: I should emphasize first that for me, as I said at the beginning of the interview, the defining characteristic of capitalism is the market dependence of the main economic actors. Of course wage labor is the market dependence of laboring classes taken to its ultimate and extreme conclusion. But market dependence, and the subjection of people to market imperatives, can happen—and historically has happened—short of the proletarianization of labor. Direct producers like those tenants on economic leases I talked about before were market dependent and compelled to respond to market imperatives. In fact, the emergence of a large force of dispossessed workers obliged to sell their labor power for a wage was historically the result rather than the cause of those market imperatives, as competitive pressures, and also landlords responding to those pressures, forced many small producers off the land.

The second point I would emphasize is that, as I said about slavery, capitalism has made use of various kinds of dependent labor, in various ways. We have to make a distinction between, on the one hand, the basic conditions, the social property relations that create those market imperatives I keep talking about and, on the other hand, how those market imperatives can be imposed on various kinds of labor, not just capitalist wage labor. In the early days of capitalist development in the U.S., for instance, southern planters were inserted into a growing capitalist economy and a world market, and—though there's still debate about this—they, at least for a time, successfully exploited slave labor in response to those economic imperatives. It would take too long here to consider how and why the employment of slave labor became less viable in the context of a capitalist economy, but the point is that capitalism could and did make use of it, as it can and does make use of other forms of extra-economic dependence and coercion. Capitalism wouldn't be capitalism if the basic relations of market dependence didn't prevail and impose their requirements on the economy in general; but this doesn't mean that those imperatives can't act on other forms of labor than wage labor or that various forms of extra-economic oppression—whatever happens to be available in any given historical context—can't be exploited to respond to market imperatives.

Of course, wage labor has the distinct advantage that it doesn't require constant extra-economic coercion, constant political or military oppression and vigilance. Economic compulsions are enough to make the workers sell their labor power for a wage and, in normal conditions, to keep on working and producing capital. So, whatever economic benefits capital can derive from forms of oppression like apartheid in the right historical conditions, those economic benefits can't survive changing political conditions, like the powerful anti-apartheid resistance. And it's no surprise that big capital in South Africa decided it wasn't worth preserving the system.

In the twentieth century, and specifically after the Second World War, you suggest that capitalist imperialism emerged in a mature form.
EMW: Yes. I think that it was not before the end of the Second World War that it actually emerged in a mature form. What you get is a two-pronged strategy on the part of the Americans, which on the one hand establishes economic hegemony through the Bretton Woods system, in which the U.S. effectively set the conditions of economic development throughout the world, and on the other hand, the U.S. establishes itself as the overwhelming superior military power during the war, capped off by dropping the bombs in Hiroshima and Nagasaki towards the end of the war.

So you have this two-pronged strategy, which has effectively been pursued from then until now. So you might want to ask, what's the connection between this economic hegemony and the military? If the United States is depending on economic hegemony in a way that an ideal capitalist imperialism should do, why does it need this massive military power? Well, it's a curious thing. In earlier forms of imperialism, the purpose of military power was pretty obvious. If you were out to capture territory or to defeat imperial rivals, it's clear why you needed an overwhelming military power. But if you're trying to establish hegemony over the world by means of your economic power, then why is it necessary to have the most hugely superior dominant military power the world has ever known? I think that here we come to an important anomaly in the capitalist imperialism that we've been seeing.

I don't think it's just a matter of the U.S. building up its military power just to compensate for its declining economic power—though that's certainly part of it. What I've been arguing is that capitalist imperialism operates by means of economic power, which is more or less separate from political, military, and legal power. In other words, unlike the feudal lord who depends on his military, legal, and political powers to extract surpluses from the peasant, the capitalist supposedly doesn't. And that makes it possible for capitalist power to extend far beyond the reach of any political or legal or military power. But this doesn't mean that capitalists don't need the support of political and military powers to maintain the conditions of capital accumulation. The trouble is that there is a growing disparity between the global scope of capitalist economic power and the more local powers of administration and coercion that it still needs.

I simply don't buy the argument that we've been getting from globalization theoreticians and from people like Hardt and Negri that the more global the economy becomes, the less relevant the nation-state is. I think the contrary is true. The global economy is being managed through the medium of the global state system. I think what's really characteristic of globalization is the growing disparity between the global reach of capitalist economic domination and the persistence of the territorial state which it still needs, because capital needs an orderly, predictable legal and administrative apparatus more than any other social form has ever done.

We shouldn't be fooled by capital's constant whining about government interference and regulation. Capital accumulation, especially because the capitalist market itself is so anarchic, is a very demanding process that needs lots of legal, political, and administrative order, as long as it's capital friendly; and in the foreseeable future, it's impossible to imagine that this kind of close legal and administrative regulation is possible on a global scale. So I don't foresee the day when capital will be able to organize the world without the aid of territorial states. But of course once you acknowledge that capital still needs this system of multiple states and that the political form of globalization isn't a global state, but a global system of multiple states, you can see that it creates some real possibilities of instability.

In other words, you believe that these local states, these poorer countries where the U.S. is trying to exert its economic hegemony, aren't necessarily going to remain loyal to its cause.

EMW: That's right. The point is, though, the U.S. needs their states to organize an orderly global economy. The U.S. depends on them all to do that. And the capitalist power, the imperialist power, is constrained by that dependence. It can't be going to war with every one of these powers or trying to coerce them by military means, because that would upset the whole climate for capital accumulation. So it has to find ways of imposing this coercion to keep these states in line without depriving them of their capacity for organizing the world for global capital. And this is a real problem for capital and a real weakness, I think, in the long run. It creates whole new spaces for opposition.

What I think has happened—especially under Bush, though the thinking behind it has forerunners as least as far back as Ronald Reagan—is that in dealing with this contradiction, the United States has adopted a military doctrine which justifies permanent war very often without any specific objectives, a kind of infinite war, a war without end, in purpose or in time. The Rumsfeld, Wolfowitz, and Perle crowd surrounding Bush actually devised a plan they themselves called "Operation Infinite War"; and for them one of the principal functions of war, as they understood it, was the so-called demonstration effect, where you show your massive military superiority without really seeking any particular objective in the way that old imperialist powers did with their military force. You're not necessarily seeking a specific territory, but you want to create a cautionary atmosphere by means of this demonstration effect: shock and awe. I think that what happened in Iraq was not just a question of the most obvious impulse to control the oil supply. It was also just to shock and awe the world, not least Iran.

The U.S. doctrine of demonstrating enormous military capability and a willingness to use it, in order to deter efforts or any temptation to think about contesting or equaling U.S. military power—would you say that this is directed at both "rogue states" and industrialized states that have been longtime U.S. allies?

EMW: Absolutely, but the problem with capitalist competition is that it's not like inter-imperialist rivalry of the traditional kind. I mean, if you're fighting over trade routes, you go and you conquer your rival and the objective is pretty clear. But you don't have that luxury in advanced capitalism because you need your competitors' markets as much as you're endangered by their competition. So you have to find a new way of controlling allies which doesn't at the same time undermine your own economic power. It has been a longstanding policy of the United States to demonstrate that it is the overwhelming supreme military power which is hardly worth trying to challenge or even to match. And if the truth be told, other major capitalist states have generally ceded that supremacy to the U.S.—something you couldn't imagine in old inter-imperialist rivalries.

Some commentators have argued that the doctrine of perpetual war represented a clear break from prior U.S. policy, that U.S. empire has taken a new turn. Is there any truth in such claims?

EMW: Well, it's very tempting to say that it does represent a huge break because these people were so extreme, it's hard to find any comparison in the recent past, not just in foreign policy but on the domestic level where they introduced restrictions on civil liberties in ways that were not only reminiscent of the Cold War but perhaps in some respects even worse. So on that front there obviously were certain discontinuities from the recent past, and the ostensible territorial occupation of Iraq does suggest that they were reverting to an older form of territorial imperialism, but I've already discussed why I don't think that was their objective.

So despite the extent to which they took their doctrine to unmatched extremes, you can't make sense out of what they were doing if you don't consider what went before. For example, that two-pronged strategy that I talked about before, that's been in place since the Second World War: on the one hand, economic domination, through the control of a global commercial and financial systems, and on the other hand, its absolutely overwhelming and unmatchable military power. There's no way that Bush could have done what he did if those forms of dominance hadn't been a longstanding objective, if the construction of this overwhelming military power hadn't already been in place. I think that the logic of the American empire and the contradictions that I've been trying to explain that prevail in it are longstanding, at least since the Second World War. You might say that Bush followed it to its ultimate and irrational extremes, but it doesn't make sense unless you see it against the background of what went before.

Where would you situate U.S. empire under Obama?
EMW: It's a really tough question where we should situate Obama in relation to his predecessors. I have no doubt that he's sincere in his more progressive rhetoric, as far as it goes, and he's certainly not George Bush. But it's not clear to me that his view of the world and the place of the U.S. in it marks as much of a break as he no doubt genuinely believes it is. We should probably listen to the alarm bells set off by his domestic economic policies and the extent to which they tread the Wall Street line or by the people in his administration who belong to that milieu. Or, for that matter, the healthcare reform fiasco and the ways it was driven by the interests of insurance companies; I don't think that can be blamed entirely on Congress. So why should we be confident that Obama's foreign policy and his attitude to war will represent a sharper break from his predecessors? Two wars don't inspire much confidence. I'm sure he believes what he says about the doctrine of "just war," which he invoked in his Nobel speech. The trouble is that this doctrine is notoriously flexible, and it's been invoked for centuries by some pretty rapacious imperial powers.

One thing you could maybe say is that Bush was so beyond the pale that even this flexible doctrine wasn't flexible enough for him. I mean, the doctrine of just war, in all its traditional versions, required some idea of finite ends and means and some proportionality between them, and it's impossible to apply those principles to a doctrine of infinite war, war without limits in time or geography. How far Obama has moved away from this is hard to say, but at least he invokes those principles of ends and means, and he may have some sense of limits—maybe like Colin Powell did with his Powell Doctrine, alone in the Bush administration.

Obama has supposedly been strongly influenced by the theologian Reinhold Niebuhr and what's known as Christian realism, which acknowledges the tragedies of war but recognizes its occasional necessity. But one interesting thing about Obama is that he seems far less concerned than Niebuhr was about the arrogance, the hubris, of U.S. power, which Niebuhr explicitly warned against. If you're going to argue that war is sometimes necessary to combat evil, a lot, of course, depends on what you think is evil, and there's always been a temptation for U.S. presidents to think that what's bad for the U.S.—or U.S. capital—is by definition evil. The other side of that coin has been to believe that what the U.S. regards as good should be imposed on everyone, everywhere. That kind of arrogant moralism can always be a dangerous thing, but, of course, it's even more dangerous when a state has the military power to act on it. I'm not convinced that Obama has strayed very far from that course. He certainly isn't about to give up the military supremacy of the U.S., any more than what's left of its financial dominance; and he isn't, after all, just acknowledging that its military dominance should make the U.S. state more, rather than less, cautious about using its power. I'm afraid he really buys into the view that the U.S. does and should lead the world and sometimes, even if reluctantly and conscious of the tragedy of war, impose its ideas of good and evil by military means.

I'd like to turn to the ways in which earlier Marxist thinkers have thought about imperialism and tried to describe its contours. You point out that we are now in a world of universal capitalism—that capitalism reaches all over the globe in a way that perhaps Marxist theoreticians might not have anticipated.

EMW: I wouldn't say that Marx didn't foresee the universalization of capitalism, but he actually never talked much about it. He gave us a vivid conception of its expansive qualities already in *The Communist Manifesto*. You get a sense of its incredible powers of expansion. But he himself was primarily interested in exploring the internal logic of the system. So in *Capital* he uses as his model the most advanced capitalist economy, Britain, and constructs a theory of the internal logic of capitalism.

But his successors did get more interested in the external relations of capitalism and the assumption that they all seemed to make was that capitalism never would become so universal. It required noncapitalist entities to exploit, and capitalist powers would engage in wars with their imperial rivals for control of those noncapitalist areas. But somehow you never get a theory which takes account of the universalization of capitalist imperatives as the dominant imperial form, and that's where we are today.

Are the theories of Lenin and Rosa Luxemburg, which were written during the classic age of imperialism at the turn of the last century—at a time when capitalist social relations were incipient or had not taken hold in most of the world—still valid?

EMW: They're obviously important to build on. I wouldn't say that they're lacking in validity. They're just incomplete, you might say. They give us a very good account of the exploitative character of capitalist power and its need to extend its exploitation on a global scale. I don't see how they could have at that stage envisaged a situation in which the capitalist imperatives are the principal mode of domination throughout the globe. This isn't to say that prosperous capitalism exists everywhere—on the contrary—but the capitalist powers do exercise their domination by means of manipulating these economic imperatives of capitalism and that's become the dominant form of imperial domination. And we don't really have a theory for that.

You write in *Empire of Capital* that this current form of imperial domination, while it may appear all-powerful to some, is potentially quite vulnerable. And the vulnerability stems to some degree from global capitalism operating through a system of multiple states.

EMW: One way of looking at it is to contrast my argument with the arguments made by Hardt and Negri. They suggest that we're now in a situation where empire is everywhere and nowhere. "There is no place of empire" is how they put it, and they themselves tell you what the political implications of their arguments are. And if you think about it, it's very politically disabling, because they say we don't really have visible concentrations of capitalist power and visible targets, that's effectively what they're saying, because capitalist power is everywhere and nowhere. That means, they say, that you can't really create an oppositional force in the form of a counter-power, and that's why working class movements and socialist parties and so on are basically a total irrelevance. Now opposition can only take the form of some mystical force and transformation of subjectivities, or whatever it is, but a counter-power to visible concentrations of capitalist power is no longer a possibility, according to them.

Well, I'm arguing just the opposite. I'm saying that there are indeed visible concentrations of capitalist power, that the territorial state may be more than ever the point of concentration of capitalist power, that global capital needs the power of the state, and depends on this global system of multiple states. And that means that, although obviously oppositional forces in the main imperial powers will be the most effective, nevertheless other territorial states have their own leverage too because the system is so dependent on them.

The reason I say that the state is perhaps more than ever the point of concentration of capitalist powers is because, if you think about it, global capital—capital itself—can't organize globalization. It just can't do it. It doesn't do it and it depends on states to do it for them. So its dependence on this form of territorial and localized power is a vulnerability and it creates direct targets for opposition in a way that hasn't existed for a very long time.

CHAPTER TWO

David Harvey: The Rise of Neoliberalism and the Riddle of Capital

Neoliberalism has left its indelible mark on our world for more than three decades. How would you define neoliberalism?

DH: There are two things to be said. One is, if you like, the theory of neoliberalism, and the other is its practice. And they are rather different from each other. But the theory takes the view that individual liberty and freedom are the high point of civilization and then goes on to argue that individual liberty and freedom can best be protected and achieved by an institutional structure, made up of strong private property rights, free markets, and free trade: a world in which individual initiative can flourish. The implication of that is that the state should not be involved in the economy too much, but it should use its power to preserve private property rights and the institutions of the market and promote those on the global stage if necessary.

What are the intellectual origins of neoliberal thought?

DH: Liberal theory goes back a very long way, of course, to the eighteenth century: John Locke, Adam Smith, and writers of that sort. Then economics changed quite a bit towards the end of the nineteenth century and neoliberalism is a really revival of the eighteenth century liberal doctrine about freedoms and individual liberties connected to a very specific view of the market. And the leading figures in that are Milton Friedman in this country and Friedrich Hayek in Austria. In 1947 they formed a society to promote neoliberal values called the Mont Pelerin Society. It was a minor society but it got a lot of support from wealthy contributors and corporations to polemicize on the ideas it held.

Did this group see their role as promoters of these ideas in the political realm?

DH: They took the view that state interventions and state domination were something to be feared. And they weren't only talking about fascism and communism; they were also talking about the strong welfare state constructions that were then emerging in Europe in the postwar period and also talking about any kind of government intervention into how the market was working. They saw their role as very political, not only against fascism and communism but also against the power of the state, and particularly against the power of the social democratic state in Europe.

The welfare state was characterized by a compact of sorts between labor and capital, the idea of a social safety net, the commitment to full employment—you call this "embedded liberalism." Up until the 1970s it was supported by most elites. Why was there a backlash against the welfare state and the push for a new political economic order in the 1970s that gave rise to the political implementation of neoliberal thought?
DH: I think there were two main reasons for the backlash. The first was that the high growth rates that had characterized the embedded liberalism of the 1950s and 1960s—we had growth rates of around 4 percent during those years—those growth rates disappeared towards the end of the 1960s. That had a lot to do with the stresses within the U.S. economy, where the U.S. was trying to fight a war in Vietnam and resolve social problems at home. It was what we call a guns-and-butter strategy.

But that led to fiscal difficulties in the United States. The United States started printing dollars, we had inflation, then we had stagnation, and then global stagnation set in, in the 1970s. It was clear that the system that had worked very well in the 1950s and much of the 1960s was coming untacked and had to be constructed along some other lines. The other issue which is not so obvious, but the data I think show it very clearly, is that the incomes and assets of the elite classes were severely stressed in the 1970s. And therefore there was a sort of class revolt on the part of the elites, who suddenly found themselves in some considerable difficulty, for economic as well as for political reasons. The 1970s was, if you like, a moment of revolutionary transformation of economies away from the embedded liberalism of the postwar period to neoliberalism, which was really set in motion in the 1970s and consolidated in the 1980s and 1990s.

What do you think was the underlying reason for the falling rate of profit in the 1970s, the symptoms of which you've just described?
DH: There were a number of other reasons connected with it. The postwar compromise had certainly empowered labor and labor organizations and therefore labor contracts were relatively favorable for those who were in the privileged unions and again that put certain stresses in the system. That is, if wages go up, profits tend to go down. So there was an element of that in the situation in the 1970s as well. In many ways the neoliberal argument that the labor market should be flexible and open and free of any union constraints became very appealing in the 1970s, as you can imagine.

The intellectual fathers—and I think they were primarily fathers—of neoliberalism clustered around monetarist Milton Friedman at the University of Chicago had a chance to put their ideas into action following the U.S.-backed coup against the Socialist Allende government in Chile in 1973. What's your assessment of this first application of neoliberalism to a country's economy? DH: This arose after the coup against the Socialist, democratically elected government under Salvador Allende, and Pinochet and the others were faced with the dilemma of how to reconstruct the economy along lines that would revive it. For a couple of years they didn't know what to do, and then Pinochet turned to a business elite in Chile that had been very important in the coup and who had established relationships with economists who were Chilean but who had been trained in Chicago under Milton Friedman. Those economists came into government in 1975 and completely restructured the government under neoliberal lines, which meant privatization of all state assets except— in the Chilean case—copper, opening the country to foreign investment, not preventing any repatriation of profits out of the country. So it just opened the country to foreign capital and opened everything to the privatization, including, interestingly in the Chilean case, the privatization of social security, which we have been hearing about in this country over the last year.

What were the consequences for both the Chilean people and the accumulation of capital in Chile following those reforms? DH: It went very well for a few years and then ran into serious problems in 1982. But when I say it went very well, it went very well for the political and economic elite. It was one of those situations where the country seemed to do well, but the people were doing very badly because of course after the coup all labor organizations had been destroyed, all social welfare structures had been dismantled. For the general population things did not go very well, but for elite they went very well, and for foreign investors things went very well for few years. And then they ran into a serious crisis and it was at that point that they started to realize that neoliberal theory in its pure form didn't necessarily work that well. And there were some major adjustments that occurred in the theory after that, which led into a different kind of neoliberalization practice.

A second example of the application of at least some of the ideas associated with neoliberalism came about in New York City in the mid-1970s, which then provided critical lessons for neoliberalism. What were the roots of New York City's fiscal crisis, and how was it resolved, as it were? DH: In the New York case, the city was heavily indebted for a variety of reasons, which are rather complicated to go into. And at a certain point in 1975, the investment bankers in the city decided not to roll over the debt, that is, they decided not to fund New York City debt any more. Now, I don't think this was an application of neoliberal theory; I think it was the way in which the investment bankers were beginning to think about the city. And it was a kind of major experiment, in which the investment bankers took over the budgetary structure of the city. It was a financial coup as opposed to a military coup. And they then ran the city the way they wanted to do it and the principles they arrived at was that New York City revenues should be earmarked so that the bondholders were paid off first and then whatever was left over would go to the city budget. The result of that was that the city had to lay off a lot workers, had to cut back on municipal expenditures, had to close schools and hospital services, and also had to make user charges on an institution like CUNY, which up until that point was tuition-free.

What the bankers did was to discipline the city along ways which I think they didn't have a full theory for, but they discovered neoliberalism through their practice. And after they had discovered it, they said, ah yes, this is the way in which we should go in general. And of course this then became the way that Reagan went and then it became, if you like, the standard way the International Monetary Fund starts to discipline countries that run into debt around the world.

You argue that a major shift in political economic practices, such as neoliberalism, could not come about—at least in democracies like the U.S. and United Kingdom—without some degree of consent, not just from traditional elites but also the middle classes. How was this consent engendered in the 1970s?
DH: There was a concerted program that worked at a number of levels. To me, the beginning point was a memo that Lewis Powell, who became a Supreme Court justice shortly afterwards, sent to the American Chamber of Commerce in 1971. What he said, in effect, was that the anti-business climate in this country has gone too far, we need a collective effort to try to turn it around. After that we see the formation of a whole set of think tanks, the massing of money by various organizations to try to influence public policy and to do it through the media, do it through think tanks. We also see the formation in 1972 of something called the Business Roundtable, which was a very influential organization. They were very concerned to try to roll back that legislation which had emerged during the 1960s and early 1970s that set up things like the Environmental Protection Agency, OSHA, consumer protection, and all of those sorts of things.

And of course they gained considerable influence in the press through the *Wall Street Journal* and business pages and business schools and the like, and through their think tanks they started to influence public opinion. But then they also needed to be able to get a hold of the political process. This was a very interesting process where the Political Action Committees that got set up in the 1970s were very active and there was a tremendous formation of them and they started to get together collectively to fund the Republican Party.

So what we see is the corporate takeover of the Republic Party along neo-liberal lines, conservative lines, rather than the liberal Republicans like the Rockefellers, who were the old-style Republicans. There was a takeover by Reagan and people like that in the 1970s of the Republican Party. But then the Republican Party needed a mass base and one of the things that then happened was that they turned to the Christian Right. Remember it was Jerry Falwell in 1978 who formed the Moral Majority. There was a coalition that then emerged, a popular base amongst the evangelical Christians on the one hand and then tremendous corporate funding of the political process on the other hand, which made the Republican Party solidly behind the neoliberal agenda.

You posit that a fundamental feature of neoliberalism is the disciplining and disempowerment of the working class. Paul Volcker, who headed up the Federal Reserve first under Carter and then under Reagan, played a pivotal role in doing this in the United States. What were the conditions in the U.S. in the 1970s—the array of class forces, so to speak, at that time—and how did Paul Volcker help shift the balance of power?
DH: There had been, during the late 1960s and throughout the 1970s, a steady process of deindustrialization, that is, the loss of manufacturing jobs. It was a slow process and in many areas of the country that process was held back by an increase in public expenditures. This was true, for instance, in New York City. Manufacturing jobs had been drained away but public service jobs were booming. And that meant that public funding was needed for that.

The federal government—the Federal Reserve—had a policy that full employment was a very worthwhile, very important objective of public policy. What Paul Volcker did in 1979 was to reverse that, to say, we're no longer interested in full employment; what we're interested in is control of inflation. He brought inflation down quite savagely in about three or four years, but in the process he generated massive unemployment. And massive unemployment of course was disempowering for workers and at the same time the deindustrialization that I mentioned accelerated. So there was quite a massive loss of industrial jobs, manufacturing jobs, in the early 1980s.

And of course that means less union power. If you close down the shipyards and the steel industry lays off people, then you have fewer people in the unions. The loss of jobs in the unionized sector disempowered the unions at the same time unemployment was rising. Unemployment disciplines the labor force to accept lower-paying jobs if necessary. So Volcker's shift away from full employment strategy at the Federal Reserve to control inflation, no matter what the impact on unemployment, was a major shift in public policy and which we still implement.

That war against unionized employment was spearheaded in the UK by Prime Minister Margaret Thatcher, whose Conservative Party came to power in May of 1979. Thatcher famously said, "there is no such thing as society, only individual men and women." How did elites respond to the power of unions prior to Thatcher?

DH: The unions in Britain, of course, were very strong and there was a very large public sector. Embedded liberalism in Britain involved the nationalization of coal, steel, transportation, telecommunications, and the all rest of it. The unions were relatively strong in the 1970s but again there was a lot of economic pressure in Britain and it ran into very serious problems in the mid-1970s. The Labour government really didn't have a good way to solve them. So the Labour government started to push for austerity in the public sector. The result of that was a huge wave of public sector strikes in 1978 and that created considerable discontent in the country in general. Margaret Thatcher came to power with a mandate really to control union power, and that is what is what she effectively did by an almost pure neoliberal strategy.

Most famously, of course, she took on the most powerful union in British history, both politically and sentimentally, which is the miners' union. There was a huge strike in 1984, which she fought through to victory for herself. That was, if you like, the beginning of the end of the real strong power of the labor movement. After that she privatized steel, she privatized automobiles, she privatized coal mining, she privatized pretty much everything in the British economy at some point. She wanted to privatize national health, but she never managed quite to do that.

She also attacked municipal government, which was a stronghold of the left in the UK.

DH: She faced significant opposition to her program by the fact that most of the large city governments were controlled by the Labour Party. And the Labour Party was not going to play ball with her program at that level. So when she started to cut funds to the local municipalities, what they did was to increase the local taxation and still keep their programs in place. What she then did was to cap the amount of local taxation they could take and that way she was involved in this huge struggle with Labour governments. In Liverpool, for example, the council there refused to cap their expenditures or their taxes and she had to have them put in jail for disobeying the national law. So there was a huge struggle on a municipal level. Eventually she reformed—tried to reform—all local finances around something called the poll tax and there was again huge resistance to this, so there was struggling going on over municipal financing in Britain in the 1980s under Margaret Thatcher as she tried to impose her will on recalcitrant municipal governments.

You see the years 1979 to 1980 as a key period for the ascendancy of neoliberalism. The Volcker shock that you spoke of earlier and the rise of Margaret Thatcher took place during this time. Another crucial event took place around those years, in 1978 in fact: the Chinese Communist Party under the leadership of Deng Xiaoping embarked on a path of economic liberalization that ultimately massively transformed the Chinese economy. You argue this event was connected in its own way to the rise of neoliberalism. How so?

DH: I think what we have to look at here is a concordance of events. It's hard to see the reforms in China were triggered by events in Britain or events in the United States. Nevertheless, the liberalization in China set China off into a market-based kind of socialism, which then found a way to integrate into the global economy in ways that I think would not have been possible in the 1950s or 1960s. Because neoliberalization, insofar as it opens up the market, globally as well as within nations, insofar as it did that, it gave the Chinese an opportunity to suddenly venture into the global market in ways that could not easily be controlled from elsewhere. I think the reforms in China were initially meant to try to empower China in relationship to what was going on in Taiwan, Hong Kong, Singapore. The Chinese were very aware of these developments and wanted to compete in some ways with those economies.

Initially, I don't think the Chinese wanted to develop an export-led economy, but what their reforms led to was the opening up of industrial capacity in many parts of China, which then found themselves able to market their commodities on the world stage, because they had very cheap labor, very good technology, and a reasonably educated labor force. Suddenly the Chinese found themselves moving into this global economy, and, as they did so, they gained much more in terms of foreign direct investment, so suddenly China started getting involved in this neoliberalization process. Whether it was by accident or design, I don't really know, but it certainly has made a huge difference to how the global economy is working.

What was the chain of events that helped facilitate the process of developing countries becoming beholden to institutions like the IMF and the

World Bank which dictated neoliberal policies—starting with the OPEC oil crisis of the early 1970s and the petrodollars that were produced by those countries in the Middle East that had oil?

DH: There's a very interesting story to be told about that and I'm not sure it has been fully elaborated upon yet. With the OPEC oil price hike in 1973, a vast amount of money was being accumulated by the Saudis and other Gulf states. And then the big question was: well, what's going to happen to that money? Now, we do know that the U.S. government was very anxious that that money be brought back to New York, to be circulated back into the global economy via the New York investment banks, and persuaded the Saudis to do that. Why the Saudis were persuaded to do it remains a bit of a mystery. We know from British intelligence sources that the U.S. was actually prepared to invade Saudi Arabia in 1973, but whether the Saudis were told: recycle the money through New York or you get invaded . . . who knows?

Now, the New York investment banks then had vast amounts of money. Where were they going to invest it? The economy wasn't doing very well at all in 1974–75, as, all over, it was in depression. Citibank head Walter Wriston came up with the comment that the safest place to invest the money is in countries, because countries can't disappear—you always know where they are. And so they started to make the money available to many countries like Argentina, Mexico—Latin America was very popular—but also places like Poland even. They lent a lot of money to those countries.

That worked out quite well for a while, but then in 1982 there was this general fiscal crisis, particularly after Volcker had raised the interest rate. What this meant was that the Mexicans who had borrowed money at 5 percent were now having to pay it back at 16 percent or 17 percent, and they found they couldn't do it. Mexico was about to go bankrupt in 1982. That was the point at which neoliberalism kicked in. The U.S. via the International Monetary Fund and the U.S. Treasury said: we'll bail you out, but we'll bail you out on condition that you start to privatize and open up the country to foreign investment and start to adopt a neoliberal stance. Initially the Mexicans really didn't do that very much, but by the time you get to 1988 they start to do it sort of big time.

But here's the interesting thing: it's unreasonable to think that actually the U.S. imposed neoliberalization on Mexico. What happened was that the U.S. was putting neoliberalizing pressures on Mexico and an elite inside of Mexico seized the opportunity to say: yes, that's what we want. So it was a coalition between the elite in Mexico and the U.S. Treasury/IMF that put together the kind of neoliberalization package that came to Mexico in the late 1980s. And actually, if you look at the pattern, it's very rare for there to be a straight imposition of neoliberalizing policies through the IMF or the U.S. It's nearly always an alliance between an internal elite, as it had been in Chile, and U.S. forces that put this thing together. And it's the internal elite who are as much to blame for neoliberalization as the international institutions.

That point turns on its head many of the assumptions the left tends to make about neoliberalism being imposed on countries solely by the United States. One of the cases where this also was illustrated was Sweden, which had one of the most socialistic welfare states, and where ruling elites forced through neoliberal policies.

DH: There was a really serious threat to the ownership structure in Sweden during the 1970s. In effect, there was a proposal to buy out ownership entirely and turn it into a sort of worker-owned democracy. The political elites in Sweden were horrified by this and fought a tremendous battled against it. The way they fought was partly, again, through ideological mechanisms. The bankers controlled the Nobel Prize in economics, that went to Hayek, that went to Friedman, that went to all the neoliberal figures to try to give legitimacy to all the neoliberal arguments. But then also the Swedes organized themselves as a confederacy of industrial magnates, organized themselves, built think tanks and the like.

And every time there was any kind of crisis or difficulty in the Swedish economy, and all of these economies run into difficulties at some point or other, they would really push the argument: the problem is the strength of the welfare state, it's the huge expenditures of the welfare state. But they never actually managed to make it work too well. So they came up with the interesting strategy of going into the European Union, because the European Union had a very neoliberal structure—through the Maastricht Treaty. So the Swedish Confederation persuaded everyone they should go into Europe, and then it was the European rules that allowed the more neoliberal policies to be introduced into Sweden in the 1990s. It hasn't gone very far in Sweden because the unions are still very strong and the political history is very strong over social democracy and the like. But, nevertheless, there has been a process towards a limited neoliberalization in Sweden as a result of the activities of these political elites and their strategy of taking Sweden into Europe.

You argue that neoliberalism plays two roles: either to restore high rates of profitability for capitalism or to restore the power of the capitalist ruling class. Could you explain that distinction and why they don't necessarily go together, as one might think?

DH: The first burst of neoliberalization in the 1970s and early 1980s occurred in a situation of very low rates of capital accumulation, and therefore the general argument was made that we need to change the way the economy is organized in order to get growth back on track. That was the general argument that was made. Now, the difficulty was, that actually the first part of the Reagan administration was in serious economic crisis, Margaret Thatcher didn't do very well in terms of transforming the economy there, and as I mentioned in the Chilean case, things didn't work out too well in Chile either by the time you get to the early 1980s.

Neoliberalism was not doing very well in its pure form, in terms of regenerating capital accumulation, but what it was doing very well was redistributing wealth towards the upper classes. You see in all of the data now that from the late 1970s onwards, those countries that turned towards neoliberalization actually achieved tremendous increases in the wealth of the elites. In this country, for example, the top 1 percent tripled its share of the national income from about 1970 to say 2000. Mexico was another case where in a short period after neoliberalization, suddenly fourteen or so people appeared on the Forbes billionaires list globally—suddenly billionaires erupted in Mexico. The market shock therapy that was given to Russia after the collapse of the wall ended up with seven oligarchs controlling about 50 percent of the economy.

So wherever neoliberalization moves, you see this tremendous concentration of wealth and power occurring in the top echelons. It actually occurs in the very, very top echelons—in the 0.01 percent. For instance, there was a little piece in the *New York Times* that said: what's happened to the four hundred richest people in this country over the past twenty years? And it turns out they were worth $600 million apiece in constant dollars back in about 1985 and they are now worth something like $2.8 billion. They have quadrupled their wealth over this period. What neoliberalization has been very good at is restoring or reconstituting class power in a very narrow band of the political economic elite.

In *A Brief History of Neoliberalism* you maintain that neoliberalism functions by redistributing wealth, as you've just said, rather than generating it in the first place, what you call "capital accumulation by dispossession" rather than accumulation by the expansion of wage labor. What are some of the forms that accumulation by dispossession can take?
DH: Accumulation by dispossession is, to me, a very important concept. And it doesn't simply apply in the periphery of the global capitalist economy. For example, in Mexico, the reform of the land system there, privatizing land, has forced many peasants off the land. The result is the land has gone into few people's hands. So you get concentration of wealth and power in agriculture in Mexico going on very fast and the creation of a landless proletariat as

a result. Now, in this country we have analogous things going on in terms of what's happening to family farming. That lot of family farmers can no longer make it and they're being taken over by agribusiness. One of the mechanisms there, of course, is through indebtedness, that people borrow, they get into debt, they can't pay off their debts, and in the end they have to sell out sometimes at rock bottom prices.

Accumulation by dispossession takes many local forms. I think, for example, the whole use of eminent domain in this country to dispossess people of their housing is a very good example of this. But then also we have the loss of pension rights. People who thought they had very good pensions with United Airlines suddenly find they don't, because the company went bankrupt and then shed its pension obligations. The same thing happened through Enron and the like. So there's a tremendous amount of dispossession of wealth and assets going on around the world. And then when you ask yourself the question, how is it, for instance, that healthcare has become less and less affordable in this country, more and more people are being dispossessed of the right to healthcare? You ask yourself the question, who is getting rich in this situation? Well, it's those very, very small elite who are getting so much money they don't know what to do with it. You look at the Wall Street bonuses, or something of that kind, you say, how come they're getting bonuses of millions of dollars when people are losing their healthcare? And I want to say we have to connect those things.

Things are going on in this country where people are being dispossessed, and things are going on in China where people are being dispossessed of their rights. There's dispossession going on in Africa, as people are being deprived of their resources, the genetic materials which are around them are being patented by corporations. There's a general kind of process of dispossession going on, which I think is very important to look at politically and to resist politically as much as we can.

Dispossession, at least on a global scale, makes one think of empire. What is the relationship between neoliberalism and imperialism, as you see it?
DH: Imperialism today is very different from the sort of imperialism that existed at the end of the nineteenth century, say in Britain and France, and so on. Imperialism today does not work through actual active control of territories. The single exception to that, of course, is the venture in Iraq, which is rather different; it's a sort of reversion to an ancient style of imperialist venture.

But what this means is that, for instance, the U.S. is an imperialist country, it has an imperialist agenda, and the way it has sought to gain its power is by a double strategy. First you try to gain power by economic influence, by economic power, by economic institutions, so that the fact that the United States controls the International Monetary Fund and the World Bank, the fact that it can actually work through those institutions, that it can exercise immense economic influence and power, is one of the means by which U.S. imperial strategies operate. The U.S. can force markets open in countries, through things like the WTO, through things like bailing out Mexico or bailing out South Korea. So the economic influence is very important.

The other strategy, which has been longstanding in U.S. imperial history, is to find a local strong person—usually a man, a strong man—who will do your bidding and you will support him and you will give him assets and give him military assistance. This is what they did in Nicaragua in the 1920s and 1930s, and they found Somoza—the older Somoza. This is what they did with the Shah of Iran in the coup that deposed a democratically elected government. This is what they did in Chile with Pinochet, again deposing a democratically elected government.

The U.S. has had this indirect form of imperialism through these two mechanisms of vast economic power and also through these characters who are supported through the coups that the U.S. supports. So this has been the U.S. imperial strategy. Now, it connects to neoliberalization in the following way: that when the investment bankers in New York got all that money in the mid-1970s and started investing it in, say, Mexico and so on, it became very important that whoever was in government in Mexico was friendly to the United States. If they were not friendly to the United States and also if Mexico got into debt, then of course you could use your economic power to make sure that you had a friendly government there. So neoliberalization connects to this imperial strategy in very specific ways. In particular now, it's very mixed in with the way in which financial institutions operate.

We saw a bit of a shift in U.S. policy with the rise of neoconservatism, epitomized by the architects of the invasion of Iraq. These neoconservatives differ from neoliberals to the extent that they appeal to a need for order and morality, rather than individualism, freewheeling cultural expression, and the chaos that the market can bring. So would it be fair to say that neoconservatives are in favor of the market, have a great deal in common with neoliberals, but just want a greater degree of social control?

DH: I think that's the way I would put it. I think that neoliberalism is a pretty contradictory form. It's not stable, and so there's a tremendous volatility that occurs through neoliberalization. That volatility means there's a good deal of insecurity and a good deal of uncertainty, and I think out of that comes a wish to somehow or other get on top of the market monster and impose some order on it from the center, and to do it by military force if necessary. I think the neoconservatives have taken that view very strongly. And I think they have also taken the view that the market ethic, insofar as it's an anything-goes ethic in itself, also needs to be countered by the imposition of some kind of moral purpose upon what this is all about. The neoconservatives are very much in favor of the market, but they recognize that the neoliberals' way of doing it is unstable and therefore it needs some sort of control. They're, in a way, control freaks sitting on top of this neoliberalism agenda—or trying to sit on top of it and as I think we see they're not being very successful.

The Hungarian economic historian Karl Polanyi represents a counterpoint to neoliberal economists like Hayek. Polanyi wrote in his book *The Great Transformation* about a process that he called "the double movement," how when market forces are unleashed on a society eventually they fray the social order to such a point that elites may call for social welfare provisions and restraints on the market, as happened after the upheavals of the Great Depression and World War II. Do you see any potential amongst elites for that sort of counter-movement now?

DH: I think there are signs. You look at the politics of George Soros or somebody like that who seems to me to be moving a little bit in that direction. Even some of the economists who were very strongly in the neoliberal camp at one time, I think of Joseph Stiglitz and Jeffrey Sachs, who are now calling for a more institutional approach to how the world economy is going to be orchestrated. They're not neocons. They're trying to come up with some sort of institutional framework that is going to be more about social justice and more about poverty, questions of that kind. I don't agree with the way they've set this up, but I think it's interesting to see how public opinion and some thinking in these circles is beginning to move towards an alternative economic and political framework that can do a better job of creating greater equality in the global system in the future. So there's a movement away from neoliberal orthodoxy right now in certain circles, and I think that movement away is also supported by certain of the political and economic elites.

In your book, you assert that U.S. military hegemony and the deficit spending that has accompanied it—not very neoliberal in fact, although Reagan did the same—has put the U.S. in a vulnerable position. What is the basis of that vulnerability and does it imperil the current political economic order on a global scale?

DH: If you look at the position of the U.S. say in the late 1960s, around 1970, it was dominant in the world of production, it was dominant technologically, it was dominant with respect to global finance, and it was dominant militarily. What has happened under neoliberalization is the U.S. has lost a lot of its dominance in the world of production. Production, its capacity, has disappeared to places like China and the rest of East and Southeast Asia. It's not totally lost it, of course. Technologically the United States still has tremendous power, but that is slipping away very steadily, particularly towards East Asia. If you look at the world finance, yes, the U.S. was very powerful in the world of finance in the 1980s and early 1990s. But now you look at the huge deficit that the U.S. has both in terms of its internal budget but also its indebtedness to the rest of the world, and you see that the U.S. is not in such a good position financially. We're actually at a cusp right now: the amount of money the U.S. is going to have to pay out to the rest of the world, in order to fund its debt, is equal to the amount of money that is flowing in from its global operations.

The only thing that the United States has got left where it's really dominant is in terms of its military capacity. But here we also see a limitation, because what Iraq shows is that the United States can dominate from thirty thousand feet up but it's not very good at dominating on the ground. It doesn't know how to dominate on the ground. So the U.S. has a rather more limited position than many people like to think, right now, which is not to say that it's subservient to the rest of the world, but it's no longer as dominant as it once was. And I think that also the huge deficits which the U.S. is now running, in relation to the rest of the world but also internally, are indeed a threat to global stability. And this is being said by Paul Volcker and quite conservative people like that, and even being said by International Monetary Fund economists, so there is a threat here because I think the U.S. is playing with fire in terms of its current policies.

I'd like to turn to what the left can learn from the rise of neoliberalism and problems with the ways the left forms its opposition to it. You make a very interesting argument about how the contradictions of the New Left, following the explosions of social protest in the 1960s and '70s, to some degree allowed for the rise of neoliberal ideas.

DH: The movements of the 1960s can be broadly divided into, for instance, the student movement, which was after much greater liberty, much greater freedom from corporate domination and state domination, and of course was very much against the war policies of the U.S. government and the way in which global capitalism was destroying the environment and so on. So there was that wing of the movement. And then the other wing of the movement was, of course, organized labor and the groups around what you might call more traditional working class organization. The movements of the 1960s had that dual character. During the 1960s they could sort of combine rather uneasily around the idea that individual liberty and freedom and social justice and sustainability and the like were things we were all collectively concerned with.

But in some instances there were real schisms within that movement. I think what happened in the 1970s is that when the neoliberal move came in, the idea erupted that, okay, neoliberalism will give you individual liberty and freedom, but you just have to forget social justice and you just have to forget environmental sustainability and all the rest of it. Just think about individual liberty and freedom in particular and we're going to meet your desires and your interests through the individual liberties of market choice—freedom of the market is what it's all about. In a sense, there was a response by neoliberals to the Sixties movement by saying, we can respond to that aspect about what the Sixties was about, but we cannot respond to that other aspect.

And I think therefore what we see is a movement in the 1970s where many people who were active in the 1960s were co-opted into the neoliberal train of thinking and neoliberal ways of consumerism as part of how neoliberalization established itself. It is a very broad way of looking at it, but I tend to think that that is what happened. That then leaves us with the question right now, what are we going to do about social justice, what are we going to do about equality, what are we are going to do about environmental sustainability, all those things that neoliberalism cannot confront.

One answer to that today on the left has been the use of the legal system. I know you're critical of this kind of approach that dominates much of the left and particularly emanates from non-governmental organizations, or NGOs. What are your views on the use of the legalistic framework of universal human rights and of nonprofits as the agents of change?

DH: I'm not against much of that. I think some of that is okay, but it has limited purchase because it's trying to fight neoliberalism with neoliberalism's own tools. It's attempting to roll back a market ethic by a logic of individual rights, when the market ethic is based on the logic of individual rights. When you start to look at the details, what you find is that, first off, the NGOs are not democratic institutions. There are good NGOs and there are bad NGOs; there is a vast array of NGOs doing very different things. The problem with the rights discourse is that as soon as you get into the judicial world, you find yourself having to actually try to prove things through the law, and the law is not exactly an unbiased institution. It has certain kinds of ways of looking at private property and individuals and so on.

For example, I think it's wonderful that in New York City, in Rockefeller Center, there is this bronze plaque where Rockefeller writes his personal credo. And his personal credo says he believes in the supreme worth of the individual. Well, all of us should know that legally the corporation is an individual. So maybe we should go out there and say, do you realize that what Rockefeller means here is that he believes in the supreme worth of the corporation? And so when I go into court and I take on a corporation, there is an asymmetry of power in this whole system. And this even works at the world level. For instance, if the state of Chad doesn't like the fact that the United States is disobeying WTO rules in its subsidies to the cotton farms of this country, Chad has to mount a case against the United States, but in order to do this, it needs at least a million dollars. But the budget of Chad is very small, so a million dollars out of the budget Chad is huge, whereas a million dollars out of the budget of the U.S. is almost nothing. So Chad cannot afford to actually mount a campaign against the United States in the WTO and claim its rights under the WTO. This is the sort of problem we run into at all levels: as soon as you go into the legal system there is an asymmetry of power and the like.

While I'm not against some of those things that are going on through the pursuit of human rights, what I'm saying is that there is limited purchase to that. What we have to look at is the construction of alternative forms of social and political organization, social solidarities, and we have to really reevaluate what is meant by democracy and what is really meant by freedom. I don't think the world is free if there's no healthcare. I don't think the world is free if we have to pay immense amounts for what should be public education. I think the current questions are what is freedom, what is democracy, how social solidarities can be built—those are the issues we should really be concentrating upon in terms of left politics.

Moving away from the idea of universal human rights, which in your book you mention has been used to justify all sorts of imperial excursions, I wonder if, on the other hand, you don't think there is equally the danger of the left celebrating fragmentation, in effect making a virtue out of weakness by elevating the notion of a multiplicity of struggles? Doesn't this approach in some ways parallel neoliberalism with its celebration of diffusion, difference, and an endless profusion of flows?

DH: Yes, I object very much to that angle of left thinking these days that says, let us just simply rely upon all the local, specific movements here, there, and everywhere, to somehow or other generate a complete change in the world without confronting state power. I think this plays into the hands of the neoliberal ethic, and I think it plays into the hands of the neocon use of neoliberal tactics in its own pursuit of power. I think that it is disempowering for the left to take that line of approach.

But again I think we also do have to recognize—and this is what I really am concerned about in my book and elsewhere—a tremendous diversity of struggles which are going on out there: struggles against dam construction in India, or the struggles of the landless peasant movements in Brazil, the struggles going in Bolivia, the struggles going on in Venezuela, the struggles going on in Sweden, the struggles going on in Paris right now. All of these struggles are very specific and we have to acknowledge their diversity and appreciate their diversity. I don't think it's a matter of saying to people, forget your specific struggles and join the universal proletariat in motion; I don't think that's what it's about at all. What we have to do is to find a way of politically uniting those struggles, and that's why I think something like the concept of neoliberalism and its penchant for accumulation by dispossession provide a kind of vocabulary to start to bring together those struggles around a more general kind of theme. So that an Iowa farmer who's just lost his farm can understand how a Mexican peasant feels, can understand how the struggles going on in China are parallel, so we start to see a certain unity in all of the struggles, at the same time as we acknowledge their specificity.

Taking the example you gave of the Iowa farmer and the Mexican peasant: on the one hand, you could say that we need an umbrella that can unite people as disparate as these groups across the world. But then doesn't that gloss over the divisions that exist, say, when the Mexican peasant ends up as a farm worker and works on the farm of that Iowa farmer. Can't the attempt to have this broad umbrella of movement of movements make for strange alliances on the left?

DH: It can and indeed I'm not arguing for a nostalgia for things past, that nothing should change—the famous Maoist adage that you can't make an omelet without breaking eggs. And so any kind of revolutionary movement has to be prepared I think to undertake some major transformations. But one of the things I think is interesting is that a lot of movements that are peasant movements or something of that kind are not against modernization, are not against transformation. What they are interested in is that they get some benefits from it. And if you look at the dispossession of the Mexican peasant or even the dispossession of the Iowa farmer, it's one thing to say that the reorganization of society is such that you have to give up your traditional ways of doing things and doing things in a very different way—it's one thing to say that. It's another thing to say, you're going to give up all your rights and you're going to lose to the point that you just become a disposable person.

And I think the struggles going on—for instance the landless peasant movement in Brazil or the movements against the Narmada dam in India—are not on the part of people who do not want change. They are people who want change, who are interested in modernization, interested in new technologies, interested in doing things in a different kind of way, interested in decent healthcare and decent education, and things of that kind. But what they are concerned about is that they are losing everything or being deprived of things in such a way that they do not get any benefits at all from it.

And that is what encourages me to think that there is more unity here than simply people saying, I want to defend my ancient ways and I don't want to be disturbed. Actually you find very little of that going on. That is a sort of romantic construction which it seems to me is present in certain segments of the left, rather than actually amongst populations themselves. I think a lot of populations want development, they want development on their terms, they want development that benefits them and not the corporations and not the elites around Wall Street.

Right, but zeroing in on the issue of class, which obviously plays a very important role in your argument, you're talking about alliances of people, who, while they may have similar interests in opposing, say, the influence or domination of corporations, may not have the same class interest amongst themselves.

DH: Well, you don't build a movement based on the divisions, you try to build a movement which incorporates difference, at the same time as it tries to recognize that in order to get something to happen, we have to transcend those divisions. For example, in this country, I think if you asked the question, who would benefit from a universal healthcare system, I think the answer would be, it would go across all groups: men and women, gays and straights, ethnic minorities, religious groups of different kinds. So you have a universal project, which is a universal healthcare system, within which there would be a variety of problems about how you designed it. You could design it to be sensitive to difference, but nevertheless the universality of it is something that seems to me could come out of many, many different groups getting together and saying, yes, we'll get behind that. Then you would need a political movement, a political organization, around universal healthcare, which means a political party that is going to advocate it in some way, bring it through Congress, pass legislation, which you would not get from remaining fragmented. And it's that kind of transcendence of the particularities and the willingness to move to the universal level which seems to me to be absolutely crucial in politics right now, which a lot of the left is reluctant to do.

*   *   *

Before we talk about the recent crisis and the obstacles that capitalism faces when it produces crises, how would you define the basic nature of capitalism? What does it need to survive and perpetuate itself?
DH: I think the simplest way to define capitalism, is that it's simply about money being used to make more money. There are various ways to do that. There are plenty of illegal ways and a lot of those are very important to the global economy right now. But if we think about legal ways, there are a variety of ways to do that: you can lend your money to someone else and get it back as interest, you can buy a piece of land and rent it out, you can buy a piece of equipment and lease it out—all kinds of ways in which you can make more money.

But the way in which Marx set it up is to say, the one in which we should be concerned about and think about most, is the one in which you take some money and you go into the marketplace and you buy labor power and means of production. You select a technology and you put people to work and they make a widget or commodity of some sort. And they take it into the market and they sell it for more money than you started out with. So that's if you like one of the ways that you make money and it's the one Marx argued means that everybody who is a capitalist could make money. The others often, it's robbing Peter to pay Paul. That's the way that he set it up. And I think we can see that going on around us all of the time and in a sense that's the central way that capitalism works.

You've just spoken about a process for individual capitalists. What does the system as a whole require to keep ticking over?
DH: Well it requires that there is always sufficient labor to keep the expansion going, because at the end of the day when you get more capital, certain pressures exist of completion and all the rest of it, that force you to reinvest and expand your business. So you need more labor: where's that going to come from? You need more means of production, which means more raw materials, more stresses in terms of extraction of things from nature and the like. You need an adequate technology and if the technological apparatus is not there, then that can be a serious problem. You need compliant laborers, both in the marketplace so that they don't make too much demands in terms of wages, and they don't get really bolshie in the labor process and start putting sand into the works, this kind of thing. And of course you need a market. So

the capitalists when they go out into the world, need all these things in front of them as it were in order to be able to continue to accumulate their capital.

You write the whole economy needs to grow minimally at a particular rate—for profits to be sufficiently high for most capitalists—which you say is about a 3 percent compound rate of growth. Why that number?

DH: The problem when you fix on a number is that everyone thinks it's some sort of God-given number. Historically the rate of growth has been around 2.25 percent but that encompasses years like the 1930s when there has been almost no growth whatsoever, and the recent couple of years when growth has been very low. But the other thing you notice when you read the financial press is that when the growth rate is 3 percent everybody seems okay; when it's less than that, they say it's not doing too well. When you turn to the business page and it says the U.S. GDP only grew by 1.4 percent, everybody seems to be very concerned about that. Now at some places and some times, it's much higher. So that right now we have a very low rate of growth in the United States and in Europe, but of course we've got an 8 or 9 percent rate in China. I don't know where it is right now, but it's coming back towards the 3 percent global average again.

So you have to be careful. I fixed on 3 percent because it seems the minimum rate of growth. But it's a compound rate of growth and you have to remember that because that means that as time goes on you need more and more profitable investment opportunities, otherwise you're really running into difficulties.

And presumably some of that has to do with the productivity and population growth rates of the workforce, with which employment must keep up.

DH: Yes, the population growth side of things. Global population has to be absorbed and so one of the reasons the 3 percent comes in is because of global population growth. But also the capital accumulation rate has to be at least parallel with that, if not in advance of that, if people are going to get richer over time and have more material goods and services to live on.

What compels an individual capitalist, who may not be thinking of the big picture, to not simply take whatever profits he or she is making and spend them lavishly? Why this intense impulse to invest?

DH: Well, the answer is as individuals they sometimes do. They sometimes say they're tired of all this, and they have a great time and just consume it up and go live on a yacht in the Caribbean or wherever. I mean, they've got enough.

But there are a couple of things here: one is that money is a form of social power and there is a lust for social power no matter what. You can see that in the way that people who have billions of dollars are interfering in elections and orchestrating things. And of course they love to be grand donors to the opera and the ballet and art museums and so on. So it's a lust for social power. And the thing about that is that other people have social power, but you want more than they've got. So there is a sort of lust of certain kind that exists there.

But the other thing is what I like to refer to, following Marx, as the coercive laws of competition. That if I don't reinvest part of my capital in expansion and my competitors do, then I don't remain a capitalist for very much longer. Therefore, in order to remain a capitalist and continue to make money I have to always keep up with my competitors. So there is a competitive edge that pushes me. Which also tells you something: that the state of competition in an economy is very tightly connected to this necessity to define the channels of reinvestment. If you've got monopoly power then you don't need to reinvest because you've got no competitors.

What about the barriers that capital faces that might impede it growing at this compound rate of approximately 3 percent? You have mentioned several of them, but let's start with workers themselves and the labor process. To what degree is that a barrier that capital has to figure out some way to overcome to be able to bring in the profits that it finds necessary to keep growing?
DH: It's an absolutely critical barrier. If there is a scarcity of labor, then capitalists have to start to bid up and wages become higher and higher. And as they become higher and higher, less profit is left over for the capitalist. The workers get a big chunk of the extra that is being produced all of the time. So this is a crucial aspect. And workers become scarce not simply in their absolute numbers but also in terms of their organizational power. When workers are well organized and relatively scarce, then that can become a big barrier.

If you look back you to the end of the 1960s and early 1970s, there were scarcities of labor around and labor was relatively well organized. And one of the answers to that—this is kind of very curious in the present climate—was to import labor. So the Germans were importing the Turks, the Swedes were bringing in the Yugoslavs, and the French were bringing in the Maghrebians. And in this country, the reform of the Immigration Act of 1965 opened up, as it were, the labor reserves of the whole world so you could bring in more and more people.

That solution didn't work too well, partly because organized labor didn't like it and there was a lot of struggle going on at that level. So they went the other way. In the mid-1970s, they started to offshore. The capital went to where the labor was: it went to China, it went to the *maquila* zones of Mexico, it went to the Philippines, it just dispersed. So it broke the power of labor, in part through that.

But then of course politically there was this assault. The crisis of the 1970s was generally attributed to greedy unions. Wherever you were, the problem was the unions—again and again you heard this right throughout Europe and right throughout North America. The result of that was that you had to get people in who were going to break the unions. And who were they? Well it was Thatcher and Reagan who did a pretty good job of breaking the political power of unions. So what was a very significant barrier in the late 1960s and until about mid-1970s, gradually dissolved. So part of the argument I make is that the labor question, as far as capital was concerned, was solved by 1985 or 1986 or so. It was no longer a big barrier.

You write in *The Enigma of Capital* that as capitalism overcomes certain barriers, it may create other ones. In the case of labor, by reducing its social power and driving wages down, it created another problem, which was that these workers could not longer afford to buy the products that capitalists were selling.

DH: One of the things that happens when you have wage repression—as we've had throughout much of the capitalist world over the last thirty to forty years, where the share of wages in national income has gone down almost everywhere—is that workers generally spend their money immediately because they have to. Whereas if more and more money is going to rich people, they don't necessarily spend it. How many pairs of shoes can you buy? I sometimes think what we should do with very rich folk is, instead of paying them in money, we should pay them in pairs of shoes and see how much they really want. If George Soros got $3 billion in one year and we gave it to him all in shoes, what would he do with them all?

So what comes out of this is since workers are getting less and less, then one of the big engines of demand—which is the demand coming from workers—is diminishing. And as a result of that, at the end of the day you've got to sell your product to someone who has money. But if the workers don't have money, who are you going to sell it to? You can do all kinds of things, like again you can find external markets; you can sell to the other part of the world, or find a market somewhere that hasn't been tapped yet. But at some point or other you have to come back to the mass of the workers and the answer there was: give them credit. So one of the big pushes that came in the 1980s was this rise of what we would call a credit economy in which households got more and more indebted to the point where household debt tripled over these years. So in some ways, the gap between the demand in the market and the level of wages was covered by the fact that people increasingly became indebted.

Other barriers that capitalism perpetually struggles to overcome are thrown up by nature. The concept of nature is complicated and fraught. That said, could you explain how nature acts as a barrier to steady accumulation and how capitalism then helps reshape nature to overcome it? There are of course people who believe, in light of the ecological crisis, that nature is an ultimate barrier.

DH: The relation to nature has a very interesting history. Capital again and again has confronted limits and barriers there and has been very sophisticated about overcoming them.

There are two things here. Take for example the question of oil. There are many people who say the world is running out of oil and there is something called peak oil, and we are past it, and we're about to diminish, and so on. I've been around long enough to hear these predictions about we're going to run out of oil in fifteen years' time—and it always seems fifteen years later we're going to run out of oil in another fifteen years' time. I'm not saying it's infinite, but I'm saying you have to be very careful about attributing it to nature itself.

For example, a couple years ago, when oil went up to $170 a barrel and gas was $4 or heading up in that direction, there was all this chatter that peak oil is here—see it's here. Then about six months later, the oil price collapsed. That tells you something: that scarcity of so-called natural resource is not natural. It depends on who controls it. So at this point you're looking at the power of *rentiers,* if you like—the landowners and resource owners—to manipulate markets to their own advantage. So many of these scarcities, which seem to be due to nature, turn out not to be due to nature at all. They're due to the power of a particular class of people who control that resource—the energy companies and the like.

Now having said that, I'm not saying there is an infinite capacity. The capacity of the atmosphere to absorb greenhouse gases or to absorb toxic wastes and so on—I think those are becoming very serious problems. But over the past twenty years, there's been some recognition of that and so environmental technologies have become big business. So what happens is that a new type of capital emerges which is going to actually tackle that kind of problem and turn it into significant advantage to itself. So there are all those sorts of issues.

And then there is that other issue: the degree to which human action has actually transformed what was once a natural environment into something that is more amenable to production. So you have all of the agricultural aspects, which are transformed environments for the production of food for us. And there can be scarcities of that, because there are certain controls that exist. And this goes to the way in which, for instance, the housing market and land prices has moved over the last fifteen to twenty years. Again, it has nothing to do with absolute scarcity. It has to do with the way in which certain people were using control over land as a means of gaining very, very high rents. You think of it and you say, why do we have to pay so much to live in the Bay Area? Why do we have to pay so much to live in Manhattan? This has nothing to do with natural scarcity—this is a scarcity which is created socially by certain processes of domination of certain basic means of production by a certain class of people who will not release those means of production except at a reserve price and that reserve price can go higher and higher. In fact, I think the *rentiers* these days are doing extremely well.

Clearly capitalism is a crisis-prone system by its very nature. And it's become even more crisis-prone, it appears, since the 1970s when there was a shift from what you call embedded liberalism to neoliberalism. How does capitalism survive? You've mentioned some of the barriers that it must overcome. But how does this system manage—at least up until now—to transcend these different crises that emerge? And what are the outlets for capitalism to get beyond these crises?
DH: There are a number of different outlets, but to be honest I don't have a complete accounting of how capital survives. I have a good idea on some of the aspects of it. For instance, one of the things that confuses me, particularly in the present situation, is the ideological means by which capital manages to convince everybody that this is the best system that could possibly ever be created by humanity to feed, clothe, house ourselves, and to live a decent life.

The lack of any major response to the crisis this time—when we've gone through a very serious crisis and are not going to come out of it easily at least as far as I can tell—the lack of any big response and search for some alternative—I don't understand. I don't understand why more people are not thinking about it, I really don't, nor how it gets inside of people's heads. How, for example, you can get a movement like the Tea Party, making all the ruckus that it's making, which is basically saying things that are completely inconsistent yet somehow or other doing a very good job of disrupting the search for any kind of alternative. So I'm not sure I can answer those sorts of questions.

But what I think come up with is that there are various tactics—some of which come from individual capitalists, confronted with a difficulty—which will find a way around it. I mentioned earlier the movement into environmental technologies, that individual entrepreneurs will see an opportunity and will move in. I think others will always see that there is always a market for something new: iPods and iPads and cell phones. There is a dynamic which is inherent it seems to me in the entrepreneurial character of capital, that many people see as praiseworthy. And I myself concede very happily that it has brought up many wonderful things that we can use—dishwashers and all those kinds of things—to make life easier. So there is an individual response. One of the things that come from the dispersed character of power within a typical capitalist system is that if these inventions are not made in the United States they will be made in Japan or made in China. The fact that a lot of it is going to be decentralized does indeed allow for a considerable adaptation of capitalists to the situation.

Now whether that individual activity can actually get you out of a crisis is a real problem. In many instances, what we see is individual capitalists, operating in their own self-interest, engage in actions that actually drive you deeper into a crisis. For example, one of the things happening right now is that capitalist profits are reviving, in part by engaging in further labor repression and laying off more people. In other words, they're not dealing with the effective-demand problem; they're solving their own problem and perpetuating the big problem that led us into this crisis.

It's at that point that government policy becomes crucial or general social thinking becomes crucial. And here you see policies get implemented by government that can identify some barrier and say, okay, here's what we can do about it. This is what Keynes did in the 1930s and Roosevelt took some of those ideas and so on. So I think at this point we need to look at the possible lines of exit from the crisis and the degree to which policy is actually addressing them to pull us out of this particularly crisis. Although part of my thesis is that, as you pull yourself out of this crisis, you're almost certainly going to be confronted with another one down the road which may be different from the one we're now in but will probably be equally severe.

You suggest that crises are not just inevitable, but they're actually necessary for the health of the capitalist system—even though they may be devastating for individual capitalists and obviously devastating for everyone else. How do crises help restore the health of the system?
DH: Crises have this way of expressing what I think is one of the fundamental characteristics of the capitalist system: which is that it is a permanently revolutionary force. If I say, I am a revolutionary, everyone says, oh my, what a terrible person. But all the capitalists are really revolutionaries. Margaret Thatcher said she was a revolutionary and she was. So it's a permanently revolutionary force.

It always engages in what Schumpeter calls creative destruction—that in order to create the new you have to destroy the old. For example, when we basically depended upon the railroads for communications—railroads and the telegraph—you had certain kind of a landscape that emerged. But when the automobile comes in and soon trucks come around, railroads become much less significant. What happens is that places that were once hubs of the railroad system decline and new places which are hubs of the highway rise up. So this process of creative destruction is part of the way in which the 3 percent compound growth is realized, that something new has to be created and the new usually means a new technology and a new configuration of class relations and social relations and all the rest of it.

These crises become vehicles by which those transformations occur—it's very hard to engage in these transformations in a smooth way without it being disruptive of existing social relations and existing patterns of activity. For example, when we talked earlier about overcoming the power of labor by offshoring, that meant the deindustrialization of much of the United States. You find many kinds of cities, like Buffalo and so on, completely destroyed by this deindustrialization. But that was very important in keeping capital in motion, keeping it going, so that capital could go to China and go to all these other places where labor costs were much lower. But it left behind communities that were destroyed. You find old steel towns where pretty miserable conditions still prevail. And then that forces adaptations in those cities.

This is, if you like, the long history of capital that has always been about doing these kinds of things. And it's not a frictionless process. Some processes operate slowly, but others are kind of stuck and then it has to be broken apart. And a crisis sort of breaks it apart.

What role does urbanization play in both the growth of capitalism and crises of capitalism? What do Paris under Baron Haussmann in the mid-nineteenth century and the New York metropolitan area under master planner Robert Moses in the twentieth century illustrate about the importance of urbanization in those processes?
DH: What happens in a crisis is that you get surplus capital and surplus labor side by side and nobody knows what to do with them: I have this money, where's it profitable to go? That means that very often you design a new project and one of the projects that is often utilized to absorb the surpluses of capital and the surpluses of labor is urbanization.

Under Second Empire Paris there was a crisis in 1848—massive unemployment of capital, massive unemployment of labor, and a political crisis. And Louis Bonaparte comes to power and declares himself emperor. But he knows he's not going to stay emperor for very long unless he actually then gets the surplus capital and the surplus labor back to work. So what does he do? He had several projects. One of the big projects was to rebuild Paris. And Paris was a mess, so he brought in Baron Haussmann to rebuild the city. They rebuilt the boulevards and you can still see them to this day. Within four or five years they'd absorbed a lot of the surplus capital in building the boulevards.

But it wasn't just only building the boulevards—it was rebuilding a whole way of life. In fact, one of the things he mandated, which was a very neat way of putting all of the seamstresses back to work, was that everybody who went to court had to wear a completely different set of clothes. It was a new design of court clothes. So there were unemployed seamstresses there in 1851–52, and he becomes emperor and decrees this, and all of a sudden they're fully at work again. And then the boulevards also became fashion places—you then get department stores and the outdoor cafés. It was a complete change of lifestyle, which absorbed a lot of the surplus capital. Now what happens when you do this is that it can work for a while, but then it runs out of steam. And so Paris went into crisis in about 1868.

The same thing happened after World War II, when there was surplus capital and surplus labor. It was absorbed in World War II. Then that's all over and you see this strike wave forming in 1945–46. There was tremendous unrest. Everybody starts to get very nervous about what all these returning soldiers who know how to shoot are going to do when they find themselves unemployed like they were in the 1930s. So one of the things they did was to absorb it in the suburbanization of the United States and the rebuilding of the metropolitan areas with Robert Moses and the highways and all this kind of stuff. But it also transformed a way of life. In building the suburbs you create a whole new set of demands for all sorts of things. I jokingly say to my students that in 1945, if you'd been smart, you would have gone and started making lawnmowers. There was a huge demand for lawnmowers in the 1950s and 1960s because that was a suburban lifestyle. And of course everybody had to have their own lawnmower. You didn't have a collective lawnmower down at the end of the block—everybody had to have their own lawnmower. So it's not only the building of the highways and the building of the housing and the building of the all the infrastructure, and the sewers and water supply systems. It's also the creating of a new lifestyle that generates a whole new set of demands for products: cars and lawnmowers and all the rest of it. This is one of the ways that capital has absorbed a lot of surplus capital over the years.

But by the time you get to the end of the 1960s, this is running out of steam. What was interesting about the crisis of the 1970s is it was triggered by a property crisis, an urban crisis, much as this last one has been for us has been an urban crisis, particularly located in Southern California, Arizona, Nevada, and Florida. The role of urbanization in all of this is something that is a bit of an untold story, and I wanted to tell it in the book so that people could make a connection between the macroeconomic process and this urbanization story.

Yet that story continues in different forms within cities today, in ways that might be more aesthetically pleasing than suburbanization: a turn towards reviving city centers, the preservation of old buildings, restored neighborhoods full of boutiques—all following the same thorny capitalist imperatives.

DH: Yes. Gentrification movements, for example, become one of the ways of the transformation of inner-city areas, depending upon where you are. You don't see much of it in Baltimore, but you certainly see it in New York and San Francisco. But there is also something interesting here about the consumption side of things: the length of time that a commodity lasts. I'm still using my great-grandmother's forks and if capital made things that lasted two hundred years, they wouldn't have a market. So they've become quite sophisticated about making things that don't last or things that get outdated. But they've also moved to create things that are instantaneously consumed, which is a spectacle.

And actually urban life has been more and more caught up in this notion of spectacle, because it's instantaneously consumed; you can't sit there and continue using it for two hundred years like I can with my knives and forks. And the interesting thing is the mobilization of the spectacle, because in effect, people become a spectacle. So it's a mobilization of a lifestyle, which is something like Second Empire Paris, where people are out on the boulevards strutting their fashions. Urban life has changed in that way, particularly since the 1970s or so. If you think about cities in the 1950s and 1960s, people say they were rather dull kind of places. New York City had no sidewalk cafés in the 1950s and 1960s. When the sidewalk cafés came in, you started to get the spectacle in the city and all this sort of thing. There were many transformations of that kind that occur. And again, what I'm trying to do is, if you like, integrate this mobilization of spectacle into the general account of how capital tries to find new ways to absorb surpluses in various aspects of social life.

Traditionally capital has used different means to find a way out of crises. One of the most dramatic is war. Yet what's interesting for the United States—at the epicenter of this crisis—is that war has preceded this crisis or been paralleled by this crisis. Why don't occupations help capitalism sufficiently? And has U.S. spending on the military limited in any way its room for maneuver in this crisis?

DH: The kinds of wars that erupt as part of, if you like, the general structure of crisis formation, are usually wars between capitalist powers. And it's inter-capitalist rivalries that spark the wars. The war in Iraq is not that sort of war and certainly the war in Afghanistan is not of that sort. So I don't see those kinds of wars as somehow or other fitting into that scenario. However, they have certainly played a crucial role in draining much of the surplus out of the U.S. Treasury and contributed in a major way to the indebtedness of the United States. I remember when the war began, somebody at that point said it was going to cost $200 billion, and the administration jumped up and down and said that's stupid, that's ridiculous. And of course, here we are much later and it's up around $2 trillion or so that it's cost. And a lot of that is debt-financed and the indebtedness of the United States to the rest of the world has increased remarkably because of these military adventures.

In a sense, these wars have played into the crisis, rather than helped to exit it. And I can't see any continuation of those wars as helping to exit it at all. It's not as if you're hindering Chinese expansion and development, or the development or expansion of productive capacity in Brazil. That's not what is happening at all.

Now the question also is whether an inter-capitalist war is feasible in these times. There are suggestions of a looming conflict particularly between the United States and China. Frankly, I don't see it. I think one of the telling moments when Bush took power was that spy plane incident, when an American spy plane collided with a Chinese plane. There was a big fuss about that and the impression was that the administration was going to go hard on China and use that as a provocative incident to discipline China. But my guess is that folks from Wal-Mart and General Motors, who actually make most of their money out of China, said, for God's sake don't do that—otherwise we're lost. So I think the possibility of an inter-capitalist war, given the inter-linkages that exist now in the economy, is probably less.

What is, I think, more likely—and we're seeing elements of that—is unrest in cities. And I think the techniques of urban warfare pioneered in places like Fallujah and Baghdad in Iraq, but also by the Israelis in Ramallah—and suppression of uprisings in urban areas are more likely to be the story of future military actions. And I don't see them as playing the role inter-capitalist wars played in the past. I see it more as an extension of repressive apparatuses. Which we're seeing all around us all the time right now in urban areas—social control and political control all in the name of anti-terrorism. I think we should see it in those terms, rather than a way of getting out of the current mess.

Before we turn to possible avenues of exit from this crisis, I want to ask you what you see as the explanation—if there is one explanation—for this crisis that we're living through. Within Marxism, there are a number of differ-

ent theories to explain crises. Often people are quite partisan about their particular explanation: you have the profit squeeze—an explanation you touched on earlier about the 1960s and 1970s, the fact that workers were demanding higher wages; the notion of the falling rate of profit; other theories around the idea that if you depress wages, you're not going to have enough consumption. How do you see this crisis?

DH: To write this book, I had to rewrite a lot of Marxian crisis theory away from the idea that there's a single explanation, to the idea that crises get moved around from one typology to another. So that if the crisis of the late 1960s was fundamentally that of labor, the crisis we've hit right now is largely one of effective demand, which is being compounded by financialization, both of demand and capital circulation in general.

So I don't see that there's one singular form of crisis at all. And I think there are many people on the left who are rather disturbed by that view. But to be honest, I can't see how we can explain the current crisis by appeal to a theory that does not recognize that 70 percent of the driving force in the U.S. economy is consumer confidence and consumer demand and the mess we're in certainly has its locus within the financial system. So we need to integrate both of those into a theoretical structure which is consistent with, if you like, the general economic theory that I work with.

It wasn't too hard to do that, once I dropped the idea that it had to be understood as a falling rate of profit, or it had to be understood as a profit squeeze. All of those things can happen, but they happen differentially. I think that for me this was one of the more important theoretical shifts that I found myself making. And as I made it, of course, you have to go back and justify it in relation to the sacred texts (*laughs*). And it's not hard to do, actually. It's all in the *Grundrisse* or it's all in *Capital* if you care to look for it. And it wasn't hard at all to justify this particular take on things.

As the crisis started to unfold, there was a fair amount of talk about this being the end of neoliberalism. And there was a lot of speculation that there would be a shift over to a more Keynesian way of structuring the economy and stimulating demand. Yet what we are seeing coming through the crisis is that most of those in power have opted for a strategy of austerity, rather than one of stimulus. What do you think this means for the ability of those in power to get out of this crisis, given the lack of demand you just mentioned? And what does it mean for the next crisis?

DH: I think over the last three years we've seen an attempt to come up with a collective solution, which is why they started forming things like the G20, bringing everybody together and saying, look, we've got to have a collective solution to this crisis. But what's pretty clear is that there is a big disparity within the G20 as to how people think about getting out of the crisis.

China for example is getting out of it in very broad terms via Keynesian strategies—interestingly, heavily dependent upon urbanization, reurbanization, and massive investments in infrastructures like water, high-speed rail, highways, all the rest of it. So in effect, China has taken pretty much a Keynesian path, including most recently allowing strikes to take place, which have resulted in increases of wages of 20–30 percent—in some cases even doubling. Now what that says to me is that the Chinese recognize that wage repression is a problem and that they need to form the internal market and reform it. And guess what? China has come out of the crisis fairly fast.

So they're shifting their target consumers from the United States to actually within China itself.
DH: Absolutely. They're doing that. And they're also triggering an immense demand for raw materials. Australia has hardly felt the crisis because they're supplying so much in the way of raw materials to China. Much of Latin America has come out of the crisis by reorienting their trade to China—with some disastrous effects in Latin America because the soybean producers are going crazy down there and doing all sorts of environmentally disastrous stuff. But nevertheless you don't feel the crisis in Latin America.

Now, the United States and Europe have gotten locked into this idea that the answer is austerity, which strikes me as exactly the wrong way to go. The one country that has implemented austerity measures from fairly early on is Ireland—it's no accident that it's a total disaster. And austerity measures and further wage repression doesn't get you anywhere.

Germany, for example, has taken this line, but Germany is fortunate because it's an export-led economy and many of its exports go to China. So actually Germany is booming again within Europe because of the China trade. Greece, which has no China trade, is not booming. Something very interesting has happened in Greece. The Chinese want to come in and actually turn Athens into a vast trans-shipment point for all Chinese goods coming in. The Chinese are actually colonizing those parts of Europe. So there are all sorts of shifts going on of this kind.

When we're looking at exit from the crisis we see two paths broadly, one of which is being temporarily successful—which is the China one—and one which seems to be me to be headed into long-term stagnation—which is the U.S. one and, to some degree, the European one. So this is a problem.

The other thing, however, is who are we talking about in terms of coming out of the crisis. One of the big features of neoliberalism all along has been you save the banks and you sock it to the people. This is what happened with the Mexican debt crisis of 1982. Mexico was going to go bankrupt. So the U.S. Treasury and the International Monetary Fund bailed out Mexico so they could pay off the New York investment bankers who had put all their money into Third World debt. So the U.S. investment bankers were saved. But they then said to Mexico, well, now you have to pay. So the standard of living of the Mexicans declined by about 25 percent in the next five to ten years.

Now, what have we done in this country? We've bailed out the banks. They are rich. And the bankers that have lasted are superrich. The leading hedge fund managers in 2008 hauled in $3 billion a piece. They're exiting from the crisis fine. We've done the first part—rescue the banks and the bankers and that class of people. Now it's sock-it-to-the-people time. Here in California it's been sock it to the people by cuts and austerity. It's being done nation-wide. This is the same thing that's going on in Britain—they're doing exactly the same thing: it's sock it to the people. We've saved the banks, the banks are doing fine, that class has come out of it okay.

There's a funny saying that comes from Andrew Mellon, a famous banker who was Secretary of the Treasury way back with Hoover, who said that in a crisis assets return to their rightful owners—i.e. him. And this is what is going on right now. We're seeing an incredible concentration and consolidation of wealth and power in the upper classes. They're coming out of it okay—those who are left; some of them have lost. You see this globally. The number of billionaires in India doubled in 2009—the number of billionaires in China has surged hugely. And the billionaires in this country—well, some of them have lost a bit, but the rest of them are doing absolutely fine.

A crisis is a moment when you fight class war. You're not supposed to say that, but I did love it when Warren Buffett said, oh, of course there's class war—and it's my class, i.e. the rich class, that's fighting it and we're winning. And that's where we are at. And a crisis is a great moment to really sock it to the people on the grounds that they have been profligate—when they haven't been profligate at all. They've been under wage repression for the last thirty years. So the question of who comes out of it is also important for how the whole system comes out of it.

How should we envision a postcapitalist future and the route to get there?
DH: We have to think at some point or other that compound growth forever cannot continue—we have to think of some alternative form. In the same way that capitalism has historically been a revolutionary form of social organiza-tion, we have to think of a revolutionary form of organization that takes us beyond capitalism into something else. Now exactly what the something is, I

really don't know. But we should be thinking about it and thinking about it collectively.

What bothers me a little bit is that there are many discontented groups around, but they're very fragmented. And they're often fragmented over what I would call a fetishism of organizational form. There are still groups around that insist that the vanguard party of the proletariat in motion is going to change the world: there are Maoist groups around, and then there are Trotskyist groups around. And then there are people who don't believe in that at all. They don't believe that state power has relevance whatsoever, for instance, that no hierarchical forms are permissible at all—it all has to be horizontal and it all has to be democratic.

I think the question I wanted to pose to all those people in those organizational forms—and some are more softly oppositional than others, like the NGO world—is, in what ways does your organizational form actually have the capacity to address what is the global problem of finding an alternative to capitalism, that can house, feed, and shelter 6.8 billion people adequately in a way that is sensitive to all sorts of cultural variety? And I find it very difficult to have a conversation about that. My concluding comments have been roundly criticized, either from the vanguard political parties—the comments that say, well, you don't have the proletariat in there anymore—or the more *autonomista* or anarchist groups that say, well, you're just a hierarchical secret Stalinist, aren't you, because you think taking state power is significant. The reactions are really visceral.

But the other interesting thing is that several of the critiques I've had say, your diagnosis is fine, but you don't understand anything about organizational form. Well, it's true. I'm not deeply into organizational form, but that was not my purpose. I wanted to say, if this diagnosis is true, what you have to show me is that your organizational form is capable of transcending and dealing with that diagnosis. Otherwise it will be like somebody having a heart attack and you decide treat it as if they had a broken thumb. It just doesn't make sense to me that people are not prepared to have that kind of debate.

Behind it, of course, also lies some vision of what technical possibilities exist. There are a lot of technical possibilities over, for example, organizing exchange through the Internet, and there is a lot of experimentation of thinking in there. But it seems to me the difficulty the left has right now is to say the alternative vision looks like this—it's much more egalitarian, it's much more respectful of the relation to nature, you can specify a number of general broad aims you would want to have, but can accomplish this aim of feeding everybody. I'm scared sometimes—some of the organizational forms you see out there, well if you actually followed those through, three-quarters of the people in the world would starve. And the fact is we depend on agribusiness and all the rest of it. It's very nice to have local foods, but in the past local foods have been very susceptible to famines and disease regimes and so on. So what I wanted to do was to have a conversation about that. I don't have a prescription. I wanted to put it out there and say, we need to talk about these things.

What about the role of the state in fundamental societal change? Some radicals believe that we could achieve a postcapitalist transformation without seizing state power. You clearly disagree with that.

DH: One of the interesting things here is that the state is almost reified as a singular thing and you are either for it or against it. I think you actually have to unpack exactly what the state is. The thing about, for instance, anarchist forms of organization—if you read Murray Bookchin or someone like that—is that there is a territorial form of organization in which people come together in an institutional framework of some kind to reach collective decisions that are sensitive to bioregional requirements and all the rest of it. And to me that looks like a state. It's a particular kind of state.

Part of what I would want to say if we are interested in these forms of organization is that we need to think about the reform of the state. There are certain aspects of the state that can be used more than others. I think, for example, one of the things I pinpoint in *The Enigma of Capital* is the crucial power that this state-finance nexus has within the state apparatus, which I think has to be broken. No question about that. If we're going to demolish anything, we have to demolish that power. But that power has been going on since the sixteenth century. And think we saw it really physical terms in the midst of this crisis: who was on television telling us what was going to happen? It was the pinnacle of the banking system—Bernanke and Paulson, the secretary of the treasury—that was the state-finance nexus in motion and it was making all the decisions. We didn't see Bush; we didn't see anyone else. They were coming on and saying, this is what we're doing, this is how we're doing it, now we're doing that, now we're doing this, now we're doing that—coming up with the three-page document saying this is what we have to do. They were making all the decisions.

So there is a state-finance nexus that really needs to be broken. But if that is broken, then we need to understand some things like, what are we going to do about money and monetary transactions? We need to come up with alternative forms of money, which are not susceptible to that kind of manipulation and the like. So there are technical issues of that sort.

So I'm neither in favor of nor against state power. I'm arguing that we have to think about the form of organization that can actually take us into it. And some aspects of the contemporary state may be usable in that transition and other aspects need to be broken.

It was interesting reading Hardt and Negri's recent book *Commonwealth*: on a certain page they say smash the state and on the next page they say the state should guarantee a universal minimum income. I think I know what they mean and I sympathize with the idea that certain aspects—the militarism of the state and the state-finance nexus—we need to smash and all sorts of other things. But there are other aspects where, no, we want the state to respond to human needs and be reformed. Will we do that by totally demolishing the state apparatus and the inter-state system? Again, if we do that, frankly, I think so many of us will starve that it's not a feasible thing. I think it's not that taking state power is the be-all and end-all of a political project—it's not—but it's necessary as part of a transitional movement in which you can, as Marx argued long ago, ultimately envisage the withering away of the state. But the idea that somehow you can actually change the world without dealing with state power right now, and occupying certain key aspects of it, seems to me to be a bit la-la.

CHAPTER THREE

Leo Panitch and Doug Henwood: Demystifying Globalization

We regularly hear that globalization is historically unprecedented from the likes of opponents such as Jerry Mander of the International Forum on Globalization. Is that actually the case?

DH: Yes and no. Financial markets probably move more quickly and are much more instantaneous than they ever were in the past, but on the other hand, the late nineteenth and early twentieth centuries were times of incredible freedom for the movement of capital. Nation-states were much, much weaker than they are today. Britain, in particular, had vast foreign holdings, far larger relative to the size of their economy or the world economy than anything we see today. It was a time of classical colonialism, when whole countries were owned outright by imperial countries. Even subordinate countries in global systems today have more power than a colonial government did a hundred years ago.

So I think it's a little misleading to talk about this as unprecedented. There are aspects that are new, there are aspects that are not new. I hate to use this word because it's kind of an ugly cliché, but it's disempowering to a lot of people because if they think that they're up against unprecedented forces, that makes them almost feel that they're unprecedentedly weak. So I would think that we need a much more subtle and nuanced analysis of what's new and what isn't, and really chuck out all of this kind of breathless stuff like Jerry Mander is speculating.

Are you suggesting that the anomaly in the past century is not the emergence of globalization in the last three or so decades, but what might be seen as an idealized period in the 1950s and '60s?

DH: I think that's absolutely fair to say, because I think people still think of that as kind of a norm against which the last thirty years have been an exception, when in fact that great boom—which was really worldwide and included almost everybody at every income level—that was the really unprecedented period. I think we need to step back.

The period of deglobalization was nothing to get too romantic about. It was the period of a depression followed by world war, so I wouldn't want to get too nostalgic about the closed national spaces of the 1930s and early 1940s either. Latin America had a better time of it, but in the Northern Hemisphere those were pretty hellish years. So I don't want to get too nostalgic at that period of the return of the local that Jerry Mander likes to talk about.

Antiglobalization proponents often argue that national boundaries have been largely obliterated by the actions of transnational corporations and the policies of multilateral institutions like the World Trade Organization, the World Bank, and the International Monetary Fund. Let's begin with the notion that these forces have eroded national sovereignty and that countries are no longer able to control their economic policies. Is this an accurate assessment, Leo?

LP: No, it's not. It's an illusion. Back in the late nineteenth and the early twentieth centuries, the fact that there were capital movements does not mean that it was a period in which states didn't have power. We see that time as the era of imperialism and where the confrontation between state forces led to horrific world wars. And in today's world the fact that there are capital movements and so much trade, which there is indeed, does that mean that the American state is not an imperial state? This notion that because of this movement of capital we don't have an extremely powerful American state would be considered an absurdity, once one puts it that way.

And this kind of language, of course, when it comes from the left serves as a means of occluding and avoiding the enormous imperial power of the American state in the world. But even beyond that and the very active role the American state plays in freeing capital movements around the world and forcing free trade on its terms, even beyond that, the places to which capital moves are not places where states are weak: they are places where states have the capacity to guarantee property rights. So states are crucial, and the power of states is crucial, to this whole phenomenon of globalization.

I might just add that you are right to point to the 1950s and '60s as the source of this illusion. But it goes back to the whole history of the left, which tends to have illusions about the nature of the state and a very state-centric conception of what the left is, what socialism is and so on. The notion that in the 1950s and '60s states were free of the influence of capital would have been considered absurd by those of us who were around in the 1950s and '60s. It was certainly true that there had been certain reforms in that period which, insofar as they benefited the working classes, have been eroded in recent years. But the state in that period was still a capitalist state—very much so—and the whole New Left that developed in the 1960s saw it as such. So it's an illusion to imagine that the state of that era was in some sense free of capital or controlled capital, et cetera.

We get into this because we try to respond to the neoliberals when they say states are bad or governments are bad. We want to say: states are good. But their very categories are confused and we don't want to adopt their categories. We need to blow past that kind of construction of the world in terms of states versus markets. States construct markets and markets depend on states and that's what capitalism is all about.

Would you say then that what has been seen as the state retreating and being replaced by the market is not accurate, but that in fact the role of the state has just changed from what perhaps might be called a positive role to a more negative role?

LP: It all depends—positive for whom and negative for whom? It's very positive for capitalists and it's played a very active role, as indeed the nineteenth century *laissez-faire* state did in constructing markets, in establishing the legal rules within which markets operate and need to operate, guaranteeing property rights and contracts and so on. In that sense, the states have been very active in a positive sense. Of course, that has negative consequences because we're dealing with markets which are not abstract technical means of passing goods and money around, but markets that are made up of unequal social relations in which there's exploitation embedded between classes, and in that sense those on the receiving end of the exploitation of course experience that kind of active and positive role as a state as a harmful thing. So, in that sense, I think you can say it was negative, yes.

At the heart of much of this discussion is the extent to which capital has become international. One frequently hears of single products made from components produced in assembly lines all over the world. How much production is manufactured in this way? And is it correct to say that transnational companies span the globe without allegiance to any one country?

DH: This is a complex area because in some industries that's true—the auto industry, electronics—there's worldwide supply chains for that, textiles as well. But then some industries, that's just not true. And when we talk about the global reach of these production chains, that's some exaggeration too. It tends to be much more regional than that. For example, U.S. corporations source things from Mexico, Western European corporations source things from Eastern or Southern Europe. So there's much more in the way of regional integration going on than this truly seamless global integration.

It's also important to remember too that the dominant industries in the world today, and most people in the First World countries are employed by these, are the service industries and those are highly national, even often quite local. So the idea that we're all just in the midst of this seamless web of global production relations is extreme exaggeration. I think sometimes people on the left and elsewhere read capital's exuberant account of itself and take it all very literally. I think they would like to see a world without boundaries, they would like to see themselves doing things seamlessly and friction free, but the world is a lot more complicated than that.

And money is still a very national institution. We still deal with U.S. dollars and Canadian dollars, so we're a long way before having a single currency in North America. And if we look at what the European Union has been going through, the project to create one currency there even for a continent that has very close economic, political, and cultural ties and which has been tending towards economic integration for fifty years now, they're still having a hell of a time with this, this new currency. So there's an awful lot of economic activity that is circumscribed within national boundaries. I wouldn't want to get caught up too much in the dominant celebratory narrative of capital itself.

LP: I agree with Doug. I think he's put it very well, but I would say this: that American multinationals are involved at the center of much of this regional integrated production that Doug is talking about and to some extent European and Japanese multinationals are involved in other regions as well. So increasingly, what you get is General Motors trying to place itself in Korea, let us say, or China, to engage in the kind of integrated regional production that Doug is talking about. This has been going on for quite a while, of course. The Japanese were coming to North America and engaged in the kind of regionally integrated production here in North America that the big three U.S. automakers have been engaged in for so long. So in that sense you do get world corporations, each of which has a national belonging, playing this role in different regions.

And related to that, you also get the Japanese and European multinationals, themselves dependent on the American states who protect them in the final instance. That is, if Lula in Brazil were indeed to try to do something very radical, let us say with foreign capital, given all the German capital there, the German multinationals would be depending on the American state to do something about Lula in the way of military intervention, much more than on the German state. So you begin to see that Doug is right that overblown conceptions of worldwide production are wrong. There is a global system in the making in which, again, states are very active—especially the American state is very active—and the multinationals that are playing on a world stage are very important.

DH: Could I add to something that Leo just said from a slightly different point of view? A lot of Canadian and Western European leftists criticized the U.S. for its military and political ambitions around the world, but I think, to use the language of economics, in lot of cases Canadian and European capital are "free riders." Sometimes they can take a rather a superior moral tone about how their regimes are better because they're not off launching wars against poor small countries, but in fact they benefit from it as well. They benefit from the global hierarchy that's ultimate enforced by the U.S. military and there is this kind of collegiality among the world's privileged. They're certainly in most cases willing to let the U.S. military do the dirty work.

LP: And even to go further—it's not only at the military level. I had a research trip to Germany and the United Kingdom to interview people at the central banks and the treasuries, the finance departments, and so on. I was really struck by the degree of coordination and integration in policymaking with the American Treasury and Federal Reserve. They act together to try to stabilize the tremendously unstable system that globalization is, especially financially under the umbrella of the American agencies. The G8 countries are heavily involved on a daily basis in doing that kind of managing and firefighting and they're doing it together of course, as well through the World Bank, especially trying to reconstruct Third World states so that they will play this kind of role in managing capitalism as well. So I think Doug's absolutely right, there is a degree of integration with the American imperium that is very, very deep.

Would you say then that there's a difference between this period and the late nineteenth century–early twentieth century period of capitalist expansion that Doug described previously? Radicals from that era argued that national capitalisms were in competition with each other and would be propelled ultimately towards conflict. Do you think that approach has value now?
LP: People on the left still have that conception for the most part, I think wrongly. When they hear the world imperialism, they think still today of inter-imperial rivalry and they think therefore when they speak of American imperialism that it must mean that there's a European counter-imperialism or a Japanese counter-imperialism. And I was exactly trying to indicate that I think that's a misconception today, that the dominant capitalist classes of Japan and Europe and the states of those countries have been since 1945 oriented to being an element in the formation of what now is the greatest empire in the world history.

That isn't to say that there might not be at some time in the late twenty-first century a Chinese counter-imperialism, but that's too far in the future to speak about. So I think that you're right, that that was what imperialism was about in the late nineteenth and early twentieth century, but that the left still walks around with a theory of imperialism that is borrowed from that era and I think is wrong to do so.

DH: I would agree with just about everything that Leo said and add that, as Keynes famously said, a lot of practical people who imagine themselves exempt from intellectual influence are often just slaves of some defunct economist. And I think an awful lot of people who may not even know it are the slaves of Lenin's conception of imperialism from his famous pamphlet *Imperialism* and these notions of rival empires redividing the world as being the nature of imperialism just don't apply these days. The United States certainly is a dominant power, but it has in most cases the active consent of its junior partners, the other G8 countries. It's almost the reverse of the vision that Lenin marked in his *Imperialism* pamphlet; it's that summed up by Trotsky of all the rich countries of the world pleasantly dining together on the poorer countries of the world.

You have both mentioned imperialism in this conversation. Has globalization become a euphemism for imperialism or are these distinct phenomena?
LP: I think one should try to retain these terms in somewhat of a separate way. I don't think that we should transfer all the meaning that the word *capitalism* or *global capitalism* or even *globalization* has to the term *imperialism*. I think imperialism is very much a state thing. It is associated with the stage of capitalism we're in, and its global nature, but it's not quite the same thing.

I think globalization or global capitalism is about some of the things that Doug referred to at the beginning, this massive increase in the proportion of world gross national product that is traded internationally—the enormous flow of capital, including foreign direct investment, both of which entailed therefore the need for the flow of money for financial capital to grease the wheels of trade and foreign direct investments and of course on the basis of that, one gets a whole lot of financial capital feeding on itself. Not all of which is speculation. Some of it is risk management and so on. So you get this enormous body of financial capital at a global level, always centered primarily on Wall Street, to some extent, and the City of London. And a lot of the surplus of what is produced in the world ends up back in those places where it's reallocated, even if it's produced in China or wherever.

So I think globalization is a real thing and I think it's also associated to some extent with this fourth industrial or technological revolution we're living through—the digital revolution or the computer revolution. I don't think it's caused by it but it's an element in it that is part of this process of globalization. And a lot of people point to that calling it things, like Manuel Castells does, the "network society" and so on, which may be going too far, but it's an important element in it.

And then I think another element is the internationalization of the state, which doesn't mean that the United States or even the Canadian state is being bypassed by the World Bank or the WTO. But it does mean that each of these states has a role, not only in managing its own economy in society but in taking responsibility for helping to manage the global economy. That's what the internationalization of the state means. And even Republicans who come in as America-firsters and unilateralists learn very quickly that the United States can't avoid its central role in globalization, and that is managing the global economy or being most responsible for managing it.

The flipside of the antiglobalization thesis, as espoused by many on the left, is that we should return to governance and economic systems at the local level, such as encouraging small business, developing local curren-cies, and so on. Might something be wrong with a society based on small private ownership and local trade?

DH: There are a number of things wrong with that idea. I think first of all we look back on the nineteenth century to when business was much more local, there's also a case of a lot of local monopolies, so I wouldn't want to get nos-talgic about nineteenth-century small business. It's not only historically inac-curate but I just think that's not a very inspiring vision. Here we are, we're speaking on a telephone, one of us in New York, one of us in Berkeley, and one of us in Toronto. We're far apart and speaking to each other, and I think that's a good thing.

I would think that one of the many things wrong with this reckless use of the word *globalization* as an epithet is that it ignores the positive aspects of internationalization. I think we want a good kind of internationalization and certainly the antiglobalization movement, the post-Seattle movements, what-ever you want to call them, these are extremely global and depend upon very advanced technology for their organization and propagation. So I think there's some good things that we should preserve in this idea of globalization, as well as try to tease out the critical parts of it.

Also I think if we want to have a complicated industrial society and don't want to go back to a hunter-gatherer phase, I think it's absolutely impera-tive, just for technical reasons, that we have large-scale organizations that are spread out over space and time. I don't think it's possible to have railroads or telephones or computers or any kind of reasonably advanced technology based on local production and local money. The local money thing is sort of a pet peeve of mine. I just don't understand how you could do anything terri-bly complicated with just relying on local currencies. An example I like to use is that it would be okay for a haircut, but it wouldn't work very well for steel or scissors. So I don't think we can think seriously about organizing an econ-omy on this kind of very local level unless we want to take many, many steps back in technological complexity.

And there are deeper social relations of exploitation that would not be addressed by just shrinking production and trade to the local level.

DH: Yeah. If we talk about just locality—we're talking strictly geography—we're not talking about the social relations that would prevail within those local areas. If we go back to the periods of more localized production, there were owners and workers in those days, too. There's certainly a more direct relation when you know that the mine owner who is exploiting you lives on top of the hill, but still you're being exploited and there's a vast social gulf, even if there's not a great physical distance between boss and worker. I think we should think more about the social relations and less about just the physical configuration of it.

Leo, what's your assessment of calls to retreat to the local?

LP: I do think that the only democracy that we have—and heaven knows it isn't all that great—but the only democracy we have is at a national level or a subnational level and I think whatever power that people who are progressive are going to be able to exercise is going to be exercised at that level. That's not to say that transnational protest movements aren't very important, but I think they are important in the sense that people come home and struggle for the things that are articulated at, say, the ports of Algeria or Rio or wherever else. So I do think what has to think to some extent about how one can enhance and preserve and carry much further a democratization that is nationally and subnationally based.

I don't think that means that one goes down to the local level and I think Doug's critique of that is right. I do think that we would want to look towards promoting a less export-oriented system of production and try to encourage people who, after all, do still have national identities and national and local structures to try to see whether they can't be more self-sufficient. They can't be entirely self-sufficient, but that would entail less exploitation of the Third World. It would also entail, I think, on the other hand, if one was to be really genuinely internationalist and egalitarian, an enormous transfer from the rich world to the poor world of resources. Otherwise, you would just have Canada taking care of itself—or even worse, British Columbia taking care of itself, which is the greatest danger of this localism I think.

So I would like to see a reinvestment in local and national democratic structures but that then was linked internationally through the types of treaties that are the exact opposite of the treaties that bring us free trade and free capital movements, et cetera—rather treaties where people commit themselves to one another to cooperate and redistribute the world's resources in a more egalitarian way. Now I know that's very idealistic but it seems to me that's what we're aiming for.

Are there any opportunities that globalization creates for the left and the labor movement?

DH: Yes, but they have to be recognized and taken advantage of. I said earlier, for example, that the protest movements that we've been talking about are internationally connected and depend upon advanced technology for those international connections. That's one example of the kinds of advantages that can be taken. I wouldn't want to see us all retreat to our little corner of the world and just lobby our city council. In New York City, lobbying the city council would be a very depressing thing to do.

This is not easy by any means, but there are great potentials for a cross-border solidarity among workers and unions. In the case where they do have these regionally integrated supply chains, a strike in a plant in Mexico could interfere with production in Ohio; similarly a strike in a plant in Spain could interfere with production in Britain. So if there are unionized workers left in the world in ten years, I think that this is a point of extreme vulnerability. Add to this the fact that most manufacturing operations these days operate on very short inventories using just-in-time production techniques, coordinated strikes or targeted ones can be very, very disruptive. So, we need much more solidarity among unions of the world than we've seen in the past, certainly. For example, the United Auto Workers in the States has not been a very inspiring example of labor internationalism, but there are great potentials there.

So do you think that the way "globalization" has extended and integrated systems internationally should be rolled back?

DH: Well, I don't know how it can be rolled back. And the periods in history when internationalization was rolled back were not always pretty ones, so I'm not sure that that's possible or even terribly desirable strategy. I think we need to promote much more, to use the old language, a revolutionary consciousness that just is very out of fashion right now.

Do you see that globalization might present any opportunities for the left, Leo?

LP: Well, at least in the sense of overreach, I think it does. Paul Volcker was the head of the Federal Reserve and probably more responsible than anyone else for laying the strategic foundation of neoliberal globalization back in the early 1980s. I heard him speaking to the Toronto Board of Trades of the Canadian ruling class here in Toronto. And he was saying, look, the gloss is off democratic capitalism and we can't go around the world talking about how crony capitalism exists in the Global South. People are laughing at us and pointing to Enron and Worldcom and so on. We need to do something about that.

So I think that to some extent the gloss is off. The kind of triumphalism that Doug referred to on the part of the apologists for cowboy capitalism around the world, that day is over and they've overreached themselves, and more and more people are recognizing, especially in the Global South that this type of globalization is not going to develop the South or most countries in the South easily. So that overreach is important and we may see this with the imperial overreach in Iraq.

That said, I think it is true. I don't know how true it's been of socialism in general, but it's been true of Marx's accounts of capitalism. I think capitalism— by turning people into wage laborers and to proletarians who otherwise are marginal to an economy or even engaged in self-sufficient production of an almost feudal kind—capitalism does raise their standard of living. It increases their exploitation but it does raise their standard of living. The trouble is, it does that in ways that are quite horrific very often. Arguably the Chinese communist-capitalist elite is right in thinking that the Chinese people will be better off in a material sense, richer by virtue of the capitalist path they're treading, but the misery that is being imposed on Chinese working people in that transition is horrific. By official accounts, there are two hundred thousand strikes a year in China as people inevitably react to this.

So that is the contradiction of capitalist history, that it does drive people out into a higher level of consumption and even production and productivity, but inevitably produces misery and struggle and contestation in that process. And socialism emerged on the basis of people engaged in that contestation saying, yes, this is a very dynamic and productive system; it's one that we want to use to build a better type of society on. And I guess globalization is all part of that and I'm optimistic that it is going to lead people to make that claim globally. Finally they will make it on the basis of saying, we need to control these capital movements. Doug's right about wanting internationalism, but people will say, we want the democratic right to decide what's invested, where it's invested, how it's invested and that entails having capital controls—not only over capital flows, transnationally, but within one's own borders.

DH: I think that's an important point because if we had capital controls on just national capital movements, people would still have no say about where capital is invested—if it were organized on a local or regional or national level. And just restricting the scope within national borders doesn't tell you much about how the capital would be allocated within those borders.

I would also add that from the point of view of the people from the Global South, they need their own kind of counter-globalization. There's no way that even a country as large and potentially rich as Brazil could really go it alone right now. If they wanted to cancel their debts or try some kind of alternative development model, it would be nearly impossible for just one country to do that. You would need extensive collaboration among members of, say, Latin American countries to present a common front negotiating with their creditors and also developing their own internal trade relations. The United States, for example, was just furious a few years ago when Brazil was promoting the idea of a regional trade association as a counterbalance to the Free Trade Area of the Americas. But that kind of regional approach and kind of solidarity among the poor counties of the world is absolutely essential if they're ever going to challenge the broad global hierarchy.

Antiglobalization as such is not simply the domain of the left, but it also very much comes from the right. Pat Buchanan for example regularly criticizes the presumed erosion of U.S. sovereignty by multilateral institutions and calls for economic protectionism. Should this be of concern to the left?
DH: Well, I think it should force people to ask themselves some questions. Why is a racist like Pat Buchanan so anti-imperialist and anti-global at the same time? And in some ways, there's a great deal of consistency. He just doesn't like foreigners and he doesn't want to have them within his boundaries and he doesn't want to trade with them. He doesn't want to have anything to do with them; he wants to retreat into this idealized world of pre–Civil War small-town white America. And that's certainly not something that would inspire me or anyone else on the left. I think there's some consistency in his position that it would bear fruit to examine. So I think we need some kind of really progressive internationalism, not that kind of reactionary xenophobic turning inward, which certainly appeals to Buchanan but not to me.

LP: Well, here I might have some difference from Doug. I think that both in North America and in Europe, and I'd even say around the world—this is even the case with Islamic fundamentalists—the inability of the left to speak to people's sense of "I live in this place and I know these people and this is my neighborhood," is a big problem and if the left doesn't have an answer to national identity, doesn't speak to it at all, just treats it as in itself xenophobic, which not all of it is by any means, then I think we're in big trouble. I think that's why I was trying to get at some way of thinking about how democracy, if it does exist anywhere, exists at a national or subnational level and how the left needs to be able to, at least in democratic terms and certainly not in xenophobic terms, try to speak to people's rights to control the resources of the democratic arenas that they operate in and to some extent recognize that national and even local identity is not always racist or exclusionary. That's what the left ought to be appealing to.

DH: I don't know how you have national identity or local identity that isn't in some sense exclusionary by definition though. You're defining A against all that is not A, and that act of defining "not A" always makes me a little uncomfortable. And then the three of us, we're all speaking from three extremely diverse metropolitan areas. You know, we may talk about localism in each of our three areas but you know these regions are all products of intense migration.

Given this alternative understanding of globalization that you've been posing, what strategies do you think the left should adopt in opposing capital?

DH: This is a very ambitious and inspiring project you're undertaking and I'm very pleased to be part of it. And you don't hear very much of it in left circles and most of our publications are not devoted to this kind of serious reflection. So this is a very good start.

I think the broader movements need to do something very similar. I mean, I love the radical cheerleaders and I love the Black Bloc and I love a lot of the styles and even the content of the demonstrations that we've seen all over the place in the last few years. But there really does need to be some more serious talk about how the world works and what kind of world we would like to see and how we get from point A to point B.

I know about a hundred years ago, the farmers who made up the Populist movement in the United States were avid students of monetary economics. It would be nice to see something like that happening again. Political economy or at least economics in particular is often surrounds itself in a shroud of mystique and tries to convince people that everything is just way beyond their understanding. And it's certainly not the case and it certainly is possible for large numbers of people to understand how the world works and then even to think beyond how to make the world a better place, but we do need to have this kind of serious analysis and conversation about it as a starting point.

CHAPTER FOUR

David McNally: The Global Economic Meltdown

Frequent economic turbulence and crises have been the hallmark of neoliberalism. What made the crisis that began in 2007 different than its predecessors?

DM: I think in the first instance it's the scope that makes it so unique, insofar as we've seen a whole series of regional crises across the last couple of decades. Some of the most dramatic ones being the East Asian crisis of 1997, which just hammered into the ground Thailand, Indonesia, South Korea, the Philippines, and Malaysia. And then, of course, the crisis in Argentina of 2000 and 2001 where we had literally the meltdown of a financial system—huge unemployment rates of 25–30 percent, shutdowns of industry, and so on. Those sorts of crises have been par for the course for some time.

But what's distinctive is that this crisis could not be regionally contained. It began quite clearly in the U.S. economy in the summer of 2007, but since then it has gone global in the fullest sense of the word, from the U.S. to Europe to Japan to other parts of East Asia. So the scope is both system-wide in terms of the economy—it's gone from the financial sector into manufacturing and now into services—and it's also gone global in a geographic sense. And that's unlike anything we've seen in a quarter century.

On the left, this crisis tends to be explained in two ways. One focuses on the deregulation of financial markets over the past three decades, which allowed for wild speculation and the incredible proliferation of financial transactions and therefore led to great instability. The other argument is one about a long-term crisis of profitability that started in the 1970s and had been postponed until the present by injections of credit into the system. Why do you take issue with both of them?

DM: The regulation and deregulation argument is the weaker of the two, although I have my own disagreements with both. The problem with the deregulation argument is that it does not identify a systemic fault line: it simply attributes the crisis to a series of neoliberal policies that allowed first the commercial banks and then investment banks and other sorts of shadow banks like hedge funds to run wild. As a result of deregulation, it is claimed that they could do whatever they wanted; they could take on exorbitant debt and make absurd loans and so on. So, if we could just put the genie back in the bottle, the argument goes, we could reregulate the banks and get rid of financial crises like this.

I've got a couple of problems with this argument. The first is that when I look at it, the evidence is not compelling. The deregulation of financial services really followed structural transformations within the world capitalist economy. As capital went global, particularly in the form of the multinational corporation, it encouraged the growth of lending institutions which could operate outside of national boundaries, in the so-called offshore banking system. Particularly through the Eurodollar market, in which banks could deal in dollars in unregulated spaces, like the Caymans, we got a financial system that was responding to a much more internationalized production system. As a result, regulated financial markets like the U.S. and the UK were losing a lot of business to these offshore banks. Sooner or later they pressed to have liberalization and deregulation so they could get into some of these financial operations from which they had been excluded.

What I'm tracing for you here is a process by which first comes the great global reorganization of manufacturing industries through the multinational corporation, then come forms of financing that fit that new world economy, and then comes the deregulation in the major centers. To reregulate you have to imagine that somehow you could wind it all back and that you could have capitalist economies that were predominantly national again—not based on multinational production and the financial arrangements that go with it. So I think the problem for the people that emphasize deregulation is that they are really unable to account for these structural changes—not just policy changes by some evil characters in government. Of course, I do think they are quite evil characters in government, but they were responding to structural changes. If that's true, then no attempt to reregulate could possibly work in a new world of globalized production and finance.

Now, the other approach at least has the merit of saying we have to look at great developments in the whole process of capitalist expansion, accumulation of new production facilities, new plants, mines and factories, and so on. We need to look at corporate profitability. The great strength here is that they're looking at those kinds of phenomena and not just focusing on the financial sector. However, I think there's been a problem with many in this camp of looking at just two or three of the major capitalistically developed economies of the North. The typical frame of reference is to look at the U.S., the German, and the Japanese economies and then to show that profit rates started to come down in the late 1960s.

Well, that's all true. I have no doubt that the rate of profit for all corporations was falling from the late 1960s to the early 1980s. But I think the evidence shows that this was then reversed. To make sense of this, I think we need to look at two really crucial transformations, which are often ignored. First, we need to see the impact of the two great world recessions of 1974–75 and 1980–82 and the way in which they provided the framework for a neoliberal offensive against labor in the North and powerful capitalist restructuring that restored profitability. Then, secondly, there is the neoliberal offensive against the Global South generally and the way in which this led to a geographic reorganization of capitalism, centered on China and East Asia.

When I speak of neoliberalism, I'm talking about a package of policies— if you were going to date it, the transformations begin in China in 1978, and accompany the election of Margaret Thatcher in Britain in 1979, and Ronald Reagan in the U.S. in 1980—where, under the banner of rolling back socialism and the welfare state and letting markets reign supreme again, they cut back social service spending dramatically. They privatized state-run utilities, industries, and so on. And they attacked the power of unions. In the British case the battle over the coalmines was crucial in terms of rolling back the unions and driving down the wage levels that workers in the North can command.

That's the first side of the neoliberal agenda. The second is the attempt to impose enormous hardship on the Global South—to use the debt crisis, which comes to a head with the recession on 1980–82, to go in and essentially rewrite the rules of the game in the Global South through structural adjustment programs orchestrated by the International Monetary Fund and to some degree the World Bank. Where they literally go and say, "You have $450 million in debt that you could never possibly pay with your little economy; well, guess what? You can have new loans that will allow you to make your payments, we'll lend you the money, but you're going to have to do all the things that I've just described and worse. You have to lay off 20 percent of all public employees. You must get rid of any subsidies for fuel and food for the poor. You must massively privatize, you must open up your financial industries, so that Western banks can come in and essentially gobble them up."

That offensive against labor in the North and against the peoples of the Global South generally did lay the basis for a new wave of capitalist expansion. They boosted profits by cannibalizing the South on one hand and by driving down wages in the North on the other. And then they began to relocate production facilities to low-wage zones of the South.

And all of that did produce quite a considerable period of expansion, from at least 1982—the end of the last global recession—to the East Asian crisis of 1997. This is the period in which you see enormous development of manufacturing in a number of these sorts of countries that I've already mentioned: South Korea, China, Indonesia, Malaysia, Taiwan, and so on. East Asia becomes the center of a whole process of global capitalist expansion.

And you can see it in the profitability rates. Profits do start to rise again quite systematically in the 1980s for corporations in Japan, the U.S., Europe, and so on. I say that in opposition to the view that there has been a crisis that began in the 1970s and just persisted for forty years, with no way of getting out of it. In that argument, all that keeps things going is credit expansion, the injection of large amounts of debt into the world economy.

The problem with that argument for me is twofold. First, it ignores the very real material effects of what I'm calling this neoliberal offensive against workers in the North and the people of the Global South generally, the way in which that does boost corporate profitability. It does enable enormous restructuring, particularly of manufacturing industries throughout the world and the geographic reorganization of production, especially in East Asia. As a result, the "forty years of crisis" argument ignores important global transformations. There's a tendency still for a lot of commentators on the left to think about capitalism as North American and Western European, with some reference to Japan, and not to take seriously the way in which the most dynamic centers of growth in the capitalist system have been outside those traditional corridors, particularly in East Asia. That's not to say the capitalist transformations elsewhere are a good thing. China, for example, has probably the most unequal distribution of income of anywhere in the world. But it is to say in capitalist terms—not in decent human terms—these have been growth centers. So I think we need to recognize that and then understand that the neoliberal expansion did begin to falter in 1997 with the enormous meltdown in East Asia. And since then credit and debt have been used to prop up the system until we began to experience this latest crisis in 2007.

If we can't explain the meltdown as part of a longstanding crisis of profitability dating back to the 1970s, how should we understand the roots of the crisis?
DM: What we need to do then, if I'm right, is recognize the ways in which capitalist growth invariably undermines itself. So the expansion from about 1982 to about 2007 lays the basis for a new slump.

The nature of capitalism is that expansion happens in a competitive context. And by that I mean, you have multiple manufacturers of automobiles, cell phones, computers, LCD TVs, whatever, and they are all trying to get their product to market with the best quality at the lowest price. And this means that they are constantly having to find new technologies that will give them a slight edge on the competition. If they can produce the same goods with slightly less labor, with slightly lower costs, they can then undersell their competitors, they can expand their market share, and so on. What this means is there is a frantic drive on the part of all those corporations to build new capacities, to build new state of the art factories, to retool them regularly with the latest computerized production systems. As they do this, they develop much more productive capacity for a specific good—let's say it's cell phones or cars—than can, in fact, be justified by the existing market demand.

In the jargon, this is known as a problem of over-accumulation, which is to say they've accumulated too many factories, too much machinery relative to what they can actually sell. That's the inevitable result of a long period of expansion, just like the expansion at the end of World War II that begins to pick up around 1946–48 and then really runs for the next twenty to twenty-five years into the late 1960s–early 1970s, before we get a global crisis yet again in the 1970s. Similarly, the neoliberal expansion does begin to run out of steam by about 1997 and I don't think it's an accident that as you get this problem of over-accumulation, profits start to turn down again. So it's true that there's a crisis of profitability, it's just that it's been much more dynamic than simply one crisis since the 1970s. There was a 1970s crisis, then what I'm calling a big neoliberal expansion from 1982–97 that gets stretched out for another decade, but then the East Asian crisis tells us that the expansion has generated too much productive capacity relative to what the capitalist market can absorb. There are factories that simply cannot operate profitably.

At that point, it is true that credit expansion does start to intervene. It's halting at first; it's big-time from about 2000–2001, particularly as Greenspan, as the chairman of the Federal Reserve Bank, massively drives down the rate of interest in the U.S. after 9/11 when the ruling class is worried that fear and panic, following upon crises in East Asia, Russia, Brazil and Argentina, will create a global recession.

Do you mean narrowly the expansion of credit to the average person through credit cards and mortgages, or should we be thinking of it more broadly?

DM: Yes, I mean all of that and the most esoteric stuff. And I do want to underline one thing here, because so much of the commentary in North America, and on the left as well, has focused on mortgage-related debt—and no doubt there is this enormous expansion of mortgage debt in the U.S. economy, and as you quite rightly said, Sasha, it included credit card debt. But quite often people lose sight of the fact that the biggest borrowers throughout this whole period were the financial institutions themselves, borrowing from one another. Essentially they are doing that because they get entranced by all these new exotic instruments that they are creating. But, put really simply, all that's happening here is that I'm being extended an IOU—and that IOU can be from Visa or American Express or from a bank that's giving me a mortgage. Anytime that I enter into any credit relation—that is to say I use my credit card, rather than paying cash, or I sign for a mortgage—I'm putting up an IOU. I'm saying, "Yes, I acknowledge I have this debt and I will pay it back according to terms agreeable to the lender." And that's what debt is. We need to think about it as IOUs.

But what these financial institutions then started to do was to package up all kinds of different IOUs together: credit card debt, different kinds of mortgages, and so on. They would literally sell you a whole bundle of them and they produced all kinds of exotic names to make them sound stable and profitable. Collateralized debt obligations were one of the largest of these. The banks went around buying these as well as the hedge funds that were owned by the investment banks on Wall Street. They all bought into their own argument, their own illusions about these things. So, yes, I am talking about mortgage-based debt, credit card debt, but I do want to emphasize that the financial services sector was taking on debt as manically as any other. So we need to be careful. The bubble may have burst in the subprime mortgage market, but it could have burst somewhere else.

You argue that, in the past decades, the financialization of the economy has been a constitutive element of neoliberalism. Can you back up and explain the importance of this financialization?

DM: Yes, you're right—it is really important. The way I see it, there are several elements involved here. When we talk about financialization, all we're really talking about is that the provision of a larger share of all goods and services involve financial transactions—more of education, healthcare, housing is provided through the market and through credit markets in particular— and that more of the profits made from the production of goods and services are staying in the hands of the financial sector. In fact the financial sector's share of profits rose from about 10 percent of profits some thirty years ago to 40 percent in the last few years. So what financialization really means is that financial transactions are becoming more and more prominent in everyday life and they are becoming more and more lucrative, more and more profitable.

Now the roots for that go back to when U.S. President Nixon took the U.S. economy off gold convertibility with the dollar. Let me put it this way. If you had an old U.S. dollar from 1971 or before, it was legally convertible into $\frac{1}{35}$ of an ounce of gold. In principle, I could take thirty-five of them and get for them an ounce of gold (although often only central banks could exercise that right). That provided a very serious pillar of stability to the global economy.

As the U.S was losing world market share, becoming more dependant on imports from other countries, as it began to develop trade deficits in the late

1960s, it became harder and harder to keep that convertibility of dollars for gold. In fact, foreign central banks did start to cash in their dollars for gold and there was a huge drain on gold out of the U.S.

So when U.S. President Nixon suspended that convertibility, he said you can no longer get gold for dollars, at which point the whole world monetary system became enormously unstable. What's a dollar really worth? Moreover, what is any currency really worth, because most currencies were pegged to the dollar—the Canadian dollar, of course, but that would also have been true of the Japanese yen or the German mark or the French franc. They had all been tied to the exchange rate of the dollar, which was in turn tied to gold. Once that ended, it was a field day for speculators. They could now start to speculate what the value of a given currency was. They could drive them up or down by betting one way or another. This made it incredibly difficult for businesses to operate. So business began to demand a certain kind of protection from the enormous volatility of currencies.

I'll give you an example. A German corporation could make a profit in U.S. dollars at its manufacturing plants, let's say in the U.S., but when it shipped those profits home it might take a loss in its domestic currency if the dollar had massively fallen. The book value at the head office in Frankfurt would then be a loss. So, they were worried about this kind of monetary instability. One answer to this was to create a contract which would allow you to buy a currency at a certain rate or sell it at a certain rate—and that's why currency trading just exploded in the 1970s. I won't take you through all the ins and outs of it, but this is where the so-called derivative markets also exploded. Now people were essentially trying to hedge the risk of a currency rising or falling by getting someone to agree to buy dollars, yen, whatever at a certain rate at some point in the future. They hoped, in other words, to achieve greater stability by locking in exchange rates through futures contracts.

There were enormous profits to be made as well as enormous losses to be made here. This was a field day for speculators. It was a field day for people who wanted to buy and sell currencies. It was a field day for people who wanted to buy and sell so-called derivatives contracts, which were essentially options to buy or sell a given currency. So the trading in all this stuff, all these currencies and all these contracts designed to hedge the risk of currencies rising or falling, just proliferated. That's the big structural underpinning of financialization.

Then you add to that the expansion of all the other kinds of debt we've been talking about from mortgages to credit cards to financial borrowing by banks and so on. You get a situation where more and more transactions in the economy are really paper transactions. They are just about buying and selling currencies, stocks, bonds, loans, mortgages, credit card debt, and so on. That's what drives financialization and it does mean that enormous profits flowed into that sector. But a lot of that is speculative. A lot of these profits are gained by simply betting on the movement of one thing to another.

A point can come where investors out there become suspicious of buying all these exotic sounding financial instruments. If for whatever reasons they lose confidence in their viability, then the whole system is in trouble really quickly. If a few really big institutions make bad bets and they collapse, then the question is, who can you trust to buy financial instruments from. You run the risk of buying junk. When that happens, markets really seize up. So, in the summer of 2007 the first hedge funds started to go down, then the Wall Street investment banks went down, and investors said, "We don't want to touch this stuff. It's toxic. All these collateralized debt obligations and all these mortgage-backed securities and all this sort of stuff is going to blow up in my face." And when they don't want to touch it, it means banks are left holding all these so-called assets, whose values are in fact falling on the market. So, financialization of this sort bred speculation, asset bubbles, and crashes.

How would you explain the distinction between so-called fictitious capital and real capital? How does the collapse of the former affect the latter?
DM: Anytime you buy an IOU, you have a fictitious capital. You can claim it as an asset—as banks do when they give me a mortgage and claim they have this financial asset that they can sell to someone else. But the problem is that asset is fictitious. And by that I mean it's only as good as the future payments that come in. In other words, you can give me a mortgage, but that mortgage is only as good as my capacity to pay a year from now and five years from now and ten years from now. In the here and now, if you lend me money for a mortgage, and you take that loan contract and you tell some other investor out there, I've got this loan and I'm willing to sell it to you as an asset—well, it's a fictitious asset because there's no guarantee that it's backed up by anything.

These financial instruments are fictitious in the sense that they may never become real. Of course, a lot of the time these IOUs do get paid off. There's a real flow of income and so on. The more inflated markets get, however, the more dubious some of the loans out there become. Really that is what's happened in this crisis. But they made $1 trillion of loans and then went around selling these loans as if they were assets and they have now turned out to be fictitious. That's been one of the quite revealing things.

When I first started giving a lot of talks on this, the major global financial institutions were saying there was about $250 billion of bad loans out there in the system. Well, if you take what they have written off and the predictions of what is yet to come, they've now gone nearly ten times as high. Now imagine what that tells us if the financial institutions could be off to that degree, if they could underestimate by 90 percent the actual scale of worthless capital out there. That tells you how quickly loans that they thought were sound can be revealed to be fictitious.

Of course, to the second part of your question, as those fictitious capitals collapse, and lending institutions start to go broke, they then start to put pressure on all kinds of borrowers in the so-called real economy. They want other loans paid back. They start to call loans in. They start to make it more difficult to get credit and so on. This is what was really hammering away at GM and Chrysler when they had to declare bankruptcy.

That's one side of the effect on the so-called real economy. The other is that as the financial sector gets hammered, it engages in layoffs. In 2008 alone, about a quarter of a millions jobs were lost in the financial services industries in the U.S. That's a quarter million more people right there who start to reduce their spending—they're not going to buy a car, they're struggling to pay their mortgages, or maybe they're not able to pay them anymore so they're delinquent. Their credit card debt is running up. They start to cut back on consumption and spending. That of course has a knock-on effect in other industries. So while the bubble burst first in the financial sector, it inevitably spread throughout the so-called real economy. And the more vulnerable the real economy is, the more it is suffering under over-accumulation of the sort I described earlier and declining profit margins which comes with over-accumulation, then it's really, really vulnerable to the hits that come on the financial side. And that's what we're seeing right now.

You've mentioned that the roots of financialization date back to Nixon's de-linking the dollar from the gold standard in the early 1970s. What role does the dollar play now as the default currency for the rest of the world? DM: I think, medium-term, this is going to be a hugely important issue. It doesn't look it right now for reasons I'll explain. As you say, if we look at the situation in 1971 the U.S. president says you can no longer get gold for dollars. It raises a really important question: why should economies the world over use the dollar as their international reserve currency if they can't convert it? If they accumulate huge reserves of it and they can't cash it in for gold, what are they going to do with it?

This was played out with a lot of struggle between the Europeans and the Americans in the early 1970s, because there was a push by the Europeans to move towards some alternative currency, perhaps something floated by the IMF. The U.S. government was able to defeat such moves through a combination of bullying and making sure the oil producing countries kept pricing oil in dollars. As the price of oil exploded in the early 1970s, it became clear that as long as oil was priced in dollars and as long as most countries import oil, they're going to need dollars.

So the U.S. dollar hung on as the main international reserve currency, that is to say, the currency that most countries will use between one another. After all, if Brazil and Thailand are doing trade, the odds are that when they settle up accounts they don't want one another's currencies. They're happy to take dollars. So the dollar operates as the international currency that most countries are prepared to use and most banks and corporations are happy to use.

The other thing is that there wasn't really a viable alternative to it. Now, I think that in the last decade we've seen the emergence of a potential alternative currency and that's the euro. The European Union is about the same size—population and economy-wise—as the U.S. economy. Its currency has done very, very well. What's we've seen is a slow drift away from the dollar and towards the euro, as if a lot of nations and a lot of corporations think that in case the dollar is going to go down, why don't we at least start to accumulate both the euro and the dollar? In the midst of this crisis, there has been a flight back to the dollar just as there has been a flight to gold in part because investors are so frightened by the turmoil, and because it is not clear if Europe will be able to hold together in a crisis. Investors figure that the U.S. government, the Treasury, isn't going to go broke at least. So if I just go and buy treasury bonds and treasury bills from the U.S. at least I know my money is safe. And they feel so much uncertainty about the safety of most of the global financial system that they've poured back into dollars.

But long-term or even medium-term I'm less sure that's going to be the case. You look at the huge injections of money—the bailout costs in the U.S. are about $5 trillion so far—most of that's been accomplished simply by printing money. The Federal Reserve Bank and the U.S. Treasury have been in agreement that they will print as much money as necessary to keep the banking system afloat. That ultimately is money that will flow back into the hands of investors the world over, particularly central banks in countries like China and Japan and South Korea. I'm not convinced that long-term, as we look at both of these, the trade deficits and the budget deficits in the U.S., that they're going to feel enormously secure about that. My own prediction would be whenever we start to come out of the worst part of this crisis, the U.S. dollar will probably start to fall in value again and while that can be a good thing for U.S. exporters, because it makes their goods less expensive elsewhere, it's not a good thing for the financial sector in the U.S., because it means more and more transactions are going through other currencies and not through U.S. dollars. At the same time, if Europe looks wobbly, there will not be any viable alternative to the dollar.

So I think there is a question mark over longer-term prognosis for the dollar, even though I don't expect it to be replaced in short order. You can see it already in the speeches that happened at the Davos Forum in 2009, where both the Russian and Chinese presidents were more or less saying we have to move away from a dollar denominated, dollar dominated global economy. And I think that's going to be an ongoing trend. The other side of it is that the American model of capitalism has been discredited in this crisis and I think that's not going to help the financial sector and the dollar either.

What would the decline of the dollar as the default global currency mean for the power of the United States as an empire? And how does this crisis affect the ability of the U.S. to continue extending itself around the world as an occupying power?

DM: Let me start with empire. I think long-term this cannot be good for American imperial power and frankly that's not something that bothers me. I'm quite happy to see the U.S. empire less powerful around the world. You're dealing here with an economy that was already running a current account deficit equal to about 6 percent of GDP prior to the crisis. It was buying from the rest of the world massively more than it could sell to the rest of the world and it was just shipping out dollars to cover that. That's okay as long as the rest of the world thinks those dollars are good. But if they get nervous about dollars and they start to dump them because they really don't want to keep holding onto billions and some cases trillions of them, then that's going to push the value of the U.S. currency down.

That's going to cause lots of problems when you want to carry on major military operations in other parts of the world because they literally become more expensive when you've got to do business in local currencies where you're running military bases and so on. Also, the huge deficits on the government's side that are being run up under the bailout program and the Bush-Obama stimulus package, are going to enormously expand the U.S. government budget deficit and that too is essentially covered by paper, by the printing of U.S. dollars and so that's going to be a double pressure, where I think investors are going to question the viability of the dollar.

So for the U.S., this economic crisis comes in the context of the real military debacle in Iraq and the ongoing failure of the Afghan mission. Obama thinks he can simply move troops from Iraq to Afghanistan, but all this is going to come with serious long-term costs. If they are going to be serious about what they want to do, you are talking about a couple of decades of the U.S. having to conduct occupations. These costs on the American economy are going to be really dramatic.

This is going to raise awfully big questions about the trillions of dollars that are going into military expenditure and bailing out a failing financial system, money that could otherwise be going into healthcare, social housing, and so on. That's going to be the really key political debate coming up. So I see the U.S. empire as developing less capacity to intervene whenever and wherever it wants as a result of some of the costs of this crisis. And I also suspect that the domestic debate about if we're going to spend trillions, where should they be spent, is likely to increase over the next couple of years.

You write that "crises are moments in which the subordination of labor to capital must be reorganized, and in which new spaces of resistance can be pried open." How so?
DM: We often think of the crisis as just a crisis of some economic statistics, but I think it much more than that. It's really a crisis for the very structures of capitalism and when that happens it means the things that most people take for granted become the subject of discussion and debate. Lots of examples can illustrate this. Take the factory occupation in Chicago at Republic Windows and Doors. There you have a situation, a tactic that has not been used by working class people in the United States since the depression of the 1930s, which all of the sudden becomes a mobilizing tactic when a factory is shutting its doors without honoring its financial obligation to its employees, their severance pay, and so on. Nevertheless, one of their major owners, the Bank of America, had been at the public trough getting a bailout. I think in these crises where all of a sudden job security is up for grabs, plant shutdowns are the order of the day.

Or take the fact that the economy is being stimulated by massive government spending. That, of course, exposes the claim that free markets are the answer to everything and anything. That raises so many social questions that normally don't get addressed. In other words, for years and years the refrain of the so-called neoliberals, their claim was, you've got to run balanced budgets. Now, of course they didn't do it, but that was the claim. Fiscal prudence, cut taxes, rely on the market, and so on. That whole ideology is melting down and all of the sudden they discover trillions of dollars that they claim not to have had in the past. Moreover, they can give the Bank of America lots of money while it's involved in an operation of closing a plant, throwing workers out on the street, and not even giving them their severance pay.

So I think moments like this produce very profound contradictions for the everyday reproduction of the assumptions we have about capitalism and how it works. People start to raise questions they normally wouldn't raise and even act in ways—like occupying a plant—that they normally wouldn't. On a larger global scale I think we can see it in a whole wave of development. Think of the riots and general strikes in Greece. Or the government in Iceland that fell after agreeing to an IMF package, and after groups in civil society started to organize every Tuesday night outside the Parliament building. Eventually they started to do it every night. There was fighting with the police, there were demonstrations, and eventually the rightwing government in Iceland had to resign. And of course there have also been big general strikes and demonstrations of between one and two million in France over how the government is dealing with the crisis.

As people look at what a capitalistic economy in crisis does to their livelihood, quality of life and so on, they can begin to think and act differently about the priorities of our society and how it's organized. So I see this as a moment for real opening for progressives and leftwing alternatives. I see this as a moment in which a left that can think creatively about the challenges of the twenty-first century and not be tied to past dogmas and past formulas but can really think creatively, can perhaps begin to speak and act on a much larger scale than we have been used to for quite some time.

Many of us hope for an end not just to neoliberalism but to capitalism itself. Yet the magnitude of the crisis appears overwhelming and many are focusing on ameliorating its impact. How do you think the left should orient its organizing and demands, reconciling the tension between immediate issues and goals, such as keeping people from being evicted, and a longer-term, far-reaching agenda?

DM: Yes, there is a tension and I think we need to figure out ways of formulating responses to the crisis that combine them. I think this is tricky, but I think it can be done. I'll try and give you some examples that combine solutions to immediate issues such as loss of jobs and loss of homes on the one hand with a kind of anticapitalist thrust to them. If we're talking about something like the crisis in the automobile industry, right now the only real discussion by the unions—and I say that about both the unions here in Canada as well as the United States—is how big wage concessions should be, how may layoffs we should accept, how much we should reopen our contracts and so on. It's really vital we begin to find ways of injecting into a wider discourse the idea that bailouts, for instance, of corporations like the Detroit Three, should be based upon principles of no layoffs, no wage cuts. And if it can be demonstrated that the factories themselves are in fact surplus, then we need to talk about actual conversion programs in which these plants would be redesigned for the so-called green economy, producing solar panels, diesel buses, that sort of thing.

Secondly the bailouts should operate on the principle that if you're investing public funds then this should be joined to public ownership. So as government intervenes and buys up banks and corporations, it effectively social-

DAVID McNALLY

izes them and moves them into the public sphere and out of the private. This
would also mean subsidizing them where necessary, which means moving out
of the logic of the market economy. If we're going to produce solar panels
in a plant in Dearborn, Michigan, that used to produce cars for instance and
it can't make a profit right away, the public purse should be made available to
keep a productive industry going based on non-market priorities, like maintaining employment and improving the environment.

Part of it is that the left needs to be much more creative and proactive
about getting an alternative, if you will, "stimulus package," which has things
like public ownership, job protection, income protection, building the green
economy, and so on really centrally built into it.

The other side of it is that we need to seize the opportunities for ongoing
popular education. One of the things we're doing, and it's really small-scale,
in Toronto is that we've brought together about six different activist organizations and movements to create something called the Popular Education and
Action Project. And we are hoping to get out into communities, union locals,
high schools, and universities doing popular education that's providing both
anticapitalist analysis and talk, discussing anticapitalist alternatives.

I think there's a real opening right now for trying to open those spaces
where the serious currents on the left, those that are nonsectarian, those that
are really open to operating on a basis of solidarity and common causes, can
create joint frameworks for action and education. Obviously this is going
to vary from locale to locale, but I would hope in the coming months that
such discussions will be happening in more and more places. I think this is a
moment to think really creatively about what this crisis for capitalism means.
And as you say, I do agree, Sasha, not simply by way of responding in terms
of the immediate demands, which we must take up—to defend people's jobs
and their houses and so on—but also to try to take up campaigns that will also
contribute to popular education and actually getting anticapitalist responses
to the crisis into a much wider discourse.

**Are you concerned at all about a crisis of ideas on the left? One segment
of the left seems to be pushing for a return to the Keynesian welfare state,
which characterized the social democracies following World War II and
to a lesser extent the U.S. And, on the other hand, you have those focusing
very specifically on local struggles and less on a wholesale, systemic agenda
for transformation. Does it concern you that there aren't ideas currently
in circulation that really would be able to address this crisis?**
DM: Yes. I think that is a real issue. There's a danger that—really just to elaborate on what you just said—those who are speaking to what we may call sys-

temic alternatives are really trying to do that in Keynesian terms. That is to say they are really imagining that we can go back to, say, 1940s, 1950s, early-1960s style of capitalism with much more regulation. I think, for reasons we've talked about already, that's a nonstarter. I think that it does not address the world in which we live. It's just a dead end for the left. You're right, the danger then is that the alternative is seen as a certain kind of local activism, and believe me, I'm a big believer in digging in and acting where we are and building resistance movements where we are and so on. But I think we can only get so far and, more than that, we actually squander certain opportunities right now if we're not putting forward a wider anticapitalist systemic approach. In other words, raising issues about how an economy might be reorganized, about how global relations between North and South might be reorganized, and popularizing ideas like social ownership, workers' self-managed production, the reduced work-week across the board, the redistribution of wealth from North to South, the green economy, and so on—really developing an integrated response which isn't Keynesian but which really does speak to the global realities in which we find ourselves today.

Interestingly, that discussion is clearly happening in other parts of the world. The statement by the World Social Movement's meeting in Brazil as part of the World Social Forum was very much exactly to that point. They are trying to move toward that kind of analysis and perspective. But I think in North America in particular we've tended to lag behind. I think the Latin American movements are ahead of us on that in particular. I think the activist left in some of the European countries, particularly France, are ahead of us on that. We need to be able to say that the local activism is crucial because that's where you build the actual resistance movements of the day, but at the same time this is a moment for the really serious left to think on a much wider scale as to how to begin to popularize alternative economics and anticapitalist forms of organization. Because this is an opportunity where we don't want our voices to be either lost because we're only doing the local activism or to be speaking in the outmoded language of Keynesianism. In that sense, the slogan which has come out of Venezuela about a socialism for the twenty-first century seems to me to be more urgent than ever before. It's an opportunity to really redefine socialism and anticapitalism in terms of its original democratic commitments and its internationalist commitments. I think there's a lot of space for that if we can figure out how to do it.

CHAPTER FIVE

Sam Gindin, Greg Albo, and Leo Panitch: Capitalist Crisis and Radical Renewal

Liberals and leftists alike argue that the economic crisis was caused by a lack of state regulation over the banks and financial markets. Consequently, they conclude that we just need new regulation to keep the financial sector in line. Why don't you think that's the case?

LP: Well, the cause of the crisis was certainly related to competition in the financial sector. But that competition was to some extent the product of state regulation. The American financial system is certainly the most regulated financial system in the world, and probably in history, if you measure it in terms of the number of pieces of legislation, the number of regulatory agencies, and the massive amounts of regulation to which finance is subject.

So, yes, there were changes that allowed for more competition in finance, although those changes were only a matter of closing the barn door after the horse had bolted. It was already the development of finance that made the old New Deal regulations impossible. The state then removed those limits and encouraged further competition in finance. So it's just a misunderstanding of what's really going on. There's a sense that the state didn't do its job in constraining markets. And there's a confusion about what a capitalist state is. A capitalist state responds to and sponsors and facilitates markets. The notion that it's there to restrain markets, to restrain capitalism, that if only it would do that it would remove the contradictions of competition in capitalism, is simply a cockamamie way of seeing the world. Although unfortunately it's the way in which it's ideologically presented to us.

Much of this may appear counterintuitive, since the dominant narrative on the left is that over the last three decades the state has retreated and let markets run unfettered. Could you give some concrete examples of the ways the state actually facilitates markets?

LP: At the most basic level, you couldn't have contracts. You couldn't have property without all of the things that the state does in the form of law, in order to guarantee to one side of a contract, or to one capitalist to another, that their deals can be validated. So at the most basic level the state is in there.

But more than that, states are oriented to facilitating accumulation on their own terrain. And some of them, the imperial states like the American, are oriented to facilitating capital accumulation and the spread of markets to do that around the world. They do that in a myriad of different ways. People think the New Deal regulations were brought in to constrain finance. Yet in many ways the Glass-Steagall Act that separated commercial from investment banking, for instance, was adopted in order to stabilize finance and to nurture it back to health. Through the whole of the postwar period there was a very close corporatist relationship between the banking sector and the regulators. The regulators were oriented to nurturing finance, not only back to health but to a new stage of development. And that's what began to happen by the 1960s.

Some of the old constraints that were put on the separation between commercial and investment banking then began to make less and less sense as finance was now very powerful and expansive and spreading around the world. And you got some removal of those. The big example was the 1975 New York Big Bang where New Deal price-ceilings on what brokers were allowed to charge for buying and selling stocks for people were broken down. They were mainly broken down because pension funds and other institutional investors were buying very large blocks of them and they wanted discounts.

Another example is the removal of Glass-Steagall, the separation of commercial and investment banking, which allowed commercial banks to be involved with derivatives, act as brokers and sell insurance, and so on. But that had already been broken down. It was never applied internationally and it had broken down domestically in the United States since the early 1980s. So it was really changing the legislation after finance had already expanded in the way it had.

Coupled with the notion that deregulation is the cause of our current economic woes is a belief that finance is simply a parasite on the real economy. What you argue, however, is that, although part of finance is obviously speculative, finance actually plays a crucial role for accumulation in general. LP: Finance is speculative and, yes, it is very much about trying to make money by trading on money. The connection between money and other commodities—money in the classic sense of contributing to producing a thing, a good— seems to have faded and I think that's where the misconception of money as *only* speculative comes from.

But no production takes place without the provision of credit. And increasingly no production takes place without the provision of credit to consumers. And finance has been crucial to the dynamics of expanded production. Especially in terms of globalization and financing the means of integrated production right around the world.

So when people for instance speak of derivatives as simply speculation, there certainly is speculation involved, but you couldn't have somebody, say

Wal-Mart, contracting with a supplier in China to produce something that will be on Wal-Mart shelves in the United States next winter, unless both parties were able to find financial intermediaries that would allow them to hedge the difference in what the exchange rate between the dollar and the renminbi is now and what it will be next winter. Or do the same with what transportation costs will be at that time. Or do the same with what interest rates will be at that time. So these derivatives are means of buying insurance in relation to fulfilling a contract for the delivery of things that are produced.

You simply couldn't have global production with out the role that finance plays just in this respect, and I'm not even getting into the role that finance plays in terms of venture capital, which was very important in terms of the development of information and technology revolution we just lived through; or the role it plays in terms of facilitating investment. You could do the same for the kind of role that finance plays in terms of making indebted consumers into viable consumers. And you see that through credit cards and many, many other aspects of the role that finance plays. And that even has to do with the role that finance played in housing, which led to the subprime crisis. People were taking out second mortgages in order to sustain their consumption in part. Now you can go even further to look at the role that finance plays via channeling workers' savings into pension funds and the role those pension funds play in investing in stock markets, investing in derivatives, and so on, which has to be traced through how that links to production.

It's an illusion to imagine that finance is out there in some greedy Gordon Gecko world and that is "bad capitalism," rather than what GM does which is somehow "good capitalism," and why GM was in the tank was because of the Geckos of this world. Not at all. This is capitalism and both productive capital, in the sense of industrial corporations or retail firms like Wal-Mart, and the big banks are part of the totality and we need to understand them in terms of the way they link with one another.

Various Marxist critics have argued that the financialization of the economy is capital's means of addressing the underlying stagnation of the "real economy," of industry in decline. The argument goes that the current crisis is part of a long downturn starting in the 1970s and capitalism's ill-health has been masked by a shift into profit-making through all sorts of incomprehensible derivatives and forms of speculation. You three see things quite differently, as you make apparent in your book *In and Out of Crisis*.
SG: To elaborate first a little more on what Leo was saying: part of the role of finance—once you see it in terms of capitalism—is to discipline and restructure the so-called real economy. It's been fundamental to that, imposing disci-

pline on every factory to be more competitive or finance will go somewhere else, to reallocate capital across several sectors, venture capital in particular, but much more generally. So finance has been fundamental to that.

The other way that finance has been absolutely crucial is to understanding capitalism in terms of its imperial dimension. It's been fundamental to capitalism actually penetrating other countries, imposing certain conditions if they want the finance, putting the United States in a position where the American state is responsible for managing capitalism more generally; and for integrating the working class in the circuits of capitalism in terms of housing and pensions and their assets rising. It's also been a socialization of workers.

Turning to the question of decline, if you leave aside looking at specific numbers for a second and just think about what's happened over the last quarter of a century, it actually looks like one of the most dynamic periods from a capitalist perspective—not from a worker perspective, but from a capitalist perspective. It's a period in which they've penetrated China. They've penetrated the former Soviet Union. They're now penetrating the enormous potential of the Indian market. We've seen a powerful commodification of things that used to be seen as part the commons. Part of what government provides has been privatized as sources of accumulation. There have been very radical breakthroughs in technology over this period in terms of that kind of dynamism.

And then when you actually look at the numbers, what you do see is that profits have actually recovered from their previous lows. They're not at the peak they were at in the 1960s, but that was a unique period. And the restructuring of the economy has been very dramatic across sectors. If you're looking at the American economy, it has restructured geographically. It has restructured in terms of what sectors are dominant right now. The importance of business services has become a very fundamental part of the economy, especially in terms of the American global role. High tech in the U.S. has grown dramatically. The U.S. has been importing a lot but it has also been exporting a lot.

So I don't think there's a lot of credibility to the argument of the American economy having declined. The real problem we have is that all this restructuring has gone on and workers have basically been pretty passive victims. They've accepted this. They haven't in any way been acting as a barrier in terms of putting other social goals or social values on the agenda. And that's allowed capitalism—American capitalism in particular—to restructure at will. And it's done really well in terms of accumulation.

You mentioned that finance has allowed the U.S. to play a particularly imperial role. How does the U.S. exercise its imperial hegemony, as you see it?
SG: The way we've been trying to think about it is, yes, there's direct involve-

ment in terms of occupation, there's direct involvement in terms of transforming so-called failed states when there's no other mechanism of doing this. But the crucial point about the American empire is that unlike national empires of the past, which actually carved up the world, this empire is trying to create a global capitalism and is acting on behalf of global capital and penetrating through capitalist institutions. That's the important element of this empire's penetration.

If more American investment is going abroad and less is in the U.S., if the U.S. share of global production is going down, that's often interpreted as a symbol of decline. But in fact what it is signifying is the spread of capitalism, its penetration into other societies, transforming social relations in those societies, transforming the states in those societies so those states actually take on responsibility for supporting global accumulation, including American accumulation within their own borders. You're creating a global capitalism within which the American state and American capital have structural power.

The structural power comes from the fact that the U.S. is still the dominant country in terms of technology. It's increasingly playing a crucial role in terms of what I raised before—business services, accounting, legal, consulting, engineering, and of course finance. There's more concentration of American power in finance then there is in other sectors. So it's very important not to see imperialism as being only about territorial intervention. And it's very important to understand that this kind of empire grows through actually spreading production, in a sense sharing production globally in a particular way.

Clearly, the type of economic regime of the last four decades is in crisis. Is the neoliberal model, in which the U.S. was in some ways the main proponent player, now dead?
GA: I think it's very hard to claim, given the way that the crisis unfolded, that neoliberalism is over or dead. Certainly we're entering another phase of it where many of the contradictions that have been internal to neoliberalism from the beginning have compounded and are now taking on a different form. One could begin, of course, with financialization and the role of financialization in neoliberalism from the beginning and financial crises being one of the elements of the developmental model of neoliberalism. And clearly the way that some of those characteristics of finance had developed in the last decade, such as the unregulated forms of collateralized debt obligations, are mutating into something quite different and we're likely to see some new regulatory forms in and around many of those markets. But we're unlikely to see those markets abandoned. We can see the way that the regulatory reform issue in Congress is going forward that these aren't radical interventions in overturning

the forms of financialization that have been central to neoliberalism. I think that's one contradiction or problem that has been present that is still there.

We see the same thing with inequalities. Wage inequalities, income inequalities, the lowering of transfers to people on welfare, and so on have been another aspect of the developmental model of neoliberalism. In many ways, that's at a crisis with the rates of unemployment being higher, the rates of people on welfare being higher, and the income inequalities continuing to expand. There are some pressures from below to address those. But as a whole, without a larger political movement we can see also that the way that the crisis is unfolding it's not on the political agenda to start overturning the income distribution dynamic of neoliberalism. In fact, the way the austerity packages are moving through the various capitalist states of the world, the workers and the poor are the key people who are paying for the crisis.

Similarly, we can see some of the tensions in and around the balance of payment issues and current account differences. There are some tensions that have been always internal to neoliberalism between the current account surpluses of certain zones of the world and the current account deficits of other parts of the world, particularly the U.S., and there's some tension in and around that. There has also been no real route out of it as of yet, with Europe in problems and not being able to move into a major importing zone and the countries of East Asia not wanting to reverse themselves either. It's likely the situation of the current account deficit of the U.S. will be continuing and some of the asymmetries in the world payment system are likely to continue.

So in many ways, we're definitely in another phase of neoliberalism as a result of this crisis. Certainly, its clear that the political forces in no part of the world have been able to break out of the neoliberal political policies or the balance of power that has backed neoliberalism, that is, the way that finance and industry have supported neoliberal policies at the level of the state.

So is this, then, an impasse based on a crisis of vision on the part of elites? Or has neoliberalism still not yet run its course as a viable engine of accumulation?
GA: Neoliberalism is linked to a particular policy framework within capitalism that tends towards a certain balance between the state and market—not necessarily, as Leo was pointing out, a withdrawal of the state, but the market playing the leading role in the determination of where investment is allocated and how incomes are formed. And within that general framework the ideas of neoliberalism can adapt to a new moment, particularly if there are no other political forces on the agenda, the ideas will be generated and something will come up and this model of capitalism will continue.

I think there's a real bankruptcy of ideas among liberals and social democrats. I think that's where the key flaw is—in the hopes that somehow state power can simply be reasserted over markets and finance constrained as a key way that an alternative of reform could come forward and, alongside that, an expansion of various regulatory structures. I think modern social democracy has failed not only at the political level, but also fails to understand many of the dynamics of contemporary capitalism.

I think the problem on the left actually is not a question of ideas as many people often put forward. I think there are many ideas on the left on how to address the crisis—from work-time reduction to various ideas about green conversion, the traditional ideas on the left on expansion of the social sector. There are many, many interesting new ideas about restructuring the state and planning. The problem really on the left is one of political and organizational capacities right now. That is just not present, so the left really isn't on the political stage as a political force, both at the level of unions and social movements. Certainly in North America we're nowhere near having an adequate political force that is capable of offering an alternative vision, an alternative agenda, especially being inventive about how new social forces might be organized.

As you're suggesting, there's clearly more than one route out of the crisis. How would you envisage a route that would benefit the working class? I would ask what route would not benefit them, but presumably that's what we're seeing now.

GA: Why don't I start with the route that is not benefiting them? Clearly, the route that is being put forward right now is that of the capitalist class and the existing states have had complete sway in setting the agenda. The initial responses that had emerged with some strike responses, some housing occupations, have largely fallen to the side, although I'll come back to the Greek case in a second. They've had a quite wide swath to cut in setting a new agenda and they're doing this with minor reforms around regulatory structure. Particularly, what they're managing to do is paying for the financial crisis and offloading so much of the bad debt into the state sector and the state sectors' emergency responses are now focused on what the International Monetary Fund has called for as a decade of austerity. Meaning that transfers to the poor are to be cut back. Public sector wages are being cut back in the order of 5–10 percent. Income transfers are being cut back. Other forms of social programs are being cut back. And this is being backed around the world by both conservative governments and social democratic governments. They've had a complete freedom to set that agenda.

There has been little response. Protestors haven't been able to push aside the move by those governments to implement these really draconian austerity packages. Right now the route out of the crisis is particularly being set by the capitalist class, in our view within the framework of neoliberalism—although neoliberalism has taken many forms, maybe we'll want to call it something different—but it was within that agenda.

It is very difficult to see any social democratic response at the moment emerging, that is, some alternative reflationary strategy that would have the tax burden shift more onto the capitalist class through various kinds of crises taxes or taxes on financial speculation of a major kind; not the small transaction taxes being discussed as basically a backstop for future financial crises.

So what you're left with is largely the question of whether you can begin engaging the union movement, the social movements, and radical political parties in a new project of organization and challenging capitalism. In an initial sense, I think that's a big question more along the lines of organizing, than per se a reform response to the crisis. It has a lot to do with new forms of attempting to organize unions and allowing much participation of workers in unions. A whole range of issues is involved there.

Within the specific ways that policies of reform could be put forward now, there's all kinds of things that could be could be raised in the context of building such a counter movement: one could be arguing for campaign around free public transit, as a way to respond to the crisis in terms of a green alternative that would have popular resonance among both ecologists and workers and poor people. Work-time reduction should be on the agenda as another response. It would be relatively easy to begin campaigns for a crisis tax—that is, a special levy on high-income groups and on the financial sector—and so on. It's easy enough to come up with a range of programs or reforms that we could struggle for. Many of our movements are putting forward some of those across North America, particularly in the major cities where there are a lot of struggles around urban reform and the whole range of housing issues as a consequence of the crisis. The question is really building a renewed left with a much different political capacity.

Sam, what have been the impediments to organizing a robust labor movement and left under neoliberalism that are obstacles in renewing the left now?
SG: One of the problems is that the argument that there is no alternative is actually a serious one—that if we don't get more radical, it's hard to imagine alternatives in the middle. One impediment is not wanting to put forth radical demands, thinking that it's better to be moderate at this time. In other words lowering our expectations. I think that's been a mistake.

The other mistake has been to think that we're going to build a movement by always predicting that capitalism is going to decline or that it will fall apart or break down. We have to be able articulate the argument that capitalism is bad even when its working well, that capitalism is now a barrier to human development.

And the third thing, I think, which relates very much to what Greg was getting at, is we have to understand that under neoliberalism it wasn't just a question of the working class being under attack, but it was also integrated into neoliberalism in certain ways. Significant sections of the working class actually increased their consumption through working longer hours and through debt. They're very much more individualized. Also, internal inequality has fragmented the working class.

When we think about all those kinds of things, what we recognize is that the working class has been shaped and formed and reformed through neoliberalism. And if we're going to overcome that, we're going to need some kind of organization that actually builds the working class, forms it in a different way. There's nothing inherently radical about the working class; it only has the potential to be radical. There are all kinds of potentials to mobilize around, from the legitimacy questions you raised, to the volatility in finance that Leo emphasized, to everything that Greg talked about. So the potential is there but the question is how do we actually build the working class into a class.

I come back to what Greg said: a critical point is that we recognize that we're fighting capitalism and we recognize how crucial the question is of building our own capacities for analysis, for understanding, for acting democratically internally.

How do we challenge the integration of the working class into capitalism through credit card and mortgage debt? What kind of politics could address that crucial dimension of the position of the working class over the last several decades?
SG: I think the poor are going to have more trouble getting credit, but the answer shouldn't be to make it easier for them to get credit. The answer should actually be to talk about things like public housing. But for the rest of the working class, I think there's going to be revival of dependency on credit, on pension funds, on trying to survive by retiring later, which there will be a lot of pressure for. I think we have to talk about breaking out of this by raising issues that may not be on the agenda today or tomorrow—but if we don't start talking about them now they'll never be on the agenda.

One of them is to start talking about nationalizing the banks. Another thing is to actually look at crises in specific sectors. If you looked at what's happened in the auto industry, without the left putting things on the table, unions end up demanding that we save our company and that we become more competitive, which essentially means: let somebody else be laid off. And the kinds of things we need to say are: the issue isn't about saving the company; it's about saving our productive capacity. It's about saving our communities. The issue isn't to be competitive but to make useful things and start thinking about developing democratic planning.

And if we link that to the environment for example, if we said that the environment means that everything is going to be changed about how we produce things, how infrastructure works, how we communicate, the mode of transportation, et cetera, then the question is why can't we mobilize around plants closing in the auto industry that have the equipment, that have these great skilled workers, and start thinking about using that in a socially useful way and converting it? If you had those kinds of structures in place, you would see workers saying, our company isn't investing or our company is starting to disinvest and move some place else—let's take it over. Let's insist it is converted to some useful ends here.

This seems commonsense in a lot of ways. But it isn't going to emerge through unions. Unions are still going to be defensive. They still think in a very sectionalist way—in other words, they represent their members or they represent workers at a particular company. That's why we have to build something that goes beyond the unions. It has to have its feet in the unions as well; unions are still important institutions. But unless we can start thinking about how we build the kind of organization that involves a cultural change and changes expectations. This will raise contradictions because the other side is going to respond, and then we'll have to think about how we go further. If we can't build those kinds of spaces—spaces which are psychologically crucial, because they make people feel like they are part of something and feel that if we aren't going to win tomorrow there's still a way of fighting back and getting someplace—I don't think we can get anywhere. Because then people will just return to saying, I have to survive and the way I can survive is by working more hours, going into more debt, hoping the stock market recovers, hoping that they fix this rotten system so that I can benefit from finance, et cetera.

Why do you think work-time reduction is important not simply for people's well-being but politically? And why do you think that it's an achievable demand to make at a time when workers often have very little leverage to shorten their hours at pay that they can survive on?

SG: That's a terrific question. I think if you look at the formation of the trade union movement, a critical demand was around work-time. I think this is generally true, but I know it's especially been true in Canada. The importance of it was that workers wanted time to read and to do other things. And I think that's of crucial importance regarding work-time today. The workforce has changed. Workers used to be able to be active by exploiting the partner who would take care of the other chores at home. That's to some extent foreclosed right now. If people can't find time to be active and to read and to think and to learn, we can't build a political movement. So politically, reduced work-time is, I think, one of the most important demands. If the only reason you're getting reduced work-time is so that you can get an additional job, that's of course a different thing.

The question of this being possible: it's only possible by building the kind of movement that can win it. It's possible technically, as we're living through this incredible period of productivity growth. Productivity has been phenomenal. Productivity growth in manufacturing is much higher than it was in the golden 1950s and 1960s. So the technical potentials are there. The question is how you organize for it.

I think a lot of that means you can't just think about winning this in your own workplace. We don't have that kind of strength. It does mean thinking about how do we actually win these things by building the class in terms of making it a class demand and thinking of the class more broadly, to that we're actually mobilizing the community perhaps in terms of arguing that this about sharing good jobs where that's the issue. But it shouldn't just be for workers who have collective agreements. It should be a general demand.

The other thing we have to think about— it's very difficult, but we really have to address it—is that it also poses the question how much we want consume and what kind of consumption and so what we think about our living standards. I'm convinced that if we only think of this in terms of consuming more in terms of the present structure of consumption and having reduced work-time to do so, that we won't go anywhere. That won't win. We have to think in terms of wanting a different kind of life, where we can enjoy life in all kinds of different ways in terms of public consumption and different forms of consumption.

GA: It should be actually one of the top things in our demands for addressing global climate change as well, because it has a lot to do with changing consumption. It's probably the most equitable way of dealing with climate change issues.

At the start of the crisis, as government stepped into rescue failing banks, you called for the nationalization of the banks, pointing out that such nationalization had partially taken place. Do you think a renewed left should still champion this demand?
LP: Yes and I actually think that the condition of achieving everything that Sam and Greg were talking about revolves around this. It's not the only condi-

tion of it, but it is a necessary condition of it—necessary in the sense that the decisions about what is produced and what is invested and how its produced and where its invested need to be democratic ones. They need to be made in a social, planned way. That can't happen unless the portion of the surplus, if I can use that term, that passes through the financial system and gives us the funds for credit in capitalism is transferred to a public decision-making process and a planned one, whereby we use the little extent to which the state is now democratized to begin a process of democratizing the economy—and in that process also much further democratize what we now know as governments or the state.

What happened with this financial crisis was there was an enormous opportunity to turn banks into public utilities. Instead we did get the nationalization of some bank—although to some extent we just got public funds put into banks without even a degree of repayment or public control. But we didn't get them changed. On the contrary, when money was put in, governments said we want to be paid back in full, we want the taxpayer to be treated as though he or she was an investor, so we want the highest return possible. Which means that you're pushing the banks to be commercially competitive. In that sense, you could say, as someone in the *Socialist Register* writes, it wasn't so much the Treasury that nationalized the banks, it was the Treasury that got privatized by the banks, insofar as their interest becomes one of getting a high return for the taxpayer—and then of course giving the banks back to private ownership.

That was a tragedy. It was to be totally expected due to the reasons Sam and Greg talked about in that we didn't have the kind of political alignment that would conceivably have led to what I'm describing taking place—banks being turned into public utilities and the whole process of investment being democratized. But that is what is needed.

It's a lot to take on, but the way we need to link the kinds of demands that Sam and Greg were pointing to with that very much larger issue of taking the banking system into the public domain and democratizing it, is to say we can't really have public transit, and free public transit, unless the state at the municipal level and at the state and federal level, can get hold of those funds that pass as credit through the banking system and transform the uses to which that's put. There's absolutely no reason why we need to think of funding this only through taxation, rather than through the savings that we all are part of. Right now, pension funds are invested in all kinds of things related to financing capitalism. Private pension funds and workers savings could be converted into a universal pension plan which is directed towards funding government deficits beyond simply the tax system.

There are all kinds of ways in which we can make people see how these things are linked. Nationalizing the banking system isn't something way out there, It's something intricately related to the kinds of reconstruction of production, the conversion of production, that Sam was pointing to. It's part of people coming to recognize that we're not so much losing a particular company as the enormous resources that these workers have as mechanics, tool and die makers, accountants, teachers, you have it. What we need to be able to do is turn the savings of our society towards the kinds of production that is socially useful, rather than is commercially driven, the way it now is.

Leo, you've stated that we're possibly living through the fourth crisis of capital in a global sense. What were the other crises and how did their resolutions affect the degree to which capitalism extended itself globally? LP: This arguably is the fourth. The first great crisis of capitalism was from 1873–96, it's often argued. The second was the Great Depression of the 1930s. The third was the crisis of Keynesianism and of profits in the 1970s. And we may be entering the fourth. Each of those crises had different causes and different outcomes. They are not all caused by the same thing and they don't all lead to the same type of outcome.

The first one produced an orientation toward internationalizing capitalism, but within the framework of competing capitalist empires. That eventually led to World War I. The second one actually broke down and stopped capitalism's internationalizing tendencies and you got the kind of beggar my neighbor protectionism that led to World War II. Out of World War II, you got the American state in particular becoming the kind of empire that was determined to get the globalizing tendencies of capitalism back on the agenda. It succeeded in that. But that led to contradictions by the 1970s, which ushered in the profit squeeze of the 1970s, partly having to do with the way which workers were strengthened under the commitment to social welfare and full employment reflecting the power of democracy that had developed within capitalism in the twentieth century. That then led to, in a sense, workers being too strong for capitalism. And it led to a profit squeeze and was resolved largely through the defeat of the working class, the defeat of trade unionism, and the further expansion of capitalist competition at a global level.

No one could say that this crisis was caused by workers being too strong. If anything it was caused by workers being too weak—too weak in the sense that they were still very much tied into capitalism. As Sam said, they were trying to be consumers by being indebted consumers. They were trying to look to their retirement by engaging in speculation, whether through their pensions or expecting that their homes would increase in value, the main asset that many workers own in a capitalist housing market. So in a sense, the kinds of contra-dictions in finance that pertain to the workers' side of the equation reflected the weakness of workers, their individuation, their fragmentation, and their incorporation as Sam said into capitalist finance and capitalist completion.

I think that, however, these are very, very contradictory processes and it isn't impossible—and you see in California the evidence of this—for indebted workers and indebted students to rise up and begin to realize what that means for them, what that means for their lives, in terms of having to pay off these debts in a way that keeps them tied in almost as debt-slaves to the system. In California, a campaign by students to have their student debt forgiven or to allow there to be no penalties for a default on that student debt would now be a very important element in the kinds of struggles that are taking place in the educational system. But insofar as that were to be viable, it would have to be connected to the much larger issues that I was talking about in terms of economic planning and the taking over of the financial system. And that's a very big political agenda.

You three have been speaking about the ways that neoliberalism has made it difficult for workers to organize in their interests, to have the time to engage in radical politics, or politics at all. Looking at the other side of the equation, what are the system's vulnerabilities that radicals should exploit?
LP: There are so many that we could go on talking for weeks and months. The vulnerabilities are of the kind that produced the great unionization move-ments and the social movements and socialist parties that emerged out of the first crisis from 1873–96. They're the types of contradictions that led people to break with the AFL unions in the 1930s and form the industrial unions that brought in everybody that was in a particular plant, whether they were highly skilled tool and die makers or whether they were janitors, into the same organ-ization. They're the same type of contradictions that led to the crisis of the 1970s, being also the moment at which the new social movements were at their height. So there are all kinds of opportunities. And to be very specific the kinds of struggles in which students and teachers are engaging in California provide an enormous opportunity to make connections between the cutbacks that are taking place, and the way in which the public sector in California is being made to bear the cost of what was a crisis not at all caused by the public sector. So the link to be made between that struggle and what we've been talking about doesn't seem to me to be too far a stretch.

It doesn't at all seem to me impossible to talk today about taking the exam-ple of the 1930s and the creation of a new type a trade unionism and, to pick up what Sam was saying, the need for the type of labor organization now, which isn't confined to a given industry but sees itself as a much broader class organization and sees the struggle for free public transit as important to the retention of their jobs—but in the way that would involve the conversion of their workplaces in a massive way. One could look at the suicides in China that led to a wage increase being given by Honda in their plant there as part of a much broader set of struggles for a working class that has grown in numbers enormously in this period of neoliberalism.

There has been massive proletarianization around the world. One could look forward, it seems to me, to an enormously heightened level of class struggle of the kind that would be enervated and encouraged by looking at what's going on in one place and what's going on in another. It's not impossible that the strikes that are taking place in Greece that Greg was referring to can have an exemplary effect. We need to do all we can to make them have an exemplary effect. So, yes, I think there are enormous opportunities. What we need much more of, as Sam was saying, are the kind of organized political forces which can intervene in a productive way to encourage this, to sustain it, to give it a broader focus. As Greg was saying, the old parties, the social democratic parties, the left of the Democratic Party, et cetera, and also those old Marxist formations that either were powerful or looked like they might be in the twentieth century, have now passed into history. We need to find substitutes and alternatives to them.

The antiglobalization movement was a very, very exciting development from Seattle on and hopefully people in it will begin to see that we need more than protests at IMF meetings and more than annual World Social Forums. Those are useful, but we need to organize out of them. They shouldn't be a substitute for building permanent organizations that can contest for power. There's been too much of a tendency in the movements of the last decade to be afraid to do that and to believe that it's enough to simply protest.

There was an interesting editorial in the *Financial Times* by the historian Simon Schama worrying that this may be the moment where people go out into the streets in protest. He made a parallel with the French Revolution and the lag that often occurs between when people are hit by a crisis and when they respond. Sam, do you think that there are opportunities now, despite the weakness of institutions of the left and labor, which we might be hopeful about?

SG: Yes and not just in terms of what's happening now. This is going to continue. There's going to be more volatility. There's going to be more pressure on people to pay for the exit to this crisis. Insecurity isn't going away. Inequality isn't going away. People see the BP oil spill in the Gulf of Mexico, they see the kind of resources the state can mobilize when it's trying to save the banks and they can contrast it to the state's intervention in other ways. They're cynical. They're skeptical. I don't think you have to convince people that capitalism isn't wonderful. You just have to convince them that there is something they can do about it.

My sense is that these things explode in unpredictable ways. But then the question is always how do you sustain it. So the opportunities are there and it's encouraging whenever you see a struggle someplace that you can learn from or be inspired by. And then there are local things that are going on. In Toronto we've all been involved in the creation of something called the Greater Toronto Workers Assembly. It was really an attempt to say, let's just not have another protest against the crisis; let's actually talk about the fact that none of the things we do right now in the movements, or in the unions, or on the left actually match what we're up against. And we need to get together in a class-based way that actually speaks to capitalism, that's actually rooted in the community, in a sense of organizing here. We're focusing on free transit as a class issue. We're focusing on how does the public sector respond in a time of austerity. And we're arguing it can't just respond by trying to get higher wages and isolating itself. It has to actually say: either we put the level and quality of administration of public services on the bargaining agenda and lead in the transformation of public services or we're going to be killed. These things evolve and they're hard to do, but the Assembly has people speaking about, and finding spaces to address, new approaches. So I'm optimistic, but not in a sense of being ready to predict that it's about to happen. But the opportunities are definitely there.

Part II
Commodification, Enclosure, and the Contradictions of Capitalism

CHAPTER SIX

John Bellamy Foster: The Ecological Dimensions of Marx's Thought

It has become an axiom of radical environmentalism that the Enlightenment, the seventeenth-century efflorescence of European scientific thought, is at least partially culpable for the destruction of the environment thereafter. Can you describe the roots of the green critique of the Enlightenment and your own appraisal of it?

JBF: The green critique of the Enlightenment argues that as a result of the seventeenth-century scientific revolution and the Enlightenment a new mechanistic world-view came into being aimed at the domination of nature. Where nature had previously been seen as a realm with which human existence was generally in accord, it was now suddenly something to be mastered, even enslaved. That's the essence of the green critique. Such important figures as Carolyn Merchant have promoted this idea, and also the idea that women lost their status as nature was demoted.

This has almost become a truism of green theory. But if you were to go back to the seventeenth-century scientific revolution—and look at figures like Bacon and the developments in science that he helped to inspire—it's really a much more complex story, because although the idea of the domination of nature originated in science at this time, you also see the emergence of the notion of sustainability. What arose was the view that human beings could separate themselves from nature, and maybe dominate nature, but that they also had to pay attention to nature's laws. And the notion of nature having definite laws was taken much more seriously than before. In Francis Bacon, both tendencies were exhibited. He referred to the domination of nature metaphorically, but he said we could only master nature by following nature's laws; and where human beings didn't follow nature's laws, they could wreak havoc on the natural environment. So you see the beginnings of conservation at the same time you see the beginnings of the notion of the domination of nature—and sometimes from the very same people.

The Enlightenment itself was about promoting reason and science in opposition to seeing nature and society in terms of faith. The scientists of the seventeenth and eighteenth centuries were primarily materialist in orientation and were in conflict with teleological views, that is, the belief that the universe had some sort of purpose to it, provided by God. The idea of evolution

was obviously not fully worked out at that time. But Enlightenment materialists saw nature as in some ways determining itself, and argued that they didn't
have to look for final causes outside of nature. This struck a jarring note in a
world that had previously rested on faith.

Francis Bacon was the leading thinker behind this change of orientation
and, of course, Descartes and Gassendi. They were the primary figures who
inspired the scientific revolution philosophically, and they had, for the most
part, this materialistic orientation—particularly Bacon and Gassendi.

The point is that in categorically dismissing the scientific revolution and
Enlightenment materialism as anti-ecological, green theorists have often
thrown out the baby with the bathwater.

**The Enlightenment arose in response to the dominant medieval Christian
Aristotelian view of the world that deemed nature as unchanging and created with a purpose. What were the fundamental assumptions of this
scholastic outlook and how did the thinkers of the Enlightenment challenge them?**
JBF: The Aristotelian approach gave a large weight to teleology, to the notion
of final causes and ultimately to God as behind everything that was happening in nature. And of course, in medieval Christianity this teleological aspect
had been given even greater weight than it was in Aristotle himself. And what
I mean by teleology is the notion that nature was purposive, that what happened was planned in some way or had some sort of divine intention behind
it. There was an order to the universe.

This teleological view, associated with Aristotle and even more with medieval scholasticism, was taken over and transformed in the seventeenth and eighteenth centuries by natural theology, which sought to reconcile science with
religion by discovering evidence of God's role within nature. William Paley, the
great eighteenth-century philosopher and scientist, saw the universe as like a
watch, which was, of course, the high tech of those days. And he said, if you
found a watch on the ground, you would realize that it had been made, that
there was artifice behind it. And he said the same was true if you looked at
various creations in nature; that nature was too complex to be the product of
accident or contingency. It has to have been created by a divine purpose, and
thus by a designer. It has to be teleological. God in this view was behind everything in nature—and this could be shown by reason and observation. But
the main thrust of the seventeenth-century scientific revolution was a breaking away from that, with the growth of materialist views.

Some thinkers like Newton and Boyle tried to bring God back into the
picture in line with natural theology, i.e. the teleological view of nature, but

their actual science was strongly influenced by materialism. Materialism meant rejecting teleological views, rejecting the notion that God governed things in nature, or that you had to resort to final causes to explain things in nature rather than being able to explain nature in its own terms. In this sense materialism and naturalism really mean the same thing. A materialist would see everything in the natural world as somehow arising out of its own development and subject to the laws of matter and motion, rather than needing some sort of divine explanation. That's really what was the crux of the matter at that time.

And the rationalism of the Enlightenment displaced humans from the center of the world—as God's special creations in the Great Chain of Being in Christian dogma—and put nature back at its core.

JBF: Yes, exactly. When Bacon came along and Gassendi came along, they not only overthrew Aristotle, but they turned to other ancient Greek philosophers, particularly the ancient Greek materialists, most notably Epicurus. Epicurus was one of the founders of the notion of that matter could be conceived in terms of atoms, but there were all sorts of aspects of Epicurus's materialism that were crucial in those days. Epicurus had said that nothing comes from nothing and a thing being destroyed cannot be reduced to nothing. These are the basic principals of conservation—that a matter can neither be created nor destroyed.

Epicurus had written after Aristotle in the third century, B.C., and the philosophers and scientists of the seventeenth and eighteenth centuries were returning to the Greek materialists in a revolt against medieval philosophy that had relied more on Aristotle and the idealist tradition. And one of the ways in which they did this is they took on the whole idea of the Enlightenment as literally bringing light. The idea was associated with the ancient Greek myth of Prometheus, who was a titan or proto-God, who had brought fire to humankind. He had brought light and reason, so that human beings could remake the world according to their reason. This is really where the idea of Enlightenment came from. It symbolized that the world was now subject to human action and reason and to principles derived from nature and was no longer the province of the Gods.

Prometheus brings Marx to mind. How did Epicurus influence Marx's thought?

JBF: Marx called Epicurus the "Enlightenment figure of antiquity" and compared him to Prometheus, the bringer of light. This emphasis on Epicurus might seem strange because people have not generally heard of him, and he is not taught in philosophy courses now. But at the time of the seventeenth-century scientific revolution and the Enlightenment Epicurus had been rediscovered. Epicurean philosophy was actually the most pervasive of the all the philosophies of Greek-Roman antiquity. Although we hear more about Plato and Aristotle nowadays, Epicureans were more common in the ancient world than were followers of Plato and Aristotle.

There were some characteristics to Epicurus's philosophy that were very important, that combined ethics and physics and so on. One of his most famous sayings is, "death is nothing to us," and what he meant by that was that once your sensations are gone, then you are not able to experience death. In other words, our whole relation to the world is a material one, carried through our senses.

Epicurus was very clear about opposing teleological views; he attacked the notion that the Gods ruled the world of human society and the world of nature. He had a place for the Gods but he placed them in the pores between the worlds without any relation to the historical or natural world. And he opposed all forms of mechanism and determinism. He had an emphasis on contingency, a very strong emphasis on human freedom and what he called "friendship," as the most important things in ordering human society. He was the one who introduced the concept of the social contract and introduced many of our sociological ideas including the idea that human society develops. But his most famous idea was the notion of the "swerve." He argued that atoms would, say, fall to the earth in a straight line but they would for some reason swerve slightly in unpredictable ways and this actually became almost a metaphor for contingency, that nothing could be predicted, but could nevertheless be understood historically. He carried that into the ethical realm and said that there was a component of human freedom, no matter how much the world and our history seems to be determined. There's always contingency—and that means there's always a realm of freedom.

Marx was extraordinarily interested in Epicurus. Epicurus is the first philosopher that we have any record of Marx referring to and he ended up doing his doctoral dissertation on Epicurus' materialism. I think that this was really very important in helping Marx deal with the idealist, Hegelian influences in his thought. But also it became a route into ecological thinking because this very deep materialism emanating from Epicurus was also fundamental to the whole development of Western scientific views and to a conception of nature that allowed for such ideas as sustainability. In Epicurus you find already a proto-evolutionary approach to nature, not a developed evolutionary theory as in Darwin, but very clearly evolutionary views.

Marx's whole complex, dialectical relation to the Enlightenment can be seen in his response to Epicurus. When Marx writes about the development of Enlightenment materialism in *The Holy Family*, and discusses such figures as Bacon, Hobbes, Gassendi, Locke, and the French materialists, it is specifically in terms of how they came out of the tradition represented in antiquity by Epicurus. This emphasis on the relation of Enlightenment reason to ancient Greek materialism going back thousands of years doesn't mean of course that Marx is uncritical of the Enlightenment itself. He understood it as a bourgeois development in the main. But he holds on to the materialist conception of nature and human history which it furthered, seeing this as vital to the development of both rational science and socialism.

Epicurus also influenced Charles Darwin.

JBF: Yes. Bacon was strongly influenced by Epicurus and Darwin took some of those anti-teleological views from Bacon. Marx too was a close reader of Bacon, as well as Epicurus. Both the young Marx and the young Darwin quoted within a few years of each other Bacon's famous statement that final causes, like vestal virgins, were unproductive of anything else. And they were very clear that the natural world changed—"evolved" as we would say now— and that this had to be explained in material terms. In many ways, Epicurus helped frame the problem that carried through in the materialist tradition.

Epicurus was also considered to be the great enemy of religion. As the greatest heretic for a thousand years or more, he was viewed as the greatest enemy of Christianity. And for Marx, of course, this was not necessarily a bad thing!

Broadly speaking, how aware were Marx and his lifelong collaborator Engels of the environment and its destruction, what we might now call "ecological issues"?

JBF: Very aware. I first became interested in Marx's environmental thought by looking at things that he wrote in the 1860s and 1870s on the environment. And it was in the process of trying to understand why Marx was able to penetrate so deeply into ecology that led me back to the origins of his ideas in the materialist tradition and to the materialist conception of nature which he got by way of Epicurus and through the science of his day. This materialist conception of nature gave him a systematic outlook that led him to core ecological issues.

But it is Marx's own direct discussion of ecology that, of course, is most important. And this comes out particularly when you look at what he wrote about the soil crisis in the nineteenth century. In Europe and in the United States in the 1840s–1870s, the biggest ecological problem—much bigger than the loss of forest and so on—was the destruction of the soil. What they discovered beginning in 1840, when Justus Von Liebig wrote his great work on agricultural science, is that with the development of systematic capitalist agriculture, crucial chemicals in the soil such as phosphorus, potassium, and particularly nitrogen were being shipped with the food and fiber from the farms to the cities and then turning into waste in the cities in the form of human and animal waste—and of course, clogging and polluting the cities in serious ways. And the nutrients were not making it back to the soil.

Marx learned about this by studying Liebig's work, but of course it was the greatest ecological crisis of the time and everyone knew about it at some level or another. One way in which the English farmers dealt with the loss of soil nutrients is that they would import bones from Europe. They took bones from the Napoleonic battlefields and from the catacombs of Europe and then used them to fertilize the soil. But another way they dealt with it by importing bird droppings, or guano, from Peru which had a monopoly on good quality guano. They discovered that the guano on the islands off the coast of Peru was the best natural fertilizer—high in nitrogen and phosphorus—and they started importing this guano from Peru on a huge scale with whole ships full of guano. They would have dozens of ships from different countries loading the guano on ships all at the same time and they would import laborers, coolies from China, to do the work under conditions that Marx described as "worse than slavery" because digging the guano and loading it into ships was so terrible.

In the United States in 1856 they passed the Guano Islands Act and the United States sent ships all over the world looking for islands with guano. They actually took over ninety-something islands, rocks, and keys—some of which the U.S. still has—because they had bird droppings. Still, the British, who controlled the Peruvian guano trade, had a virtual monopoly on the guano.

What was happening was this: the shift of the nutrients from the farms to the cities and the failure of the recycling of nutrients meant the land was being systematically impoverished. Marx, after studying Liebig, brought the notion of *metabolism*, which was then emerging as a concept in biology and chemistry, to bear on this problem. He said that there was a metabolic relationship between human beings and the soil. A metabolic rift had been created, which was a product of the extreme separation of town and country under capitalism. The rift in soil nutrient cycle meant that the "the constituent elements of the soil" were being shipped hundreds and sometimes thousands of miles to the cities, where these essential chemicals ended up as pollution, destroying the urban environment, while not returning to the soil which was therefore robbed of its nutrients. This was a severe ecological problem that had to be transcended in any society that was going to be sustainable.

Marx talked about the need for sustainability in quite modern terms. He said we need to protect the earth for future generations, which is exactly the way we talk about sustainability now. He said the soil had to be restored, but the only way you could restore things, the only way you could get around the situation, was to overcome the alienation of human beings from the land.

Many people are familiar with Marx's theory of alienation as it relates to labor; that is, that workers are disconnected under class society from the labor they do, seeing it as separate from themselves. But I would hazard that few are aware that Marx applied it to our relationship to nature as well. JBF: Right. This can be seen when you look at Marx's *Economic and Philosophical Manuscripts* written in the 1840s. What most people are familiar with is the section that he wrote on the alienation of labor, which was the core of the *Economic and Philosophical Manuscripts*. He talks about how labor is alienated from the work process.

But there's another part of the argument that's really inseparable from the argument on the alienation of labor for Marx, and that you find throughout the *Economic and Philosophical Manuscripts,* including in the section on the alienation of labor. Marx argues that human beings are also alienated from nature. And in fact, for him, these are two sides of the same thing. Separation from the land is a prerequisite in order to create a working class in the modern sense of what Marx called the proletariat, that is, those who have no way of surviving but by selling the labor of their hands—those who have no access to the means of production, so they can only survive by working for a wage and selling their labor power. This problem of the proletariat for Marx is inseparable from the removal of the people from the land, the extreme alienation from nature. And so throughout the *Economic and Philosophical Manuscripts,* and even more systematically later on in the *Grundrisse,* he talks about this estrangement of human beings from the land, from nature, as a precondition for the alienation of labor under capitalism. The labor process itself he defines in *Capital* as the process by which people carry on the metabolic relationship between nature and society. In other words, labor is how people transform nature for society and he saw this as a metabolic process. Any kind of separation or alienation, extreme alienation, of human beings from nature therefore creates fundamental contradictions.

In the *Economic and Philosophical Manuscripts,* Marx discusses the pollution in the large industrial towns. He refers to the fact that factory workers are deprived of light and deprived of air—that they're deprived of the natural means of existence. But somehow, in discussing Marx's concept of alienation, this notion of the alienation of nature, which underlay much of his analysis, has been de-emphasized. It's odd in a way. If you go back to Marx's earliest writings in political economy, he was concerned with issues such as the theft of wood in Germany. This was one of the first political-economic issues he addressed, before he wrote the *Economic and Philosophical Manuscripts*. He was concerned from the very beginning with what was happening when the peasants were being removed from the land and cut off from the natural means of existence. This kind of alienation then, the alienation from nature, is inseparable for Marx from the alienation from labor. Marx says that human beings belong to nature, they're a part of nature, and it's only a distorted society that separates the two. Later on, in *Capital,* he talks about it in terms of the metabolic rift, incorporating some of the scientific understandings of the time in making these issues more concrete. But the theme is there in his work from the very beginning.

Yet some theorists have argued that Marx's theory of alienation was an idea that he developed in his early years, during a period in which he had not yet thrown off the profound influence of Hegel, and which he abandoned later.
JBF: Yes, Althusser propounded that view. It seems peculiar to me because, of course, he wrote about alienation right through his works, from beginning to end. It's true he emphasized it very strongly in the *Economic and Philosophical Manuscripts* but he discusses alienation very extensively in the *Grundrisse*, which he wrote in the 1850s. He talks about it in places in *Capital*, although the language of alienation is not the primary way he expresses himself there. But even as late as 1881, in the last two years of his life, he was mentioning alienation in his *Notes on Adolph Wagner*.

So it's a theme that goes right through his work. He never abandoned that conception. It's interesting—a lot of people know that he was influenced by Ludwig Feuerbach in developing some of those ideas. Feuerbach read Marx's *Capital* and recognized his own influence and his own emphasis on alienation there—and even recognized the environmental aspects of the argument.

Much of Marx's thinking about nature was shaped in reaction to the ideas of the nineteenth-century Protestant cleric Thomas Malthus, who himself has had a significant—and I would say, unfortunate—impact on contemporary environmental thought. Most people have heard the term Malthusian in relation to theories of population growth. What was Malthus's argument and Marx's critique of it?
JBF: It's hard to explain Malthus's argument because so many people have heard it reported in a certain way but have never read Malthus, and Malthus over the years has been presented in a quite distorted fashion. What people know is that Malthus said that human population could increase geometrically, while food supply tended to only increase arithmetically. So essentially

you have an exponential growth in population with a weaker, incremental growth in the food supply. But he was talking about these as tendencies and his actual model is an equilibrium model; that is, Malthus believed that population never does really grow, or hardly ever can be said to grow, much faster than the food supply, because he argued that the population is always constrained by the food supply. When food becomes scarce or runs out, population growth quickly turns into its opposite.

Malthus said that in periods of ample food supply the mortality rate decreases, population tends to grow fast, as people have more children. Yet, with a big rise in population the food supply is unable to keep up and pretty soon it is insufficient. Natural checks then begin to operate. Growing infant mortality and starvation due to food shortages would limit population to whatever level the food supply had increased by. Within a very short period of time, the population growth rate would be pulled back to whatever the long-term rate of growth of the food supply was. So, the real problem, in his view, is that the food supply can't grow fast enough. Yet, he never actually explained why the growth of food supply was so limited—although he had certain broad assumptions about what degree of natural fertility you can find in the soil and limited land supply. He simply pronounced that food supply couldn't be expanded very rapidly. As Marx said, he assumed that human beings tended to multiply exponentially but that this was not possible for the rest of nature—or that part of it that constituted the human food supply.

Malthus never uses the terms "overpopulation" or "excess of population." He even says that that language of that kind is not really appropriate. And he didn't argue in terms of the whole earth. He was arguing primarily in terms of England, i.e. in a limited context. The whole argument had nothing really to do with ecology at all. For example, Malthus thought there were no limits to other kinds of material resources, other than food. He never discussed issues of agricultural productivity aside from the abstract Ricardian theory of rent, which emphasized limits on natural soil fertility and decreasing marginal returns as poorer land was brought into cultivation. Rather than making an ecological argument, what Malthus was really trying to do was to justify the class structure of capitalist society by arguing that it was necessary for a certain part of the population to remain poor—that there was only so much room at the table. And if you tried to have welfare laws, or Poor Laws as they called them in those days, which would try to redistribute wealth towards the poor, all you would do is bring down the society. So he was arguing that there has to be a group of people that are always on the verge of starvation, and others who are well-to-do; and that's what helps maintain the equilibrium in society. It was purely an economic and class argument.

It wasn't until the 1940s that anybody really presented Malthus in ecological terms. At the time of the Green Revolution, they needed an ideology to support the expansion of agribusiness in the Third World and they could no longer use eugenics, which had gone out of favor because of Nazi Germany. So Malthus was resurrected as an environmentalist, but nobody had ever really treated him that way before.

As far as Marx was concerned, Malthus was a class defender of an iniquitous position in society. Malthus argued, for example, that in the case of a mother who had a child out of wedlock, society should do nothing for her or her child but simply let them starve. Likewise he proposed that in dealing with the poor in Ireland the authorities should pull down their huts, because the poor would propagate less effectively if they didn't have houses to propagate in.

Clearly evincing great Christian compassion.
JBF: Yes, Marx complained of the meanness disguised as compassion of the Protestant parsons like Malthus. From Marx's standpoint, Malthus was an enemy of the poor and that was the main criticism. Marx saw the food problem as historical in nature. He thought that agriculture was in crisis, that it wasn't expanding as fast as it should. He focused on trying to understand the reasons why the soil problem existed and saw it as a crisis in sustainability endemic to capitalism. He therefore charted a very different approach from Malthus, one that actually did take the agricultural problem and the ecological problem seriously as historical issues to be addressed.

Let's turn to the green criticisms of Marx and Marxism. Environmental thinkers have characterized Marx as believing socialism would mean absolute abundance and the absence of natural limits on growth, like a version of Malthus turned on his head. How fair an assessment of Marx would you say this is?
JBF: If you look at Marx's writings in *Capital*, in his clearest discussions of socialism, he said it was necessary for the direct producers to regulate the metabolic relationship between nature and society. And there's a lot that he wrote on this. There are agricultural problems and ecological problems, questions of sustainability, and this was something that could only be addressed by human beings consciously trying to regulate their relationship to nature within the context of human freedom directed by the workers themselves. Those who were engaged in the work, who hopefully would come to control society, had to govern the relationship to nature in a sustainable way. He's very, very clear about that. This is not an argument rooted in some kind of automatic abundance or rejection of ecological problems.

But there are other parts to Marx. In *The Communist Manifesto*, everybody knows how he praises industrialization under capitalism. And Marx was no enemy of industry. So he didn't have the view that everything in society, i.e. society as a whole, should go back to nature as some deep ecologists do. His view rather was that sustainability meant building on the past but also creating new social and ecological relations.

Deep ecologists and green theorists in general have erected a special criticism of Marx; they call him "Promethean." But they mean something different than what the term meant to Marx and meant to the Enlightenment—and that meant bringing light to people. Now Prometheus is seen as bringing fire in the sense of a motive force—coal, steel blast furnaces, and so on—and the notion of fire as power and the growth of technology. And Marx is seen as being kind of an extreme mechanist and absolute promoter of machinery and industry without any concern for nature. And of course, that's belied by all that he wrote about sustainability and about the ecological crisis and so on.

So how did this view of Marx as a mechanistic Promethean come into being? JBF: One of the things that happened within the Marxist tradition is that right after Marx died, there were a number of thinkers like Bebel, Kautsky, even Lenin, and especially Bukharin, who developed his ecological views to some extent. These ideas were well-known at the time. But in the 1930s, Marxist ecological understanding died a double death. One was the rise of Stalinism in the Soviet Union that basically killed off ecological views. In fact, many of the leading ecologists in the world were within the Soviet Union, where ecological science developed rapidly in the 1920s—people like Nikolai Vavilov who discovered the origins of germplasm. Vavilov was purged along with many other ecologically oriented thinkers, including Bukharin, by Stalin. The Soviet Union, beginning in the 1930s, went in a very anti-ecological direction with primitive socialist accumulation, which expropriated the land of the peasantry in an extreme form of industrialization. So they were very anti-ecological and those parts of Marx's thought died out.

Primitive socialist accumulation, as it was called, was a conscious attempt to telescope the whole process of primitive capitalist accumulation by rapidly expropriating the land from the peasantry and shifting the surplus derived in agriculture to urban centers and industry. The enormous destructiveness of the displacement of the peasantry, which in the British Industrial Revolution had carried out over hundreds of years, with enormous pain and torment, was supposed to take place over a few five-year plans. Ecologically oriented scientists resisted such extreme expropriation of nature and displacement of those who worked the land. These people, including Bukharin who was the leader of the opposition in this area, were therefore purged early on in the Stalinist period. This led to a commitment to industry over agriculture, and heavy industry over light industry, which looked like a society that had gone mad from an ecological perspective. Out of this you get the idea that Marxism is a kind of extreme Prometheanism.

But Western Marxism also moved away from any kind of meaningful ecological critique in an entirely different way. Western Marxism became very antipositivist, which turned into an antiscience view in many cases, rigidly separating science and society. In the work of Lukács, Korsch, and Gramsci in the 1920s, and in the work of the Frankfurt School, Western Marxists tended to focus on the historical sciences and the humanities and to write off science, which they saw as inherently mechanistic or positivistic.

Like everyone else who studied Marxism in the West in the 1960s and '70s, I was told—supposedly based on Lukács—that the dialectic applied only to human history and not to nature. Western Marxists thus put up a firewall between nature and society. Nature was the realm of natural science exclusively, which operated under different methods. The old Marxist idea that nature itself could be approached dialectically was seen as false. Nature was the realm of the mechanical.

In contrast to nature, society was regarded as a reflexive, properly dialectical realm, and any attempt to apply positivistic, scientistic views to social relations was wrong. Critical theory, in fact, became practically identified with combating intrusions of positivistic scientific principles into the social sciences. There is no doubt that this critique was important. But the consequence was that the natural sciences—and more to the point the human relation to nature—were written off as issues by Marxists and critical thinkers.

It is true that the Frankfurt School—for example Horkheimer and Adorno in the *Dialectic of Enlightenment*—sometimes addressed the domination of nature. But nature in this perspective was almost always viewed through Freudian lens, as *human nature*. Real ecological knowledge, dealing with *external nature*, was almost always absent. Those aspects of Marx and classical Marxism that had dealt with the human relation to nature and natural science were deemphasized and scarcely read at all. Materialism gave way to idealism even in the Marxist tradition. While the materialist conception of history was discussed, the fact that Marx and Engels had also identified with the materialist conception of nature was unknown to most Western Marxists. Engels's *Dialectics of Nature* was seen as an example of the contamination of Marxism by the positivist, Promethean virus, and to be ignored.

It has taken Marxism a long time to break down this firewall and reclaim the full dialectical realism of Marx's thought. But without this there could of course be no resurrection of the classical Marxist ecological critique despite its crucial importance to our time.

What does a Marxist ecological view give us that mainstream environmental theory doesn't? Why should we care whether or not this nineteenth-century thinker recognized the importance of the environment or not?
JBF: I think that's a crucial question. The answer I would give is that Marx saw the problems that society was facing as all of one piece—they had to do with the capitalist system, with a mode of production. And the value of Marx's ecology, and the dangers that it poses for the establishment, is that it tells you that these things are problems of the system. They're related to a whole system of social classes, extreme polarization of town and country, and alienation of labor, which is also an alienation of nature. And it tells you that in order to deal with these issues, in a serious way, you're going to have to deal with the whole structure of capitalism and its transcendence.

Of course, that's very much against the ideology of our times. Not only within the establishment, but also in green thought, too, because a great deal of green thinking says that we just need to change our consciousness. We need to just think differently, we just need to recycle, change our behavior, have a new philosophy, and so on. But what Marx is telling us in terms of the metabolic rift, and in terms of sustainability and co-evolution, is that we have to address the nature of the system in which we live, and that issues of environmental degradation are tied to issues of environmental justice and social justice generally.

CHAPTER SEVEN

Jason W. Moore: The Socio-Ecological Crises of Capitalism

It's become axiomatic on the left that we're facing a twin crisis of capitalism and the environment. We tend to think of environmental crises as something fairly new, as an affliction of our modern industrial era. Why is that not accurate?

JWM: Well, there two things that are going on here. The first is the issue of a twin crisis, and the second is the notion of environmental crisis. Now the problem with thinking through and talking about this great term "environmental crisis" is it's a bit like pornography. People know it when they see it, but it's hard to define. And what I've been trying to do for some time now is to really think through how capitalism has emerged since the fifteenth and sixteenth centuries as a way of reshaping the relation between humans and the rest of nature.

Now I put it in these terms because this immediately helps us get away from the notion that in one box there's a "social crisis," and in another box that there is something that we can call an "environmental crisis." These are in fact a singular process of transformation that today we call a crisis. I think that this is what the inflationary price crescendo of 2008 with the food price shocks, the oil price shocks, coupled with a financial meltdown of that year, has really driven it home. There is a growing awareness, even if it is rarely stated in such terms, of a profound interconnection between biophysical transformations and biophysical problems and crises, on the one hand, with the central institutions of the capitalist world economy, on the other—of financial markets, of large transnational firms, of capital intensive agriculture, and so on.

So if we start from a premise that these are in fact unified processes, we get away from the notion that if we just fix the markets, fix the machines, if we just fix this or that problem that we put in a nice convenient, tidy little box—maybe it's population, maybe it's imperialism, maybe it's something else—then we open up a whole set of questions about how we are all part of nature. We open up a new way of seeing those large, so-called "social" processes that we always refer to—globalization, imperialism, industrialization—as themselves ecological projects—ecological projects that seek to rework the relations between human beings (human nature) and the rest of nature.

Much of the analysis from the left and the environmental movement tends to focus on impacts and effects. That is, that society or capitalism is the cause and the way the natural world is despoiled is the effect. In your piece "Ecology and the Accumulation of Capital" you refer to it as the foot and the footprint. Why isn't this a helpful way to understand the dynamics at play?

JWM: Yes. This is an absolutely important thing to reflect upon and there's a lot of very high-powered academic discourse that goes on around this. But I think that the central idea is that once we start to classify a certain set of social processes as social, rather than as socio-ecological, we start to create the very firewall, the very binary, the very kind of divide that we are trying to overcome. That is, we on the left are trying to overcome the creation of what Raymond Williams, the great Welsh literary theorist, called the "singular abstractions of society and nature." This is a very, very modern concept and there's no denying that a tremendous amount of quite useful science and technology has emerged out of it—this idea that "nature" is in one box and "society" is in another.

This sort of binary would have been a completely foreign notion to precapitalist societies, whether we were talking about medieval Europe or early Imperial China. There was always the notion that nature and society were inextricably connected with each other. That's not to say that these were ecological edens—quite the contrary in many cases.

However, what we see in the modern world-system, which is a capitalist world economy from the fifteenth and sixteenth centuries, is something that we all take for granted now, the tremendous divorce between an extraordinary mass of wealth in the form of money capital, and an extraordinary mass of wealth in the form of nature, including human nature. This divorce was precisely what was impossible before capitalism. Only through a socio-ecological system that systematically, progressively removed peasants from the land, and established the conditions for productivity revolutions in "cheap food," do we see the possibility for money capital to command and shape the most basic contours of life. We can think today of all the great financial flows and accumulations of fictitious wealth in the form of financial securities, and despite the recent devaluations, we can see that these flows and accumulations are pivotal to the natures that are being transformed and reworked in very violent and radically transformative ways.

So the question is: what's the problem with this divorce, this binary of nature in one box, and society in another? Well, the problem is that the starting point is precisely the sort of symbolic universe of modernity, this divide between nature and society that we see in ecological footprint discussions. And in fact if you go and you read the work of somebody like Mathis Wackernagel, who is the central figure in this tradition, there is the constant appeal to what can only be called neoliberal discourses—pleas for the efficiency of markets and for the reduction of waste, and so on and so forth. There's not this sense that the market itself is a bundle of ecological and social relations.

But that's the interesting thing. In the world left today, in a sense we do see a convergence around a dialectical sense of how nature and society are interwoven. There was a time when industrial struggles in large factory settings were regarded as social and peasant struggles or conservation movements were seen as environmental. But in fact what we see today, and nowhere more clearly than the ongoing struggles for justice around world agriculture, is a fusing of all of these moments. There is an emergent sensibility that Wall Street is a way of organizing global nature—every bit as directly as a farm or mine, albeit with different specific forms. So what I would say is that in some ways the movements are very much ahead of the scholars in this respect, that there is an intuitive and often very practical grasp of what is nature, that nature is both the state and industries in the big cities and the "factories in the field" in capital-intensive agriculture, along with global financial markets, all at once.

This way of seeing promises a way out of the great impasse that we saw in the world after 1968, which was that you had one set of movements that was oriented towards something they called environmental issues, and another that was oriented towards social issues, economic justice issues and so forth. I think that we are beginning to see a move towards a transcendence of that divide. At no time has this been more necessary.

How do you conceive of the dialectical relationship between these different elements?
JWM: What I mean is there is literally no moment that we can think of that is biophysical and not social at the same time. In other words, no one symbolic box that we can say, here's a set of *social* interactions that have to do with culture, sexuality, or identity or perceptions of environmental change, and on the other hand, here are biophysical changes that are somehow independent of all that.

This of course is not to deny the very obvious fact that there are global cycles: a nitrogen cycle, a climate system, and all manner of biophysical processes. The point is that in the abstract—and that is what they are when we are saying that there is a global nitrogen cycle—that doesn't tell us very much. When these abstractions of the biophysical world tell us something concrete, is when we understand how human societies have formed, have developed, have experience fundamental shifts, or declined, in the *relation* with those biophysical cycles. What is "concrete," then, becomes a matter of the specific ways that extra-human nature crystallizes with human transformations of all nature, both in terms of perception and material constructions.

This is very important if we want to understand the global environmental crisis, or as I prefer to talk about it, *ecological* crisis. This language, "environmental crisis," is often thrown about much too promiscuously on the left. *Monthly Review* is a good example of this. For all its brilliance in opening our eyes to real problems that are central to the way capitalism works, there is still the notion that the limits are outside of us. This means that you can have a discussion of the accumulation crisis and you can have a discussion of the environmental crisis and you don't need to connect the dots. This is a very dangerous way of moving forward, even as we recognize the great contribution of those to have set these so-called "twin crises" right in front of us.

Would it be fair to say that socio-ecological crises are characteristic not only of capitalism but of class society?
JWM: Yes. Certainly civilizations—and we know this from the work of Jared Diamond, Clive Ponting, John Bellamy Foster, and many others—civilizations have been in the business of despoiling their surrounding environments for a very long period of time. Now what capitalism does when it begins to emerge, in a very powerful and real way after 1450, is to accelerate the pace of environmental degradation, and in fact to use environmental degradation as a way to accumulation money capital. And we see this in the great sugar plantation frontiers as they move across the Atlantic world, the great silver mining frontiers in present-day Bolivia and Mexico, that there is a new pace of transformation. And essentially how capitalism works from the very beginning is a kind of ecological hit and run. It goes where the ecological wealth can be extracted fastest and most profitably. So great forests were mowed down in a matter of decades—whereas for the Romans or for the Chinese or for the Mesopotamians, that took a matter of centuries.

So there was a radically accelerated pace of transformation that goes on from the earliest moments in the rise of capitalism. What that meant is that there was a constant search for a new frontier, for a new greenfield site. They went to Madera, a tiny island in the middle of the Atlantic. The Portuguese in the fifteenth century set up plantations. Sugar is a hugely fuel-intensive crop. They cut down all the trees. Production collapsed and they moved on. They moved on to another little island called São Tomé and then to a very big continent, in the northeast of Brazil. The story goes on from there.

What is often not recognized, and this is central to what I call the industrial society myth in environmental thought, is that this was not simply the act of greedy and predatory colonialists. Now of course the colonialists were often greedy and often predatory, sucking up the ecological wealth and bringing in African slaves to work the sugarcane fields, and in themselves suffer the greatest ecological degradations, that is, death. But this was not only going on in the Americas. It was not only a colonial process. It was very much a capitalist process, because we see the very same thing going on with the greatest superpower of the sixteenth and seventeenth centuries, the Dutch Empire.

The Dutch go to Poland; they go to Southern Norway. They go all around the coast of the Baltic and cut down forests—exactly like what we see in Brazil. And of course from Brazil, the sugar frontier moves on to the Caribbean and the same process goes on again. This frontier movement is absolutely central to understanding capitalism as an ecological regime, as a way of ordering the relation betweens humans and the rest of nature.

It's the difference between what I call the five-century theory of capitalism and the two-century theory of capitalism. The two-century theory says it is industrialization. The fact of the matter is that capitalism was profoundly technologically dynamic, and highly industrial, long before the Industrial Revolution. In fact, the Industrial Revolution comes about in response to what I call a *developmental* ecological crisis. It was an ecological crisis of the mid-eighteenth century that was implicated in the shift to coal, to steam power and the profound global transformations of nature that we had seen over the ensuing century and a half.

Now this is important because today we talk about something we call peak oil. Peak oil is not the fundamental product of industrial society, so much as it is a capitalist way of organizing this human/extra-human nature relation that I've been talking about. There are a variety of theories of peak oil. The most widely circulated theory has to do with a simple relation that the pace of production is outrunning the pace of discovery of new fields; that is to say that production is running ahead of the oil frontier. And when that happens, the theory tells us, the price of oil will go up, up, up.

Now we have to be careful of how this argument is developed. The central point I would like to drive home is that peak oil, in itself, is not a novel occurrence. That what we saw in the mid-eighteenth century was, in a sense, "peak charcoal," because charcoal made from the great forests of Europe and the Americas, this charcoal was the key energy source for metal production, for glass making, for sugar refining, for the most basic economic activities of early capitalism. Until we begin to see past the surface of this resource as a geological reality, rather than oil as commodity that reveals the deeper structures of our times, then we are left with the notion that the problem is an external problem, that capitalism will collapse because of an external scarcity. But in fact there is no such thing as an external scarcity, because oil is just a goopy substance; it becomes a fossil fuel through modernity's crystallization of human/extra-human nature.

This is useful because it is a way of understanding, a way of thinking about a long history of transformations in civilization and in the modern world where historical limits of food, energy, and resources were overcome. At the time, as for Thomas Malthus in the later eighteenth century, many people believed these historical limits were in fact external, absolute limits. This is the case with much, but not all, peak oil discourse on the "end of oil" today. So we can only begin to understand the precise nature of these *historical limits* of food, energy, and resources, to understand how today might be a different sort of ecological systemic crisis, from the recognition of capitalism's demonstrated capacity, in previous centuries, to transcend these developmental ecological crises.

Now what I mean by that—let me give you an example with the great forest crisis of early modern capitalism. From 1750 to 1800, there was a tremendous problem in delivering energy supplies to the base of productive centers of world capitalism—that is, metal production, shipbuilding, various kinds of food processing and so forth. That was obviously an historical, ecological limit. It was an ecological crisis that was produced by the relations of the system itself. And what we so often forget today is that capitalism is not only a crisis-generating machine or system, but that it has developed through these ecological crises. And indeed the ecological crisis of the eighteenth century is a good example of this.

It's important to understand that there are different kinds of ecological crises that we've seen historically. The kind that I just mentioned is a *developmental ecological crisis*, that is a crisis of a specific phase of capitalism's nature-society relations, something that we first see in the middle of the eighteenth century. The other world-historical form of ecological crisis I would call an *epochal ecological crisis*. This is what we see in late-medieval Europe, in the thirteenth and fourteenth centuries. This was an ecological crisis that created so much instability, so much turbulence in medieval Europe that feudalism went by the wayside and a new order emerged. This new order was capitalism. It wasn't planned. It very much emerged out of the chaos of the situation. But feudalism was never reestablished because of the very ecological problems that it created, because the socio-ecological limits that feudalism encountered were also limits that feudalism produced.

What form did the ecological crisis take that helped end feudalism and fed the emergence of early capitalism?
JWM: That's an excellent question. If we look at what happened in medieval Europe—in feudal Europe at the beginning of the fourteenth century—

we see some very similar processes to what we see today. At the dawn of the fourteenth century, there was an agricultural system that had very much over-extended itself. That was issuing declining returns, declining yields. The climate had begun to shift, towards colder and wetter weather, at the time because of non-anthropogenic factors. The essence of the problem was that feudalism had pushed itself outward, had developed to where it was increasingly vulnerable to very small socio-ecological disturbances. When those disturbances became greater and greater, as in the early fourteenth century, the climate became colder, it became wetter, it became more difficult to grow food. There were already problems with soil exhaustion. There were already problems with declining yields, so when a shift in the climate came in—today, we call this the "Little Ice Age"—this paved the way for increasingly serious famines, increasingly serious food crises.

This in turn combined with the great commercialization and urbanization processes of the previous centuries to create a very favorable environment for epidemic disease. And as know, these conditions reached a world-historical tipping point with the Black Death in the middle of the fourteenth century. There was of course a population crash, but the main point I would like to underscore is that epidemic disease was not an "output" or a "footprint" of the feudal system and its crises—the Black Death, in itself, expressed a civilizational vortex of class struggle on the land, subsistence crises, and much beyond.

Much the same came be observed about all manner of epidemiological forces that seem to moving to center stage in recent world history—avian and swine flus, skyrocketing rates of cancer far beyond increases in life expectancy, and the rapid proliferation of all manner of "syndromes," from autism to autoimmune disorders, that no one really seems to understand very well, in terms of their root causes in their nature-society dialectic. In 2009 Obama declared a national state of emergency around swine flu. In one sense this was a singular event that passed from our memories in a few weeks. In another, however, this event speaks to a structural crisis of capitalism as ecological regime. Mike Davis has made this case in his wonderful book on the avian flu. What we see is a series of fractures and tensions that begin to multiply in the life of a historical system such as feudalism, and such as we see in the system today. Never before, certainly not for well over a century, have we seen so many points of tension and fracture in the modern world.

You argue that in history crises, both precapitalist and capitalist, have been resolved by plunder—by expansion into new frontiers as well as technical innovation—although under capitalism the speed and intensity of these processes has been accelerated. You suggest that land productivity has been

of central importance to precapitalist societies, whereas labor productivity is central to capitalist society. What's the basis of that distinction and why is it relevant in understanding the current crisis?

JWM: This distinction between the productivity of land and the productivity of labor is really one of the central dividing points between capitalism and other historical systems that we've known. The only thing that capital values is labor productivity. It's not so much that capital ignores nature. It divides nature in this profoundly alienating and explosive way—sometimes creative, sometimes destructive, usually both. The danger is always that the biophysical well-being of watersheds or of soils and many other aspects of ecological life, that those are sacrificed simply to raise the number of bushels produced per person per hour.

How I talk about this in "Ecology and the Accumulation of Capital" is that there has always been, and capitalism is in a sense defined by, this very close connection between what I call productivity and plunder. On the one hand, there are all these extraordinary technological innovations that have raised the productivity of labor power, of *human* nature. The steam engine is probably the greatest example of this. On the other hand, all of these innovations, without exception, have been premised on the plunder of nature. This is at the core of many discussions of fossil capitalism today—that when you take coal out of the ground or natural gas or oil out of the ground, it is being used to raise the productivity of labor.

So when people—and very many good people on the left—talk about the possibilities of a technological fix to today's problems, what they are doing is taking one part of this twin process and saying technology can do everything now. Well, technology has never done everything. In fact, technology, if we think of the great sort of epoch-making technologies of the modern world—the railroads of the nineteenth century, the automobile of the twentieth century—these were inventions that only existed through the massive conquest of global nature. It's really important to put these two things together.

And let me just put one other idea out there to think about. The rising labor productivity over the course of the modern world has been paired with a rising toxicity of the global environment. Every phase of capitalism is not just more productive in terms of human nature, not just more voracious of extra-human nature, but also more toxic. By this I don't simply mean there's more pollution, that more coal is burned, that more oil is burned, so there are more pollutants in a general sense in the atmosphere and the air that we breathe. I mean that what we see from the earliest moments of capitalism are new kinds toxic effluents that radically transform the existing socio-ecological order.

The greatest example of this in the seventeenth century was mercury mining. Mercury was used to extract silver from the great mines of the

Americas. And while mercury had been used by civilizations for a very long time, there was this revolution in the volume of mercury simply dumped into the surrounding environments, including the bodies of indigenous peoples. In the present moment—and we see this in calls, such as from George Monbiot, for a return to nuclear power—we see nuclear power as an example of this. You have waste that's not simply waste; it's not simply garbage. It is waste that threatens to unwork or at best destabilize the basis of human life on this planet, indeed the whole web of life. You see this also with herbicide regime of capital-intensive agriculture—in the U.S. the widely used herbicide, atrazine, demasculinizes male frogs. We might well ask if this is one of a growing number of "canaries in the coalmine." That's part of how labor productivity is linked up not only in the conquest of global nature, in the sense of how people discuss the new enclosures around biotechnology and intellectual property rights, but also that there is this powerful moment of toxifying the biosphere. There are resource frontiers, agricultural frontiers, and these are profoundly interconnected with waste frontiers. Sooner or later, toxification catches up with business as usual.

Another thing that is tied to labor productivity and the accumulation of capital is food. If food can be made available at a cheap price, workers can be paid a lower wage, and the cost of labor goes down.

JWM: Yes, the issue of cheap food is absolutely paramount to the present moment, because the big question about the crisis we are living through is this: will the crisis we are living through give rise to a new period of world accumulation? Are we likely to see a new period of world economic growth, such as we saw between the end of the Second World War and the early 1970s for example, or in an earlier era, during the apex of British world power, between the 1840s and the 1870s? Will the present "crisis" give rise to another one of these middle-run phases of world growth? Or are we perhaps in an era that looks much more like the fourteenth century in medieval Europe, where the pressures were building for an epochal ecological crisis and a transition to a new way of organizing the relations between humans and the rest of nature? As we know, that new way of organizing global nature can be very good or very bad. From this perspective, we can talk about the issue of cheap food and how it's related to neoliberalism as a phase of world history.

Neoliberalism was this phase of world economic history that began in the early 1970s and was associated with the American defeat in Vietnam, the end of the gold standard, the recycling of OPEC dollars into New York banks, the coup d'état in Chile that overthrew the democratically elected government of Allende, and much beyond this. The point that I wish to underscore is that neoliberalism, in contrast to all previous phases of capitalism, was about *taking*, first, and *making*, second. In the 1970s, everyone was talking about a new scientific-technological revolution that would unleash another revolution in labor productivity—automated factories, robotization, and all that. But it turns out that this was not at all the path of technological revolution in the late twentieth century. The one country that went furthest in automated production, Japan, entered a deep stagnation around 1990. And the greatest economic miracle of our times, China, was miraculous on the basis of labor-intensity, not capital-intensity. The greatest innovations of the past three decades are found, of course, in information technologies, especially in moving information faster and in surveillance technologies. So, it became possible for trillions of dollars of financial securities to move faster and faster and faster, and this acceleration of turnover time helped capital to move through successive financial bubbles between 1997 and 2008. It was a way of accelerating history so as to put off the settling of accounts. Today, the accounts still have not been settled. We are still in a kind of bubble, something we might call the "bailout bubble."

The only way out of this bubble, this long series of financial crises that really began in 1997, is by building a better mousetrap, finding a new combination of productivity and plunder. And this is where we see big problems around the provision of cheap food. Now, the neoliberal era, from the 1970s on, was characterized the cheap food in human history. Part of this was the result of the Green Revolution strategy, developed first in the U.S. in the 1930s and globalized, most famously, with the agricultural revolution of the 1960s in India. This second phase of the Green Revolution, centered in South and Southeast Asia, began in the 1960s and really flowered over the next fifteen years. The crucial point to remember is that this phase of the Green Revolution was not a neoliberal process. It was not a neoliberal project in the sense that it was geared toward national food security, in a sort of quasi-market way.

Now what happens in the era of neoliberalism is essentially a redistribution of power from farmers to big agribusiness. This is the second part of the cheap food story. Remember that neoliberalism is primarily about taking, and not about making. This redistribution of power and wealth from the producers of food to the accumulators of capital was a direct result of the U.S.-led "Washington Consensus," especially the neoliberal regime that reshaped the economies of the Global South after the debt crises in the 1980s. The middle-run strategy was to bring more peasants into the world market, increase aggregate production on the world market, and depress food prices. All things being equal, falling food prices were "good" for economies such as the U.S., where real wages were falling, but the full impact of this was obscured by cheaper food.

The strength of the middle-run strategy was also its weakness, and this is now becoming apparent. All of this happened without a revolution in agricultural productivity. Indeed, growth rates for the major cereal crops—corn, wheat, rice—peaked in the mid-1980s, and have been slowing down ever since. Now, advocates of biotechnology have come along to argue that this slowdown can be reversed. But biotechnology is only partly a technology—it is an effort to forge a new socio-ecological regime of accumulation. What has become clear is that the rapid diffusion of genetically modified crops since the mid-1990s has yielded absolutely zero in terms of launching a new agricultural revolution. Biotechnology has not succeeded in raising what scientists call the intrinsic yield of crops. There's been no Green Revolution–type boom in the delivery of the food surplus.

What that means is what neoliberalism did was essentially reorganize the world food system to release a huge amount of cheap food. And what we saw between 1975 and 2003 was the cheapest food in the history of the modern world, going back all the way back to the fifteenth and sixteenth centuries. This is central to the economic vitality of neoliberalism: cheap food. Cheap food is so important because it is the primary factor in determining the floor and ceiling of wages for the world's workers. Workers must be fed enough to reproduce themselves. This is why subsistence crises were abolished first, in the seventeenth and eighteenth centuries, in heavily proletarianized regions such the Netherlands.

Now there are a whole series of factors that are coming unraveled as we speak, and have been doing so with great velocity over the past few years. The era of cheap food now seems to be over. For a world-economy that is still very much faltering, moving into what looks to be a very serious depression—there's a lot of boosterism in the press, but it looks very serious still—the end of cheap food is very bad news. This is not a view limited to radicals. Even the United Nations Food and Agriculture Organization estimates that, for a basket of key food commodities, we can expect price increases 10–35 percent over the next decade. And this presumes that agricultural productivity does not decline by very much, which may well be overly optimistic. The progress of global warming has been implicated in what agronomists call "yield suppression" for the big four cereal crops—wheat, rice, corn, and soy.

Now let's put the FAO's forecast of 10–35 percent food price increases in perspective. At the end of the nineteenth century, the world-economy also experienced a great depression and it came out of this in large measure because food prices went down and they went down very sharply, by about 27 percent for basic food grains in the thirty to forty years before World War I. So we need to start sorting through the tea leaves here to really look at the significance of cheap food, and to take our recognition that the cheap food is not good quality food, that it is toxic food in many cases, and take this to the next level to understand what it is that makes the meat unhealthy or what makes the grains very low in nutrition.

On the left, we tend to think of crises of capital accumulation as crises of overproduction—that is, too many competitors producing too many goods, leading to a glut of products and falling prices and profits. But you point out that Marx also wrote about crises of underproduction, and suggest that we should dust off that concept again.

JWM: This is very important in understanding the present crisis in capitalism. This crisis, in my view, is a terminal crisis that will probably unfold over the next few decades, but one that nevertheless signifies a crisis of capitalism as we have known it for over six centuries. Now what we have become accustomed to thinking about in terms of economic crises in capitalism is the theory of overproduction. That is, too many commodities, too many goods are out there. Consumers either can't buy them or have already bought them. So you have vast warehouses, as you see today, of automobiles sitting idle. Nobody can sell them; there's no consumer market to buy them. This is an overproduction crisis.

When I started to look into the history of capitalism, and began to look seriously at what was going on in terms of the basic nature/society contradictions of the system, what I discovered was another great crisis tendency, the tendency towards underproduction crisis. Over the course of the first three centuries of capitalism, between about 1450 and the 1750s more or less, the great problem was *under*production. That is, it was difficult to get the timber to the shipyards. It was difficult to get the energy, the charcoal, to the ironworks or the sugar refineries. It was difficult to get the basic elements of production to the factory gate. This was an underproduction crisis, and it was the driving force of the late-eighteenth-century crisis, what I have called a developmental crisis of capitalism as ecological regime. I'll take up this issue and how it relates to scarcity and to Malthusianism in a moment. And let's be clear that Marx uses the language of underproduction himself, in a way diametrically opposed to Malthus; that is, Marx viewed underproduction and so-called scarcity as internal to historical capitalism.

The big question is, how did capitalism overcome this underproduction crisis of the later eighteenth century? Well, what happened was the marriage of coal-fired, productivity maximizing innovation, in the form of the steam engine, with the conquest of global nature. The great steam power and coal revolutions of the nineteenth century illuminate this marriage ever so clearly—

these great ribbons of steel, the railroads, and also steamships, were designed not just to move capital and people *to* new areas, like Australia or the American West or India; they were equally designed to suck in an unprecedented bounty of global nature, including human nature as new labor power. Remember that American industrial capitalism in the later nineteenth century was built by immigrants fleeing the great agrarian crises in Eastern Europe and East Asia; and these agrarian crises were the result of an American agricultural revolution in the Midwest combined with the global market created by Britain, and made possible by the steam engine. It was this great leap forward in capitalism's capacity to suck in nature's free gifts that allowed it to suspend this tendency towards underproduction. Indeed, the tendency was largely checked throughout the twentieth century. It is testimony to capitalism's remarkable technological dynamism that today, even most on the left continue to think of economic crises as too many goods chasing too few people.

Now what we are seeing, I suggest, are the first signs of a return to this underproduction crisis tendency. The tendency towards overproduction, at the same time, is not abolished. Both tendencies are working at the same time. We've touched on food. And I think what we are seeing is an exhaustion of the agricultural revolution model that we have known for the past five or six centuries. That is, the Dutch came to world power because they were Europe's best farmers—in any event, the most productive, the most competitive, the most dynamic. Then the English came. And of course we know from our textbooks in the U.S. that there was a great agricultural revolution in the American Midwest with reapers and mowers and threshers and the U.S. became the granary of the world. And the story has rolled on for a very long time.

But what we've seen in the era of neoliberalism since the 1980s is a real stagnation of this agricultural revolution model. So biotechnology comes in, in a big way since the 1990s, but it has not delivered a rising food surplus. In fact what we are looking at in a wide range of official reports from the United Nations, the FAO, and many others, is a forecast of declining agricultural productivity growth. Again, this looks a lot like Europe in the early fourteenth century, although for very different reasons. And we also see this around questions of oil. Now what a lot of people don't realize is that before the great price inflationary crescendo of 2008 when oil hit $147 a barrel in July 2008, that crisis was driven in part by these big oil corporations in part turning towards stock buybacks. They were taking advantage of the financial expansion to buy back their stock, with the presumption that the financial expansion would push stock prices ever higher. And on the other hand they weren't investing in oil exploration and drilling. There were real problems of investment, really since the late 1980s. The International Energy Agency, which is the rich group of countries' energy watchdog, became very hysterical in their 2008 report, the *World Energy Outlook*, where the IEA said there's too little investment going on, and the investment that is going on is often dominated by state oil companies that have different interests than what we have known in capitalism for the past five or six centuries.

There is a real breakdown of how capitalism is working in the basic sectors of the capitalist world-ecology. Not just the world-economy, but the world-ecology—that is, the way that capitalism organizes the human- and extra human-nature relationship. We see this in oil and we see this in agriculture. This is something that we all should be thinking about very seriously—the breakdown of historical investment mechanisms. When Marxists talk about accumulation, what we're really talking about—it's much more than this of course—but in simple terms what we're talking about is investment. And that was always the saving grace of capitalists. Yes, they were brutal, they were violent, they were horrible. And at the same time, the investments that they sunk into production delivered the goods to enough people to keep the system working, to deliver *enough* social goods to *enough* people that there was kernel of truth in capitalists' arguments about "development" and "progress." Now if we have an underproduction tendency that's coming back after nearly two centuries is coming back into primacy, then we have a very serious issue with the legitimacy of capitalism.

You distinguish between epochal and developmental crises. Do you view the most recent crisis of capitalism as an epochal crisis or one that will at least in the short-term develop into another moment within perhaps an unfolding crisis?

JWM: Yes, this is really the question we really all need to be thinking about. What kind of crisis is this? Will we see another wave of capitalist development over the next twenty-five to thirty years? Now the conditions for this can be summarized very glibly, which is one part productivity, technical innovations, social innovations and so on, one part plunder, expansion into new frontiers. It's a twin process, as I've indicated. Together, this movement of productivity and plunder has delivered cheap energy, cheap raw materials, and above all, cheap food and labor, for the better part of six centuries. Productivity and plunder have been so inextricably linked in modern world history since the sixteenth century that it's impossible to identify an epoch-making technological innovation that does not fundamentally depend on the movement into new frontiers.

So when we ask the question "Is another phase of global capitalist development on the horizon?" we need to right away go and ask, "Where are the new frontiers that would make that possible?" People often say to me, well, what about Africa? That's the new frontier. Well, it's hard for me to think of a region that's more thoroughly transformed by the modern world-system than Africa, from the slave trade of the early modern era to the cash-crop colonialism of the late nineteenth and early twentieth centuries to the ravages of structural adjustment of the 1980s and since. We need to look at where those frontiers are and we also need to look at where's the energy going to come from. Okay, so Africa is often regarded as a new oil frontier, but will this work if African consumption is repressed? And since oil and modern "development" are so deeply intertwined, what does this mean for capitalism's promise of a broadly defined social development?

But frontiers are not merely geographical places. They are also socio-ecological relations that uncork a new stream of nature's goodies for free or low cost: cheap food, cheap energy, cheap raw materials, cheap labor. In every great era of capitalist development, we see these four factors come together, through new technologies and new enclosures. Although the supply of one or more these factors has always flowed from specific countries or regions, the crucial point in the discussion is that cheap food, oil, and so forth benefited capitalism as a whole, not merely this or that country. So, yes, Angola may have oil; and Brazil, land; and China and India, labor. But do any of these modest energy, food, or labor frontiers promise to grease the wheels of accumulation for the next three decades? This is the big point, the systemic point— cheap food and cheap energy is a world-historical process. No phase of capitalism has emerged in the absence of cheap food and energy, and no "great leaps forward" in the provision of cheap food or energy are on the horizon.

The history of capitalism is the history of creating new commodities— and the need for them—where commodities had not existed before, such as transforming women's unpaid labor into new products. Is there a push right now, as you see it—leaving aside fuel and water—to generate new internal markets where they previously never existed?

JWM: Yes. I think that is what's going on. But it's hard to see where that will be successful. Some of the most dynamic zones of the world's economy today, one thinks of the so-called BRIC countries—Brazil, Russia, India, China (although I'm not so certain how dynamic Russia is at the moment)—these are countries with vast internal frontiers. The world-historical question is not just will those frontiers be sufficient to bring down the cost of doing business, and create new conditions of accumulation for those countries. The national and the systemic aspects of this frontier process are dialectically connected. As we know, the BRIC countries do not exist in nice, tidy boxes. We are dealing with the systemic process and the question is: will those frontiers bring down the cost of labor, bring down the cost of food, bring down the cost of energy not just on a national basis but on a systemic basis?

And let's not forget metals. For the first time in the long twentieth century, from World War I to 2008, we saw five commodity booms. The most recent one before 2003–08 was that of the 1970s. Until the past decade, these had always turned on agriculture and energy. This time however, metals were included in the mix. It's not there isn't plenty of metal of various sorts in the world; it's not that there isn't enough oil. It's that it is increasingly costly to extract these vital raw materials.

I think that's a sort of basic punch line here: that in order for accumulation to revive, in order for economic growth to revive beyond a short blip of a year or two, those vital raw materials, the labor supplies, the food supplies, the energy supplies, the metal supplies need to be delivered cheaply and indeed more and more cheaply over the coming decades.

What approaches and solutions do you think we should avoid and embrace in working for ways out of this system that creates these crises? You mentioned the nineteenth-century Protestant cleric Thomas Malthus, who argued there were natural limits built into the food supply. Are you concerned about the influence of his ideas on the environmental movement today?

JWM: I think the first lesson is that Malthus was wrong because he took the problem of limits outside of history, outside the history that women and men make in the modern world. So the issue is not that there is no scarcity—of course, capitalism is a system that is premised on scarcity. That's why markets in the capitalist era function the way that they do. So I think the mistake of the left has been in a certain reluctance to deal with the problems of scarcity, or in some cases back into an embrace of a neo-Malthusian scarcity mentality in which there are these "natural limits" that are outside of how capitalism functions historically as an ecological regime.

I think the second big lesson concerns technology. Technology is not a magic bullet. Technology is not alchemy; it doesn't create something out of nothing. So we need to understand this relationship between plunder and productivity, between technological innovation and the global conquest of nature.

Finally, there is the big question of what kind of crisis are we in the midst of. I believe we are in a crisis of capitalism as a historical system. Yes, as many people on the left point out—*Monthly Review* is excellent on this—this promises catastrophic loss of human life. At the same time, we need to take care to theorize, in a historically grounded way, capitalism and the ways that it has created new nature-society relations, repeatedly, that have overcome the old limits, the old bottlenecks of commodity production and accumulation. I like to say that capitalism does not *have* an ecological regime; it *is* an ecological regime, and this means understanding socio-ecological frontiers as forests and fields, yes, but also as, say, labor frontiers in advanced capitalist centers. Since World War II, for example, capitalism has been very good at say bringing in internal labor frontiers, and the proletarianization of women in postwar America is a great example of this. The fact that American households were able to maintain their income levels after the 1970s by adding a second wage earner was a tremendous internal frontier, if you will, of commodification in the modern world-system.

What we need to remember is that these internal frontiers are not infinitely reproducible. There's not an endless stream of frontiers. Economists talk about a law of substitution, as when cheap whale oil ran out in the nineteenth century, because they killed all the whales that could be cheaply hunted. Petroleum products came to replace whale oil as the major industrial lubricant. Well, that's not an infinite process. There are substitutions that can be made, but they are not all created equal and they are not infinite. So this is part of what sometimes gets into the pores of many very good and lively left critics of capitalism's environmental contradictions. They've lost track of the relentless fact that the law of substitution is a historical law that the conquest of nature has been a powerful way of creating growth and that it has done so through specific innovations of reworking nature. Think of coal, and of steam power with railroads and steamships, or a jet airliner today with oil. These technology-resource combinations are not infinitely repeatable. I think that's really the important thing to reflect on when we ask ourselves: is this a crisis of a phase of capitalism, or of capitalism itself? And good people will disagree on this. But until we pose the question in these ways I think it's very difficult to have the kind of discussion that we really need to open up. It's really central to open up these questions of the relations of nature and society as inextricably bound.

CHAPTER EIGHT

Gillian Hart: The Agrarian Question and Multiple Paths of Capitalist Development in East Asia and South Africa

What motivated you in the early 1990s, after decades studying Asia, to return to your native South Africa and begin the research that forms the basis for *Disabling Globalization*?

GH: I had been away from South Africa for nearly twenty years. I went back at the end of 1990 for the first time in, in fact, exactly nineteen years. Through that first part of the 1990s before the election, there were huge debates going on around what the future of South African society would look like. At that point the African National Congress had really been taken by surprise when they were unbanned on the second of February, 1990, and there was a great deal of debate particularly around economic policy which the ANC in exile had not in fact given a deal of attention to.

What was becoming evident in that early part of the 1990s was that there were very powerful forces that would press for neoliberal policies and one of the key examples that they were invoking was the "East Asian miracle." East Asia was being held up as an example of the magic of the market at work and apartheid was being portrayed as a sort of colonial protectionist set of policies that would just have to be swept away. South Africans were being told that they were going to just have to go and do like the East Asians. And what was very clear to me was that this was an extraordinarily distorted view of what East Asia was all about.

How did they define the East Asian miracle, a term used to describe the economic trajectories of South Korea, Taiwan, Japan, Hong Kong, Thailand, Indonesia, Malaysia, and Singapore?

GH: The East Asian miracle they defined as unleashing market forces and getting the state out of the market; that it was based on export-led growth, the lifting all sorts of protections, and privatization.

I was very struck when I went back to South Africa for the first time in a long time by the presence of fairly large numbers of Taiwanese industrialists in South Africa. And the places that these industrialists had gone to were also areas where there had been massive dispossession of black South Africans. In addition to historical processes of dispossession, from the 1960s onward what the apartheid state did was to rip literally millions of black South Africans from white farms and from areas that were known in South Africa as "black spots" which were areas in rural South Africa where way back in the nineteenth and early twentieth centuries, black South Africans had actually bought land. Very large numbers of people had settled there and through the logic of apartheid, what the government was trying to do was to move people from these so-called black spots into areas defined as part of the bantustans.

This mainly happened in the 1960s?

GH: This began in the early 1960s and between the early 1960s and the early '80s somewhere between three and four million black South Africans were moved from these so-called black spots as well as from white-run farms into patches of land often defined as part of the bantustans and very often these areas were within fifteen to twenty kilometers of former white towns.

So under this sort of bizarre geography of apartheid, what you had were patches of land that were defined as part of the bantustans into which millions of people were packed in different parts of the countryside. They essentially were areas of urban-like density in the middle of rural areas. And it was into these areas that large numbers of Taiwanese industrialists moved, starting in the early 1980s. What was happening essentially was that the apartheid state was offering huge subsidies to industrialists to shift to these areas and part of the idea was precisely to prevent black South Africans from moving into the major urban areas.

And precisely at the point that the apartheid government was offering these tremendous subsidies, what was happening in Taiwan was that huge numbers of small-scale industrialists who had grown tremendously rapidly through the 1960s and '70s were having to leave. Wages were going up, exchange rates were appreciating, and the sort of labor-intensive industries that they had set up were no longer viable. The Taiwanese government was trying to move them out and the South African government was trying to attract labor-intensive industries to these so-called border areas, the areas on the edges of the bantustans.

Simultaneously in the early 1980s, South Africa was increasingly being isolated internationally and Taiwan likewise was a sort of international pariah. South Africa and Taiwan had actually set up diplomatic links, so these diplomatic links facilitated the movement of Taiwanese industrialists. But there really were other basic economic and political forces that were drawing Taiwanese industrialists into these areas.

Where I became very interested in all of this was that it seemed to me that, in place of these abstract models of the East Asian miracles, it would make a lot more sense to look at what had actually happened when some of these tremendously successful small-scale capitalists had moved into the South African countryside. That was the initial motivation behind my doing this research.

The other thing that drew me into the research was that there was a huge debate going on in the early 1990s that was cast in terms that "the city versus the countryside." One group was saying that South Africa's future was metropolitan-urban and that with the lifting of controls on movement, large numbers of black South Africans would just move into the main urban centers.

Apartheid had, of course, been premised on the control of the movement of black South Africans.

GH: Yes, right up until the second half of the 1980s. It was very strong influx control through which black South Africans had to carry passes. In order to live in the main urban areas, they had to have so-called Section 10 rights, and those who didn't have these rights, well, then could be thrown in jail.

In the late 1980s, these restrictions were being lifted, but the argument was that, with the lifting of these apartheid restrictions on movement, black South Africans would just simply pack their bags, move into urban areas. In the early 1990s, some World Bank representatives and many in South Africa were arguing that South Africa's future was metropolitan.

And then there was another argument—interestingly coming primarily out of another segment of the World Bank—arguing that, in fact, South Africa should follow a peasant path of development and that there should be sort of large-scale land redistribution to create small-scale peasant farmers, who were to be more efficient than these large white farmers who had been heavily subsidized by the apartheid state.

There was, in other words, an intense rural versus urban debate. What seemed to me to be totally missing from this debate was the fact that precisely because of these processes of dispossession, there were these huge townships with urban-like density in the countryside where people had made investments in housing and so forth, and that were not likely to empty out anytime soon.

The second thing that drew me into all of this was I came across a press report of what was going on in a funny little town called Bronkhorstspruit, which is about sixty kilometers east of Pretoria. What this report said was that white local government officials had set up an area of Bronkhorstspruit called Cultura Park. There was a large Buddhist temple being built here and a visitors' center and they were making trips to Taiwan in order to lure Taiwanese industrialists.

And what made this very interesting was as follows: in the early 1990s, after apartheid had ended, the subsidies that had brought in the Taiwanese in the 1980s had been lifted. The argument was that without these subsidies the Taiwanese would just pick up, pack their bags and move off. So of course what made this report so interesting to me was that it indicated that maybe there were other things going on.

I went and visited Bronkhorstspruit and discovered that these white local government officials had actually set up a travel agency in Taipei and were bringing in planeloads of Taiwanese and were then selling them real estate in Cultura Park where there was a large stock of luxury housing. One has to understand that property in South Africa in those days was extremely cheap, so that what this also indicated was the way in which these local governments were bypassing the national government and moving directly into, not only the global economy, but some very specific places to draw in industrialists. I then discovered that this was not only happening in Bronkhorstspruit but in fact was happening in these little towns all over South Africa, that these white local governments were fiercely competing with one another in order to bring in Taiwanese, and also Chinese, industrialists.

And the third thing that drew me into this was the whole question of what would happen when democratically elected local governments came into power that would obviously be black majority governments drawn from these adjacent black townships.

These were the three questions that pulled me in, all these forces coming together in these places where you had former white towns, huge black townships, connections with Taiwan, and an impending fundamental change in local government, as well as in national government.

What sort of racial politics emerged from the white local state courting Taiwanese investors? And how did they differ from the subsequent black-dominated local state?
GH: These questions of race and ethnicity were very powerful. What was going on in South Africa at this time were a lot of celebratory discourses around the "rainbow nation," nonracialism and so forth, although it was very clear that powerful elements of racism were very firmly in place. But one of the ways in which this was manifested was the relationships of different groups of South Africans to the Taiwanese who were defined as "the other" both by the left and by the right—so the questions of these forms of accumulation, connected with race and ethnicity, was a very interesting question.

How then did these dynamics play out within these black townships that you studied?
GH: Well, I ended up working in two of these former white towns and adjacent townships in KwaZulu Natal, which is about halfway between Johannesburg

and Durban. What made these two places really interesting is that they're only a hundred kilometers apart. On the face of it, they look very similar, with a former white town and huge black township. One of them is called Newcastle, the northernmost one, and the southerly one is called Ladysmith. They were British colonial army outposts. They evolved in some fairly similar ways. At the time of my research, Newcastle was larger than Ladysmith in terms of population but just in a lot of ways, they seemed very similar.

What made them very interesting was that it turned out that the local political dynamics were very, very different. Part of my research is about how and why it is that these two places that look so similar, are both connected with East Asia, both have these huge black townships and so forth, turned out to have very different local political dynamics.

How did the differences between these two townships, Newcastle and Ladysmith, manifest themselves?

GH: I'd like to start off talking about formal politics and here the really key point is that in KwaZulu Natal, the main opposition to the African National Congress comes from a party called the Inkatha Freedom Party, or IFP, led by Mangosuthu Buthelezi, who was one of the bantustan leaders during the apartheid era. The Inkatha Freedom Party stands for a sort of Zulu ethnic nationalism and in the late 1980s and early '90s there was, as some people may know, a major civil war in KwaZulu Natal between supporters of the ANC and the IFP.

The main political difference between Newcastle and Ladysmith is that in the Newcastle township the Inkatha Freedom Party was much, much stronger than the ANC, whereas in the Ladysmith township, the ANC is much stronger.

What happened in the 1996 local government election was that the ANC won in the Newcastle township, although they won by a very small majority. What had actually happened was that one of the most unpopular of the Taiwanese industrialists had decided that he wanted to become the mayor of Newcastle and what he did was he ran for the Inkatha Freedom Party. In effect, he won the election for the ANC in an area that was regarded as an IFP Stronghold.

In the Ladysmith township at the time of the local government election, the ANC had a massive electoral victory. But what these differences in electoral outcomes reflected, were very different underlying political dynamics that you can't understand simply at the level of formal politics. You can only understand them historically.

The Newcastle townships were set up in the early 1960s and at that time was that people were being moved into these townships through what were often very brutal processes, and there was very little in the way of overt resistance to these removals. Part of the reason for that has to do with the fact that this was an extremely repressive period in South African history, but it also has to do with some longer local histories. But basically, what happened was that there was relatively little resistance to the removals into the township.

This, in turn, carried over into the nature of the youth movement. There was a small but very militant ANC youth movement that emerged in the Newcastle townships, although the large majority of people in these townships were supporters of the Inkatha Freedom Party. These were townships into which the apartheid state actually put, relatively speaking, significant resources. In addition, the labor movement historically was weak in the Newcastle industries.

In Ladysmith, the situation was very different. There was huge, very organized resistance to removals. This, in turn, was linked with the fact that in the early 1950s Govan Mbeki, who is the father of Thabo Mbeki, lived in Ladysmith for two years and was very active in local organizing. Govan Mbeki was one of the great leaders of the liberation movement, who was imprisoned with Mandela. Older people in and around Ladysmith had vivid memories of Govan Mbeki, and of how he helped them to understand the links between land, labor, and politics more generally. I have a wonderful quote from an older person who knew Govan Mbeki quite well, who said to me, when you think about land, you must realize that land, labor, and politics go together.

What was very clear was that the legacy of his organizing in this area carried over into the resistance to removals and this was made somewhat easier by the fact that most of the forced removals in the Ladysmith area took place from the early 1970s onwards, when the labor movement in South Africa more generally was resurgent, and there was just far more overt political activity.

This high level of opposition to forced removals was linked with a very highly organized industrial labor movement, and this was linked in turn with a much more broadly based and organized youth movement. So that the three key struggles around land, around labor, and the youth movement took totally different forms in Ladysmith than in Newcastle and this, in turn, carried over into local government, so that the outcome in the second half of the 1990s was that very different forms of local government emerged in these two places. Local ANC councilors in Ladysmith were highly accountable to their township constituents who themselves were organized and mobilized. One example is that a form of participatory budgeting was introduced in Ladysmith. In contrast, local government in Newcastle was totally chaotic.

Which gets to the heart of one of the main themes of your book, which is that the so-called agrarian question, these histories of agrarian disposses-

sion and struggle, are central to understanding the outcomes of politics much further down the road.

GH: Yes, the agrarian question is absolutely central and its importance is ongoing. By the agrarian question, I mean the connection between processes of dispossession and how this, in turn, links very directly with the *conditions of reproduction of labor power*—that is, the ways in which people support themselves. It means access to housing, to electricity, to running water, and so forth, and in South Africa these are very, very directly linked and connected with one another. I think there's a tendency on the left in South Africa to assume that dispossession from the land is part of what happens en route to capitalism, that it's a fairly natural process through which one has to pass as part of what is entailed in the development of capitalism.

And this, in turn, actually goes back to a very important debate that took place in the 1970s, the so-called race-versus-class debate. The big argument there was that it was very important to recognize that what was going on in South Africa was not simply the consequence of apartheid, but that it was closely linked to the development of capitalism. This, in turn, related to liberal interpretations of apartheid which basically said that apartheid was all about irrational racial discrimination and that as more and more black South Africans were drawn into the economy as producers and consumers discrimination would sort of fade away. A lot of the opposition to sanctions and divestment was based on the argument that you just had to let market forces work and that apartheid would melt away. The counter-argument was that actually what was going on here was that cheap labor was functional to capitalism, it was good for capitalism, and that what one had to focus on was capitalism rather than apartheid. That, therefore, attributing dispossession and forced removals to apartheid rather than to capitalism was a mistake and that, in fact, dispossession was what capitalism was all about and a natural part of capitalism.

As a consequence of that, I think, there's been relatively little attention to the agrarian question in South Africa in the sense that Govan Mbeki pushed it right from the 1940s onward, when he argued for the importance of linking land and labor and linking rural and urban struggles. Mbeki in the 1940s was trying to get the urban-based ANC to attend to the links between rural and urban struggles, but he was dismissed. In the 1970s and '80s, with the resurgence of organized labor, the left and liberation movement really came to focus very heavily on the urban industrial working class. And again, too, there was a relative neglect of rural struggles and of linking rural and urban struggles.

What seemed to me so important about these places was that there was this very, very direct and vivid connection between histories of dispossession and industrial labor and the conditions in which workers were living. This was part of the reason why the Taiwanese connection became so significant in my research because it really helped to make very clear that the histories of racialized dispossession in South Africa were absolutely essential and were continuing to shape the living conditions of very large numbers of black South Africans.

What were the different ways that the agrarian question and agrarian transformations unfolded in East Asia, which were then held up as a model for South African development?

GH: What was interesting about these Taiwanese industrialists who came and settled in these areas in South Africa is that many of them were actually the product of redistributive land reforms in East Asia that took place in the late 1940s and early 1950s. What had happened in East Asia was firstly, of course, mass mobilization of the Chinese peasantry, which really defined the success of the Chinese Communist revolution. Once the nationalists had fled from China to Taiwan, they were very aware of the dangers of peasant uprisings. The U.S. military at that point, of course, was heavily involved in Japan, Taiwan, and Korea. And what happened in the late 1940s and early 1950s is with the strong support of the U.S. there were major redistributive land reforms that happened in Japan, South Korea, and Taiwan. An unintended consequence of these redistributive land reforms was that by the late 1960s and early 1970s in Taiwan large numbers of these small peasant farmers started transforming themselves into small-scale industrialists and it was precisely these industrialists who, through the extraordinarily rapid growth of small-scale industry in Taiwan, were no longer viable by the 1980s. It was they who moved into these areas in South Africa.

The great irony was that these industrialists, who themselves were the product of redistributive land reforms, were moving into areas that were the site of just massive racialized dispossession and it was through these stark contrasts that I was able to use not only the comparison between Ladysmith and Newcastle, but also the South African–East Asian connections to really focus in on how and why these histories of forced removals and dispossession in South Africa have vitally important ongoing significance.

Perhaps not surprisingly, the neoliberal depiction of the East Asian model of development neglects to mention this history of land redistribution.

GH: You know, there's been a lot of criticism of the East Asian model as an example of a success of the market, which has shown very powerfully that, in fact, the state was very heavily involved in the economy in South Korea and in Taiwan. I think we've given much less attention given to these histories of redistribution.

I think what makes these histories of redistribution so interesting and compelling is that they operated in effect as a "social wage." I'm particularly thinking here of Taiwan and of the way in which a huge proportion of the industrialization in Taiwan has been in rural areas where households retained access to land and I'm thinking also of what has happened in China, particularly since 1984, when again a huge proportion of this very rapid industrialization has happened in villages and small towns where households have retained access to land. What this, in turn, has meant, is that it's possible for industrialists to pay relatively low wages, *money wages*, while at the same time, *real wages* are relatively high. That's what I mean by the social wage.

Let me give you an example of this. In Newcastle in 1995 what started happening was a lot of knitwear started pouring into Newcastle from China. What had happened in Newcastle was a lot of small-scale Taiwanese had set up, all producing knitwear—each of them producing a piece of a sweater. One little factory made shoulder pads and one embroidered pockets and another made the fabric and another sewed it up, et cetera. And they were producing mainly for the domestic South African market. In 1995–96, a lot of cheap knitwear started moving in and it was coming from Taiwanese industrialists who had moved to China. These were the uncles and aunties and cousins of industrialists in Newcastle and the knitwear was absolutely identical. What the Newcastle industrialists were saying was that this knitwear was coming in at prices below the cost of production in Newcastle and that this demonstrated emphatically that wages were too high in Newcastle. One of the issues here is there are tremendous labor conflicts in Taiwanese factories.

I compared wages paid by Taiwanese industrialists in Newcastle with those paid by Taiwanese industrialists in China and what I discovered was something very interesting, which is that if you take money wage rates, i.e., wage rates using the prevailing rates of exchange, wages in Newcastle were roughly double those of China. So that in dollar terms, Taiwanese industrialists were actually paying twice the wages that their counterparts in China were paying. Yet if you take real wages, what those wages could actually buy, what I discovered was that real wages in Newcastle were 30–40 percent lower than those in China.

In other words, the social wage was higher in China.
GH: That is precisely the issue, that these histories of redistribution had created conditions in which social wages were higher. What my research has done is to try to say something about global competition. And part of what it shows, I think, is that global competition emanating from East Asia is partly a product of a very particular set of histories that have created conditions in which very low wages contribute to the intensification of competition.

But this is not just a force of nature; it's a product of very particular redistributive histories. In the context of South Africa, for example, what it does is it enables a questioning of the conditions under which South Africa is being told to move down a neoliberal path with a history of massive inequality, massive dispossession that renders it almost impossible to compete in these conditions. The South African government has indeed conformed to a lot of the policies associated with a fairly orthodox neoliberalism. And what has happened is massive job losses, increases in cost of basic services, and very clearly, strongly increasing inequalities that have become ironically far more marked in the postapartheid period where there's been some degree of deracialization in the upper reaches of the income distribution—but in which probably something like the lower 40 percent of the population in South Africa has suffered real declines in income.

Clearly one of your intentions with _Disabling Globalization_ is not simply to look at South Africa, but to challenge much of the thinking on the left about globalization. What are the implications of the differing trajectories of South African and Taiwan for how we see "globalization"?
GH: Well, one of the big arguments of the book turns around the dangers of what I call the "impact model" of globalization. More often than not, when people talk about globalization, they talk about it in terms of its impact. And what seems to be so dangerous about this way of thinking is it conjures up a set of technological and market forces that almost have the force of nature that bear down on us—and to which we have to just bow down—which is the neoliberal argument, that there is no alternative. But it also, I think, sets up a kind of a rather dangerous notion of these forces bearing down and that all the "local" can do is then resist and react. This impact model operates through a set of dichotomies, along with global/local are active/passive, economics/culture, masculine/feminine. I think that the impact model is tremendously gendered in conjuring up these active technological and market forces that are roving all over the globe, and the local is depicted as this sort of passive, feminine recipient that has to make itself as attractive as possible in order to lure capital.

Another of the dichotomies that works here is time and space, where time is this active force, and space and place are seen as these sort of empty containers. And this tends to go along with a notion of the local as a bounded unit with lines drawn around it, which is one of the reasons why arguments are cast in terms of the local as the site of resistance to the global. It seems to be extremely dangerous because what they do is, they buy right into the impact model and they concede to all the dichotomies through which the impact model does its insidious work. This is where an understanding of place with the local—not as a bounded unit but as points of coming together, of multiple forces that are also connected and linked to other places—leads one to ask different kinds of questions. Because it leads one to talk about power and practice, and it leads one to ask questions about how is it that particular kinds of connections are being made. How is it that capital is able to exercise the power that it does? But instead of thinking about these abstracted technological and market forces, we can move into much more specific kinds of understandings in a way that it can be very powerful and useful on practices, power, processes, and connections that can also illuminate the possibilities for alliances and the possibility for change. In other words, they focus attention on how these processes that we call globalization are being produced and in this process of production, what are the slippages, openings, possibilities for alternatives.

What does this approach look like in a practical sense with regard to the work you did in South Africa?

GH: Let me take concrete examples of Ladysmith and Newcastle. What I did not do in my study was to say, what is the impact of globalization on these local places? Rather what I did was to say, look, what's interesting about Ladysmith and Newcastle is that they represent a coming together of forced removals, of apartheid geographies, to try to get industries to relocate to these places, of connections with East Asia.

They represent points at which regional, national, transnational connections were all operating. In other words, they represent vantage points from which one can see a whole lot of connections at work. It seems to me that we need an understanding of the local not as a bounded unit upon which global forces bear down, but rather understanding the local as points of connection or coming together of multiple forces and then trying to think about what are the key connections and how can we use these connections both to understand what's going on and in order to forge alliances and to think about commonalities as well as about differences, through which alternatives might be envisaged and put into practice.

Can you give some examples of these possible alternatives today?

GH: Many very interesting movements that are emerging in many different parts of the world are precisely agrarian movements and, going back to your earlier question, one of the reasons why agrarian questions remain so important is that what we're seeing in many different parts of the world is a lot of organizing going on around demands for land, but often linked with urban struggles. Of course the most famous of these is the MST (Landless Workers'

Movement) in Brazil, but there are many others in different parts of Latin America.

In Indonesia there's a very active land movement emerging. The Landless People's Movement that's taking shape in South Africa is a reflection of the ongoing significance of agrarian questions. But what is needed is an understanding that does not see these agrarian movements simply as rural or peasant movements, but sees them in their relationship to what is going on in urban areas and tries to make connections with worker's movements, with struggles around electricity, water, urban services, and so forth, which in many parts of the world are in the process of being privatized. This is one of the examples where struggles around land, struggles around livelihood, and struggles around broader living conditions might be linked and connected with one another in ways that are both attentive to historically, geographically specific conditions but are also able to see linkages and connections with what is going on in other places.

CHAPTER NINE

Ursula Huws: Labor and Capital, Gender and Commodification

You contend that what has powered the economy in the twentieth century has been the transformation of previously unpaid domestic and hence female labor. How so?

UH: I think probably the word that sums up the process I'm talking about is *commodification*. The way capitalism has developed over the centuries has been by transforming activities that used to be carried out, if you like, for their use-values in the home—were outside the money economy—transforming those activities into the basis of commodities that can be mass-produced and sold for profit.

Now, it's often a two-stage process. You don't go kind of straight from grandmother scrubbing clothes on a washboard in the kitchen to the washing machine. There's also an intermediate phase where it's a service industry, like for instance the mass laundry industries that grew up at the beginning of the twentieth century. But the inexorable process is towards creating more and more commodities that can be mass-produced.

What are some other examples of things that previously had been the domain of female labor that were then commodified?

UH: Almost all the things that used to be done by women in the home—either in the nineteenth century or in the second industrial revolution around electricity in the 1920s and '30s—became the basis of new commodities. In the nineteenth century we saw products like soap, mass-produced goods, and prepared food. Up to the eighteenth century in Britain, things like beer were made in the home—people wouldn't go out and buy them—and things like candles and clothes for the household and so on were all made in the home. As the eighteenth and nineteenth centuries wore on, they became the basis of factory-made goods. And then in the twentieth century, with the spread of electricity, a whole new wave of commodification came in, creating things like vacuum cleaners, washing machines, and a whole range of appliances in the home that we use supposedly to take the labor out of housework.

You also write about activities that aren't turned into tangible commodities, but turned into services instead.

UH: I think the way that the process tends to go is it starts off being an activity which is carried out for nothing in the home—for rich people by servants in the home, and for poor people, for themselves in the home. And that could be almost any activity. It could be like making music, like telling people what happened during the day, like making the news and so on; or, as I said earlier, washing clothes, preparing food, and cleaning.

And then in the next stage, you get the development of what you might call mass service industries. From things like just people making music in the home, you got things like orchestras or bands or various forms of performance music that was performed by people who are providing a service. You might have had to send the clothes out to a laundry or have a washerwoman come in or have food that was prepared in a restaurant or something like that, which is the service industry.

The thing about service industries is that it's kind of hard to make a profit from them above a certain point, because the workers have to be reasonably skilled. Each restaurant meal has to be cooked more or less the same way, for instance, or each shirt has to be washed more or less the same way. And so as they become the basis of large industries and then they have to compete with each other. The way to improve productivity, when technology comes in, is to find a way of commodifying it; in other words, making it so it can be a mass-produced product. And slowly the service industries give way to manufacturing industries. So the live performance by the orchestra gives way to making records or CDs or DVDs or making radio sets or television on which people can experience the music.

And capitalism makes a lot more profit out of commodified music, like selling CDs, than it does out of live music. Running the Milan Opera House or something like that requires huge public subsidies. But selling CDs of Pavarotti's greatest hits, you can make an awful lot of money on it.

You point out that pleasure, too, has come to be regarded as something that can be bought, leading to the growth of the entertainment industry, amusement arcades, package holidays, the cosmetics and fashion industries, and pornography. How is this commodification of pleasure linked to traditionally female work?

UH: It's not exclusively female work, but the tendency is that the bulk of activities that go on unpaid in the home are done by women. Housework activities historically are linked with the role of the mother or the wife as somebody, if you like, who services the family, who pleases, who gives pleasure, who entertains the kids, who gives sexual pleasure to the husband. It's a role of actually giving pleasure. If you can say that there's a service relationship in the home, it tends to be one in which more power is held by the man and the woman is doing the servicing, rather than the other way around.

We can't generalize too hard around these things and there are class dimensions to these differences, and there are ethnic dimensions to these differences as well. But generally speaking, it's been the areas of life which have been historically most protected from the market that have been the areas of women's unpaid labor and of social relations in the home. In the twentieth century particularly these became very much opened up to the market and have become the basis of new industries.

How would you say this change has affected the status of women?
UH: I think it's the constant process of renegotiation of relationships between men and women, between parents and children, between disabled people and their carers, between people who work in other people's homes and the people they work for. The home is a site of, or the sphere of, consumption, if you like. It's a site of constantly changing relationships.

One of the really interesting and scary things that commodification is doing right now is that what it takes with one hand, it gives with the other. For example, we all go out and buy supposedly labor-saving appliances to make our lives easier in the home—we buy washing machines, we buy fridges, to try to minimize the amount of housework we do, but the amount of time people spend on housework doesn't go down. In fact there's a lot of evidence it's actually going up. Part of the reason for that is that the kind of work that used to go on in the home, like the physical work of scrubbing floors or peeling potatoes or whatever it was has been replaced by new kinds of consumption work, whether waiting in line in checkouts at an ATM machines or in supermarkets or in gas stations or waiting in virtual lines in a queue for a call center. Because increasingly the purchasing of these commodities and the distribution of these products has become quite a complex process with more and more self-service involved and as the market becomes more complicated, choosing the right product also becomes much more complicated.

But also these things become harder to work and harder to learn how to work. So there is effort involved in choosing the product you want to buy, learning how to use it, getting it fixed when it goes wrong, and increasingly all these processes involve consumption work. And so the time spent on unpaid labor is just as much as it always was—it's just a different kind of unpaid labor from what it was in the past.

Who benefits from consumption work like self-service?
UH: It's to the benefit of the employers of service workers. What's happened is that the service industries have become more and more Taylorized, in order to maximize the productivity of service workers. The time they spend on each

task has to be minimized. The tasks become more and more routinized, more and more speeded up. You can talk to anybody who works in a call center and they'll tell you what the pressure is to keep the length of the calls down, to deal with as many calls a possible, to meet performance targets, et cetera. Now the way that that is done, the time that is saved hasn't just disappeared into nowhere. It's been transferred onto the consumer, so paid time has been turned into unpaid time.

The same thing has happened in supermarkets. In the early years of the twentieth century lots and lots of people worked in retailing and they stood behind counters and literally waited on people. They stood there with their aprons on doing nothing until a customer came along and when a customer came along, they said, "What do you want, Madam?" and then bagged up the vegetables, weighed them, did all the labor and handed them out and it was actually physically delivered by a kid on a bike. In my childhood in Britain in the 1950s you'd be sent down to the greengrocers with an order, and then later that afternoon a boy would come along on a bike and deliver it all.

Now all that labor of delivering and all that waiting time and all that time spent bagging up the vegetables and so on have been transferred to the consumer. And also a lot of the cost of transport and storage that used to be born by the industry is transferred to the customer. And this they call increasing productivity—it's pressurizing and Taylorizing the work of the paid workers, squeezing as much labor out of them as possible. But it's also transferring all the squeezed-out labor onto all of us as consumers.

And it's not just that it's the amount of work has been increased, but it's also the quality of that work has changed as well. So the kind of autonomy that people used to have in terms of how they structure their consumer experiences has increasingly been ironed out because of the Taylorization of service workers.

When you say "Taylorization" you mean assembly line–like pressure and standardization.
UH: Absolutely, yes. For instance, if a call center worker is working with a standard script, as they very often are, that doesn't just mean he or she has to always ask the same questions in the same sequence. It's also means that the consumer has to effectively fill in the form as well. It removes your right as a consumer to actually say what you want to say.

You know, you've been waiting in line, listening to this recorded message, saying, "Your call is important to us, please hold," and you hold and then you key one for marketing and two for this and three for that and whatever other number for customer service, and you finally get through to the right call center operator, who could be anywhere in the world, incidentally, and she says "Hi, my name is Tracy, how can I help you?" And you, at that point, are exploding with rage and you want to say, "Well, Tracy, I ordered this dishwasher and you delivered me a fridge." But you can't do that because you have to follow their script. Because first of all they say, "Can I confirm your zip code and can we confirm the registration number?" And all of this is all being done in the name of choice and consumer rights and so on.

The act of being a consumer has increasingly been reduced to effectively filling in forms. If you buy things on the Internet, it's literally filling in forms. If you're doing it over the phone, it's virtually filling in forms. Sometimes I think just this business of being a consumer—you have to remember passwords and pin numbers—it's a kind of bureaucratic nightmare. It's just as Taylorized as if you were an employee but you aren't even paid for it.

In *The Making of a Cybertariat* you point to an increased individualization and privatization of daily life, so that for example people now, instead of going to the movies, watch television or DVDs at home; they buy their own TV sets, for which they have to lay out the money. What sort of effect has this had on the culture and political activism—or the potential for political activism?

UH: Well, I think it's contradictory. At the simplest level, it's heavily eroded what used to be public spaces, where people came together, cinemas, sports grounds, and so on. I'm not saying these things have died out, they haven't, but people have all kinds of collective experiences in the past, which are now gone—even kind of isolated collective experiences. In the 1960s in the UK there were two television channels, so you'd go into work the next morning and everybody had watched the same TV program and so you had something you could all talk about. And now you have six hundred channels and so all these individual experiences have been separated. So there's a level on which it has eroded the collective and fragmented people and kept people at a distance from each other. That instead of dealing with somebody that you have eye contact with over a counter in a store or a post office or wherever, you're increasingly dealing with disembodied people over the phone or by email. And it's very easy to dehumanize someone that you're not making eye contact with and sharing pheromones with.

But having said that, just as the telephone was a completely contradictory technology—that both distanced people and also put people in touch with each other in new ways—so I think the Internet is also both distancing and at the same time quite empowering for a lot of people. It's created new ways of organizing, new ways of communicating around the world. And so for some kinds of people who are disadvantaged in the old face-to-face world, because they had physical disabilities or they didn't conform to standards of beauty or they were the wrong color or whatever, the experience of having a telemediated relationship can actually be very, very liberating. I've interviewed people who say, "It's great—on the Internet I have no gender, I have no race, I have no disability. I can be anyone I like." But just as it's empowering for some people, it's also terribly threatening to people who are used to wielding power in traditional face-to-face ways. So it's extremely complicated what it has done to human relationships, I think.

Let's return to what you were speaking about earlier, about the commodification of domestic work and what has been termed the "socialization" of labor. Socialist feminists used to argue that this socialization of housework—that is, the transformation of women's unpaid labor in the household through labor-saving appliances and services—would lead women to gender emancipation. But you argue that this labor saving has not happened.
UH: I don't want to posit some golden past where we all want to go back to emptying pails and scrubbing floors and breaking our backs. I'm not saying that. I wouldn't want to give up a dishwasher. But what I am saying is that in and of itself it's not liberating. It's possible to completely socialize domestic labor to bring it out into the market without emancipating women. There isn't a technical fix to gender power.

You see it more clearly in developing countries, but it's probably to different degrees the case everywhere, that what it's actually done is to lock people more and more tightly into the market in order to be able to buy these things, to buy a decent home or rent a decent home, and fill it with all these things that increasingly we all feel we can't live without. And life is such that we really can't live without a lot of them now. I mean, you can live without a fridge in a period when you could get food delivered from the end of the road daily or two or three times a day with no problem. Now with the need for the weekly trip to the supermarket, you can't do that. So, you need a fridge. It's become a necessity.

What that's done is it has locked people more and more into the market, which of course, also locks them into the workforce. And so women now need to work for economic survival to a greater extent than they certainly did in the 1950s and '60s, and possibly than they did for an even longer period before that, because the market hasn't actually liberated women completely. I mean, it's theoretically gotten rid of the heavy labor of cooking and housework and so on, but it hasn't solved the real problems like the childcare problem and things like that.

So it means that women have been forced into the workforce, but on very unequal terms. And so they've ended up in the ghettos of part-time work or of various kinds of contingent labor where they're earning a lot less than a lot of the average male wage or certainly less than any kind of notional family wage that people used to talk about in the 1950s and '60s. So relatively speaking, they're actually economically worse off than they were before they had all these wonderful things in their homes. They might feel better off. They might think, oh, well, my grandmother didn't have such a beautiful home as this and she didn't have all these things. But in reality, in terms of how hard they have to work to reach the subsistence level, they are probably actually as badly off, if not worse off, than their grandmothers were.

Yet socialists have traditionally argued that the socialization of labor is a progressive thing, since it breaks down oppressive traditional social arrangements and brings workers together in a way that they can exercise their social collective power. It raises the level of production to a point where socialism could be feasible. If we were to picture a postcapitalist world, would it be based on the commodification that capitalism has created? Would prepared food and consumption be socialized or should it all rest at the feet of the individual? Or is there another way?
UH: Well, I think there are different ways of socializing. I think that's the first point. And a lot of the socialist visions of the early part of the twentieth century actually were visions of service industries. They were visions of people collectively delivering use-values, not commodities. So there were public laundries, there were good free health services, good universal education systems, good social services of various kinds, food cooperatives, and so on. The idea was that these were service industries; they weren't commodities to produce a profit. They didn't have to operate by the rules of the market.

The conventional traditional socialist view on commodities was that it was the force that not only propelled capitalism forward but was also going to destroy it. The idea was that capitalism would kind of implode from its own contradictions because basically it would run out of markets. That on the one hand, as technology developed you'd produce goods more and more productively, so more workers would be laid off, and because manufacturing industry was so productive, there wouldn't be any jobs for them to do, and the unemployed people wouldn't be able to buy the products of these new highly automated factories, so there would be this crisis of overproduction and capitalism would come to its knees. That's one half of the story. The other half of the story is that it would physically run out of markets globally. Because you can only keep extending markets at the time when there were still tribes of people living in New Guinea who had never seen a car and when there were still lots of people in the world in subsistence agriculture in all these places that capitalism hadn't reached. It could go on expanding geographically and deal with its overproduction problems by bringing more and more people into the money economy. But the idea was that sooner or later capitalism would run out of markets.

Yet it seems to me that those ideas that all we had to do was sit back and watch capitalism self-destruct were actually very, very naïve because what this model of commodification seems to me to show us is that you never run out of new things to commodify. Each stage in the process generates new commodities. Each new service industry becomes a basis for new manufacturing industries, but then each manufacturing industry, as it becomes more developed in turn generates new service industries and so the wheel goes round.

Take the automobile. You had people who looked after horses until there was the automobile. There was this mass service industry of looking after horses and stagecoaches and whatever. And then all of those people got put out of work and the auto industry came along which was very much regionally concentrated in certain parts of the world and factories were created building automobiles. On a simple level, that was manufacturing jobs replacing service jobs. But then to make the automobiles and to service automobiles, you need new service industries. You need garages to repair them, you need people to make roads, you need people to clean them, et cetera. And then these processes in turn get automated, so you get the self-service gas station. And somebody has to make a machine for that, and then those making those machines in turn generate more service industries and so on.

It's an endless, endless process, and I don't believe that capitalism, while human beings are doing anything with their lives outside the money economy, will ever run out of the possibilities of new commodities, if you see what I mean. And the conclusion to be drawn from that is that we need political solutions.

You touched on one of the conventional ideas on the left, which is the argument that "robots don't buy cars"—that our society has become so mechanized that there will no longer be any people who could be able to afford to buy anything because they'll all be unemployed, and that as societies become more and more industrialized, you're going to have mass unemployment. You believe that's a misguided view.
UH: It's completely a misguided view in my opinion. Every time a major new wave of technical change comes along, that argument is put. Every time it's proved wrong. Of course, there is incredible destruction of jobs and of peo-

ple's lives with each of these changes. You may get very high unemployment. Whole communities may be decimated by technological change. We have in England, and I know you have it in the United States as well, we have these rustbelt regions where whole production industries basically have been wiped out. The people, for instance, coal miners in northern England; they didn't get re-employed as call center workers in the southeast. They got left on the dump. But if you're talking total number of jobs, more new jobs are constantly being created than are being destroyed, although they may be being created in different places and they may be being created on much worse conditions for labor than the older jobs in which workers may have developed quite good forms of organization and collective bargaining and so on. And usually capital seeks out greenfield sites for low-skilled new jobs.

Right, which we've seen in the United States, and it's certainly hurt the labor movement. Ursula, conventional economic wisdom posits the mark of advanced capitalism in the late twentieth and early twenty-first century has been the shrinkage first of agriculture and then industry and the dominance of services in our economies. This is the argument that we're in a "postindustrial society." Why don't you agree with that narrative?

UH: Well, I think a lot of that is really kind of a statistical construct. I would think a much more accurate way of describing what's happened has been that there's been a massive commodification of agriculture and a major reconstruction of industry—both of service and manufacturing industry—which has been characterized by what you might call an elaboration of value chains. Sorry, that's a bit of a pretentious phrase! I'll come back to that in a minute, if I may. But it seems to me that if you include in your definition of agriculture all the people who process food, the people who distribute food, and the people who pack it, the people who make tractors, the people who make fertilizers, the people who work in the kind of genetic bioengineering—if you include all those people in the agriculture sector, if you define the agriculture sector as the process of producing and distributing food to people, then you'll find that probably just as many if not more people are employed in it as ever there were.

The service sector is a more complicated story because this is a weird category that lumps together all kind of different things. I did some detailed research in the UK and went back through all the national censuses back to 1901 through to the end of the twentieth century, looking specifically at women's employment. And you always see these graphs showing service industries going up and agriculture going down and I realized that this only works if you leave out the domestic servants. At the beginning of the twentieth century, huge numbers of women and quite a lot of men as well were working in domestic service. What can be more a service industry than being a servant? I mean, it's the same word. But if you put them all back into the picture, it stops being a line that goes up; it's a line that stays more or less constant. But I think more importantly, this category of service industry lumps together a lot of totally different things, things which are to do with delivering services to consumers like public services, health, and education, or things like hairdressing.

Personal services are one thing, but there are also business services. A big part of this so-called rise in services that people keep commenting on is a rise in business services. And what business services are really is an expression of the more elaborate division of labor that is developing in manufacturing industry. As products get more complex, but also as companies try to maximize their profit and externalize as many costs as possible, increasingly what they do is a breakup the companies into separate cost centers or profit centers. When you have a process that's automated, you can manage it by results. You don't need to stand over people and make sure that they're doing what they're supposed to be doing. You just say, I want you to make x number of these things, and then you count the number that they've produced and you pay them. So as soon as it is possible to standardize a service function it becomes possible to outsource it.

So what happened from the 1980s onwards, really, was this massive growth of outsourcing of business services. And, of course, when things get outsourced, they get reclassified in the statistics. So if you clean the floor in a car factory and you're employed by the car factory, you get counted as a car worker, but if you are working for an outsourced cleaning company, then you get miraculously transmogrified into a service worker, although you're doing exactly the same job in exactly the same factory. The first wave of outsourcing was those kind of things. But now we've got outsourcing of actual core business functions—things like outsourcing of human resources management, you've got outsourcing of back office services, you've got outsourcing of customer services, of design, of software development. You name it.

I did a big international survey in eighteen countries a couple of years ago where we found that over 50 percent of companies are outsourcing at least one business service. Most are outsourcing a lot more. And furthermore, 6 percent of them in Europe, and I would say probably more in the United States, are outsourcing to another country. So it's exactly the same activity being done for the same capitalist employer in relation to producing the same product.

This is what I meant when I said earlier that there is an elaboration of value chains. What you're getting in the division of labor isn't just one worker doing one thing and another one doing another thing on the same production line; it's that these production lines are spread across different companies and across different countries around the world. And they involve services as well as manufacturing.

In both your analytical and trade union work, you've written a great deal about workers, many of them female, who are employed in information technology—and in fact, you're one such worker yourself. In *The Making of a Cybertariat* you write about the difficulty in conceptualizing such employees who have ultimately been called officer workers, white-collar workers, telecommuters, nonmanual workers, e-workers. What are the issues involved in classifying them?

UH: I think the traditional kind of socialist view, if you like, was that real workers were men. Or I'll modify that: real workers were people who worked in factories. In the class system, you have your capitalist class, and then you have your sort of intermediate class of professionals and managers, who were generally seen as men, and then you have your workers. And you might subdivide that, you might say, oh, you've got peasants and you've got workers and you've got a labor aristocracy, you've got a lumpenproletariat. But basically, the archetypal image of a worker is what you might call "spanner man." To the extent that there are female workers, they're "apron lady"—they're cleaners, they're low-level manual service workers, they're not seen as real workers.

Middle class workers were seen as masculine, but people were kind of uncomfortable trying to define them. If you read the early literature like famous studies of office workers, they're actually defined by their clothes and defined more specifically by male clothes. They're called the black-suited worker or the white-collar worker. And they're seen as this kind of army of clerks. Marxists used to argue about what their class position was: were they just kind of appendages of managers, or could the lower layers be seen as part of the proletariat? But in fact, while they were arguing something was happening which they were missing, which was that not only was the group of office workers massively increasing, but it was being feminized. So by the 1950s and '60s the huge majority of office workers weren't wearing black suits or white collars, they were wearing light pastel color twin sets, I guess. They were women and a lot of them were women working part-time.

Because the division of labor was changing so dramatically during the postwar period, you had the circulation of capital and the circulation of goods becoming much more complex, so lots of jobs were being created in industries like banking. And you had government becoming much more complex and routinized, so lots of jobs were being created in the public sector. You then had the introduction of early computers and keypunch machines and things like that and huge swathes of new jobs being created in the offices of manufacturing companies. And it was women doing these jobs. People in the trade union movement on the whole didn't seem to want to think about them, but by the 1970s when there was the women's movement, organizations like 9 to 5 in the United States started to try to organize women office workers. But basically they were seen as a kind of embarrassment and if anything they were even the subject of hate by working class men because they were kind of caricatured in the popular media as the secretary. You know, "Take a letter, Miss Jones." You see hundreds and hundreds of these cartoons in the 1960s of the sexy dolly bird, as they were called in England, sitting on her boss's lap taking dictation while he gropes her. They were seen as a symbol of the power and the privilege of the manager as compared to the workers. But they were also the gatekeepers to the manager. So the guy from the factory floor who wanted an interview with the manager was humiliated by this secretary who kept him at bay.

This stereotype of the office worker as a secretary meant that they weren't actually seen as real workers and in the population statistics because sociologists tended to want to look at class. Class is the thing sociologists were most interested in and their idea of the unit of class analysis was the household. Women were put into the same class as their husband, so it was their husband's occupation that was supposed to determine the class status of the woman. Which meant that it was kind of invisible, this terribly embarrassing fact, which people are still very uncomfortable with, which is that if you look at the class position of women office workers they're very often married to men or the daughters of men who are of a different social class than they are in terms of the statistics. The models say office workers are above factory workers in the statistics in class terms. But their wages are often a lot lower. The point is that nobody has really dealt with these women as real workers in a serious way until very recently.

You've studied those who work at home or away from the traditional workplace. How does it benefit employers to hire people working at home and why has it become so common?
UH: Well, it's quite difficult to generalize about because there are home workers working at every level. There are people doing incredibly poorly paid manual assembly work. Probably the most exploited workers in the world, in developed and undeveloped countries, are home workers doing assembly work or stuffing envelopes or doing routine kinds of things like that. And then at the other extreme you have people to whom being able to work from home is a kind of privilege of power. It seems to me that the best way to differentiate home workers is on the basis of their labor market bargaining position.

If you've got scarce skills and the employers really need what it is that you do, then you can negotiate a situation where working from home may be to your benefit. It may enable you to dispose your hours more flexibly, make better child-care arrangements, avoid rush hour travel, et cetera.

But more usually, the boot is on the other foot. It's a way for employers to minimize their risks. They minimize the costs of actually having somebody working in an office. They minimize workers getting together and organizing and because the workforce is so fragmented, it's much, much easier to lay off and easier to underpay.

What's the potential for cybertarians of the world to unite, given these employees' isolation from their fellow workers?
UH: Well, it seems to me that this has got to be the way forward. I've been doing a lot of research particularly in India but in other Asian countries too on, if you like, the new cybertarians who are growing up working in an offshore call centers and software development and so on. And it's clear that now, for the first time in history, we have people with a common labor process, with a common relation to capital, speaking common languages and with access to a technology that allows them to communicate around the world. Theoretically, we have the best chance ever of work that's actually organized internationally. But the reality is that there is so much division, that the local situation is so different. Somebody working in a call center in India occupies a completely different social position from somebody working in a call center in Britain, for instance. They will be much more educated, they will be much more part of the local elite, if you like, they might be from the class that has servants in India, which in England, they certainly wouldn't be. But also and even more importantly than that, there are enormous racist divisions right now, both within the trade union movement as well as within general populations.

One of the most disturbing things that comes out when you talk to call center workers in India is how much racist abuse they get on the phone from their customers in the United States and in Europe—really horrible things that nobody should have to listen to as part of their job. I think that's gotten a lot worse with the kind of Islamophobia that's around right now because a lot of people can't actually tell the difference—one Asian is like another Asian, as far as they're concerned. It goes so far that some call center workers are practically being accused of being terrorists—and they're just trying to do their job. I think those kinds of divisions are incredibly worrying. When workers are pitted against consumers and one race against another, it is going to be an unbelievably difficult challenge to develop international understanding and solidarity.

Capitalism is in crisis of a magnitude not seen for decades. How do you understand that crisis? Has capitalism run up against newfound limits?

UH: It has always been a contradiction of capitalism that it needs to expand in order to survive. As Rosa Luxemburg recognized, the sum total of the value of all the workers' wages will never be enough to buy all the stuff they produce because of the share that is taken as profit by the capitalists, so capitalism always needs a market outside of itself where people will buy the surplus products. But that isn't the only thing that drives the expansion of capitalism.

As I have mentioned, it is also looking for new spheres of life that are outside the money economy to exploit for the development of new commodities. These include natural resources, like the plants in the rainforest that can be used to create new drugs, as well as human resources like traditional music, art, creativity, sex, and tacit knowledge. Capitalism has always scoured the world looking for new sources of raw materials like minerals, energy sources, natural products, and so on. And it has also always looked outside its traditional territories for new sources of cheap and compliant and unorganized labor. These days, because of the huge quantity of goods that are produced worldwide and the wastefulness of the production processes, it is also looking desperately for new sites to dump the detritus that results from all this commodity production and to get the hazardous waste processed. In the commodification process we have seen use-values transformed into exchange-values, for instance when public services like health become commodified, producing profits for pharmaceuticals companies.

But now we are seeing a development whereby even negative use-values can become commodities that are exchanged on the market. You can see this in the Kyoto agreement that has created an international market out of pollution rights. There is one other important driver of capitalist expansion, which David Harvey has drawn attention to. This follows on from the capitalist imperative to constantly accumulate profit. This means that capitalism is always looking for new places to invest this accumulated surplus. We saw it in the nineteenth century in huge investments by Western companies in things like building railways across India or Africa or laying cables under the oceans to carry telegraph traffic that became the ancestors of today's optical fiber Internet backbones. Which, incidentally, usually follow exactly the same geographical routes. It is probably no accident that Nokia used to be a rubber company that made the rubber coatings for the old telegraph cables. Of course all these different reasons interact with each other in quite complex ways. As new groups of people are brought into the global workforce, they also become new consumer markets for global products. As surpluses from one part of the world are invested in providing infrastructure for other less developed regions of the globe, this stimulates new developments in these areas and so on.

So there are several interconnected reasons why capitalism constantly needs to expand into new territory. In the latter part of the twentieth century, the world pretty much ran out of virgin space for this kind of expansion. There are very few spots left on the planet that are not already being exploited for their minerals or their timber or their fish or the DNA of their plants or the labor of their people or the purchasing power of these people or being used as gigantic garbage dumps. Meanwhile the huge investments in infrastructure and other things that were made in South and East Asia, parts of Latin America, and parts of the former Soviet Bloc in Eastern Europe caused very rapid development in some of those regions in the last two or three decades, perhaps most dramatically in China and India but also in places like Brazil. With very low-paid workers in these countries there was no way that the huge surpluses that were generated could be reinvested locally.

So what happened? To the extent that there were still underdeveloped regions of the world left, a lot of that new investment went there. Chinese companies have bought up huge tracts of mineral-rich parts of Africa, Peru, and other spots in the poor world, but also undeveloped land in less expected developed countries like Finland and Sweden. More dramatically, much of the surplus has come back to the developed West. All the major European steel companies are now owned by Indian companies, who have also bought up several iconic European automobile brands like Jaguar and Land Rover. The IBM personal computer, perhaps one of the most symbolically important products of the information revolution of the 1980s, is now owned by a Chinese company. A Brazilian company now owns a huge chunk of the global brewing industry, including many famous so-called "national" brands of beer like Stella Artois, Beck's, Leffe, Coors, Skol, et cetera (all made on the same production lines).

The world economy is now completely interconnected, not just through patterns of ownership but also through the international division of labor, with workers in one country directly linked to those in others through complicated value chains. A shock to one part of the system will go rippling across the network and affect people in very different places. This is not intrinsically new, of course. Capitalism has always ignored national frontiers. But for many years it was possible for capitalists in the West to convince their workers that there were parts of the world that were outside capitalism, because of the existence of the Soviet Union and China with systems that claimed to be, and to some extent really were noncapitalist. So the depression of the 1930s and the crisis that came in the aftermath of the oil shock in the 1970s were not blamed so directly on the financial system itself but could be partly blamed on other factors—

including other nations. And most people still thought in terms of national economies that were to some extent under the control of national policies.

Since the fall of the Berlin Wall in 1989 there has been an enormous amount of economic instability globally. We can think of the crisis of the Asian currencies in 1997, the bursting of the dot com bubble in 2001 and so on, but the current crisis is far and away the biggest one that has taken place in a world that is now acknowledged to be capitalist all over.

I do not think that it is going to implode because of this crisis. The system is inherently instable and has always been characterized by booms and busts, and in the busts there is always a huge cost to be paid as weaker firms go to the wall and workers are laid off in the thousands. There is enormous waste and destruction involved in closing down factories, of course, but this helps to get rid of surplus supply. It creates a kind of winner takes all logic in many old industries and the winners can do very well indeed. There is also scope for new industries to emerge. There are still plenty of new things to commodify. One of the new goldmines for capital is the uncommodified parts of the public sector. In the last few years we have seen a tremendous wave of expansion of aggressive new multinational companies that make their profits from the outsourcing of commodified public services—anything from care services to IT support. These companies are growing exponentially, partly through transfers of employees from the public sector and there is no sign of them being negatively hit. In fact only recently I read in a specialist IT newsletter that the UK government wants to make savings of £5 billion and one of its plans to achieve this is by outsourcing more of its back office processing and IT support to low-cost destinations like India. It's business as usual for companies in this field, and there are also rich pickings to be found in areas like armaments manufacture and space exploration where there is a continuing demand for developing ever more sophisticated new products that don't depend on consumer markets.

So I really don't think this crisis is going to end the capitalist system, although it will undoubtedly generate a lot of human suffering. But there is one big "if." If enough workers around the world react to this situation with a realization of what's going on and understand that it really is a global system and that it can only be tamed if they all get together and do something about it then there could be scope for real changes. A more pessimistic view is that in crises like these workers are so grateful for the chance to have a job at all that they get their heads down and put up with worse working conditions and harsher management. Instead of holding hands across the ocean—which is something that requires enormous courage and optimism, especially for people who have dependents to think about—they are much more likely to fall for protectionist rhetoric. We are seeing a very worrying rise in Europe right now in support for far-right xenophobic political parties. In the U.S. I expect you have the slogan "American jobs for American workers." Here in Europe we have "British jobs for British workers," "French jobs for French workers," "Danish jobs for Danish workers," and so on, right across the twenty-seven member states and no doubt elsewhere too.

Part III
Alternatives?

CHAPTER TEN

Vivek Chibber: National Capitalism in the Third World

How would you define national capitalism?

VC: Well, it's true that most capitalisms historically have been national capitalisms, and almost all of them still are. And what it basically means is that while countries share certain characteristics with capitalist economies elsewhere in the world—patterns of development, policies that undergird the development and which oversee them—they tend to be peculiar to the national economy and hence dissimilar. So that the national capitalism of France is not the same as that of Sweden or the United States, and Brazil is not the same as Argentina or India. So, the basic idea is that countries still have some kind of independence and autonomy to set their own trajectory of development, albeit in a capitalist path.

What would motivate a country in the developing world to follow the path of national capitalist-led development, rather than that of international capitalist investment?

VC: Well, the two aren't exactly counterposed. All national capitalisms have to partake in some way of the world economy, and especially poor countries, they have to acquire technology, sometimes capital, certainly managerial expertise and things like that from the outside economy. So when we talk about national capitalism, the idea isn't that countries cut themselves off from the international economy. The idea is simply that the trajectory of development is decided by local actors instead of international actors and that really would be the motivation to have some kind of national capitalist development.

The truth is that people reside in localities, in particular spaces, and you want your economic development to be of a kind that's conducive to people's welfare, people's well-being, which means that you want to be able to exercise some sort of control over how the local economy is growing. The chances of having more control over your economy are greater if the state has the ability to control capital flows and has some kind of say over local investment decisions, et cetera. Which means that if all of the investment in your economy is coming from multinationals whose headquarters are thousand of miles away, and who are impervious to the control of the national government—which is sort of the dream behind NAFTA and the WTO now—in that kind of situation, the needs of local population aren't going to have very much to do with the path the development takes.

So, if you have to live with capitalism, the chances are the kind of capitalism that's least corrosive to communities, to people's well-being, is one that's subject to some kind of control by your national government.

State-led development had its heyday in the Third World in the 1950s and '60s. In what historical context did these policies arise in Asia and Latin America?

VC: They were pretty much the rule across South Asia, East Asia, Latin America, and even the Middle East. And what brought it about is, I think, a combination of several factors. One was the Great Depression, at the end of the 1920s, which temporarily broke off links between especially South American countries and the Northern, the more advanced countries—which sort of forced the South American countries to develop their local industries because suddenly they couldn't import a lot of the goods that they had been acquiring from northern countries so far. That set them on a path of what's called import substitution. Now, import substitution basically means that goods that you've been importing into your economy, from the outside, goods that you've been purchasing from other countries, can now be substituted by local production.

That started off as a kind of a necessity for these countries, because they were cut off from the United States, from Europe, and they had to suddenly produce their own goods. But it got a big boost from local entrepreneurial groups, local capitalists, who were now mature enough and big enough to contemplate producing goods which earlier they really couldn't because they couldn't compete with the imports flooding into their economies.

So they gave political support for this project to be more than just a temporary respite from links to the world economy and they wanted it to be a more ongoing long-term project for building local industry. And the best way to build local industry is if you create a market for it. The best way to create a market for local industry is to keep foreign goods out.

So, the shock of the Great Depression turned into a more long-term project of import substitution. Now, this was given its final boost after the Second World War, because what happens in the Second World War is that European economies were utterly devastated, and the United States turned its attention away from developing countries and towards Europe, which it saw as the linchpin of the world economy. So once again, countries in the South, South America, India, countries like that, saw for themselves an opening to develop their own industries because the U.S. was exporting most of its goods to Europe and Europe was in no position to export goods to the South.

The final ingredient to all of this was that the war also put into place in all of these economies, a huge apparatus, a huge machinery for wartime economic planning, and when the war ended, a lot of this machinery for planning was still in place. So left groups and political elites, politicians, bureaucrats, saw for themselves an opportunity to not only develop local industry but to also have some degree of control over how private investment was going to be made, where private investments would flow, and the conditions under which capitalists could be allowed to make profits.

So you had this combination of capitalists wanting to protect the local domestic market for themselves, politicians and bureaucrats seeing an opportunity to control what capitalists were doing, because quite often capitalists couldn't be trusted to make the right kind of investment. They would make it in high profit, short-term industries instead of industries that were more conducive to long-term growth. They said, okay, now we've got to plan some kind of investment. And unions on the left saw this as one step towards socializing the means of production, because planning was associated with socialism.

All these things came together, so that by the 1950s what you had was import substitution being the linchpin of development strategies all over the developing world and it was married to some kind of attempt at national planning, economic planning. And that lasted into really the late 1970s–early 1980s.

Why has it been that the left historically, including much of the Marxist left, has tended to see the national capitalist class as an important force for the economic development of countries in the Global South?
VC: The basic aim of the left, whether Marxist or non-Marxist, whether socialist or anarchist, was to do away with capitalism, to have some kind of movement towards socialism, and this was especially strong in the first half of the century when the left worldwide was really powerful.

But there was also a sentiment amongst Communist parties, especially the ones associated with the Third International, that's the Communist International started by Lenin and then taken over by Stalin; parties associated with this tendency had the opinion that while socialism was desirable, in any of these countries capitalism hadn't yet developed far enough to put socialism on the agenda. They were still too poor, their economies were basically agrarian, and basically dominated by peasants, and labor as a consequence was too small and too weak to really put any kind of noncapitalist alternatives on the agenda.

So in the foreseeable future, the idea was, there would have to be some kind of accommodation to capitalism. And there was a variety of sort of strategies behind why the accommodation would have to be made and the conditions under which it could be made. But there was a kind of agreement amongst big chunks of the left that socialism would have to be put off for a while.

Well, if you had to live with capitalism, it meant you had to reach some sort of accommodation with the agents of capitalism, which is capitalists, the bourgeoisie.

Now on this the socialist left tended to break down local capitalist classes into two groups. One was what was called the *comprador bourgeoisie* and this was capitalists who were subordinate to, and linked up with, multinational firms. They were junior partners with them; they were local traders with them. They were people who sort of warehoused the goods made by multinational corporations. These capitalists, it was thought, really had no direct interest in developing the national market and the national technological base because they were linked up with agents whose main interests were in other economies.

The second group of capitalists that Marxists tended to identify was what they called the *national bourgeoisie*. And this class, this group, this segment of the capitalist class, had two characteristics which set them apart from other capitalists. One was that unlike comprador capitalists, these were supposed to have been oriented towards and produced for the domestic market. So they made, for example, garments, textiles, sometimes automobiles; often times, they were in food processing. They produced for the local market. So they had an interest in the development of indigenous capitalism, because you have to remember that the left thought you had to develop capitalism so that socialism could be put on the agenda. So you need to find capitalists who have some kind of interest in the quality and the advancement of local capitalism.

This is one characteristic that national capitalists had. The second one was precisely because they were interested in developing national capitalism, they also might have had an interest in pushing back the power of precapitalist agrarian elites who were thought to be an obstacle, again, to the development of local industry. They wouldn't release peasants from the land. They sucked up a big part of the social surplus. They were accustomed to labor-repressive techniques and hence got in the way of technological advancement. So there had to be some sort of strategy that got rid of the local agrarian class and it was thought that national capitalists would be an ally in this fight. So you have the national bourgeoisie, on the hand, the putative agent for dissolving pre-capital agrarian structures; on the other hand, an agent that would have some reason to oppose multinational capital because multinational capital was encroaching on domestic markets and these capitalists supposedly wanted to protect their own domestic market.

So if capitalism was to be what you had to live with in the near future, the national capitalist was the segment of a capitalist class with which the left thought it could make some kind of pact, some kind of alliance to develop local industry, so that at some point down the road it could fight for something more. The compradors were then thought to be, as it were, in the other camp, as were the agrarian classes.

So this ended up being a strategy for an alliance between labor, the national bourgeoisie, and some segments of the middle class. This was what social scientists of the 1950s called a *modernizing coalition*. And the national bourgeoisie was at the heart of it, because labor was too weak to fight its own fight and comprador capitalists were thought to be opposed to any agenda to modernize the economy.

What was the actual experience of these Import Substitution Industrialization regimes in the 1950s and 1960s? On what alliances were these regimes built?
VC: The basic political structure of national capitalism—of what's called now developmentalism or state-led capitalist development—the basic political structure was one in which national capitalists and politicians, the local political parties, had the uppermost position. Labor and the middle classes were included to some degree in the coalition, but basically sidelined politically. They had very little say in what went on.

This was the first rude surprise for labor which thought that because there would be some kind of planning and because a lot of the political parties that initiated this economic strategy, because a lot of the political parties had left rhetoric, labor across the South had thought that it would have a seat at the table, as it were. It became clear this wouldn't happen. In some countries, there was outright repression and smashing of unions, very quickly. But in other countries, it wasn't so much a smashing as a sidelining of labor by either making them completely dependent on the state for any kind of increases in wages and safety conditions, et cetera, or by getting them mired in very complex, corporatist structures inside the state so that they became absorbed by the bureaucracy. The end result of both of these was that the organizational basis for labor's strength—which was the autonomous, independent power of unions—steadily eroded over time.

In India, for example, labor legislation passed right after independence made it almost impossible for labor to get any of its gains out of collective bargaining—collective bargaining means basically you negotiate with your employers over conditions of work and for wages, et cetera. Instead, the government took it upon itself to revise wage schedules, to send any kind of labor disputes into immediate arbitration, things like that, so that within twenty years the labor movement had no reason to be a movement. Any time something went wrong, they would simply go into arbitration or petition the local politician. This happened everywhere. It happened in Brazil, it happened Argentina, it happened in Egypt. Everywhere labor was sidelined and over time lost its power.

So the basic political structure was one in which national capitalism was on top. The other rude surprise was that the whole period of developmentalism ended up being one in which the state basically handed over enormous quantities of public money to local capitalists, either in the form of subsidies, cheap credit, tariff protection, in order that local capital could develop. The idea was that through planning, in exchange for getting all these subsidies, capitalists would agree to giving up some of their control over investment decisions. And so planners would tell them, "All right, we'll give you all these subsidies, we'll give you really cheap interest loans, but in return don't invest for example in very high profit luxury automobile industries, invest instead in say a steel plant, invest instead in making some sort of infrastructure deals." These would be over time profitable, but they would also have very beneficial effects for the economy.

This required that planners would have some ability to monitor, to regulate, to channel the flows of investment in one direction or the other. Now what happened was, in case after case, capitalists were very happy to take whatever subsidies, whatever help, the state gave them, but fought very, very hard to not give up unilateral and complete control over investments. And what planners, bureaucrats, and politicians found was that when they tried to make their state apparatus, their state machinery, powerful enough and efficient enough to actually oversee what capitalists were doing, capitalists fought them at every step and pretty successfully pushed back any attempt to make states more efficient at planning, to put apparatuses in place that could regulate planning.

So what had ended up happening was you did have at first a fair amount of success in changing the industrial structure of these countries over three, four decades—but mainly because of the efforts of the public sectors, state enterprises, and mainly because politicians and the state subsidized capitalist projects so heavily that capitalists really were guaranteed to make no losses. So they went into sectors, basically with a complete guarantee of not making any losses. In exchange, they had to give up very, very little.

By the 1970s and '80s one of the main components of the fiscal crisis of these governments in South America, South Asia, et cetera, was that the subsidies that they had been giving to capitalists didn't generate revenues coming back into the state, because capitalists refused to be taxed; they refused to make investments in their right sectors. The second consequence was that all the imports that were coming into these countries—remember, they didn't have their own capital goods industries, they didn't make their own machinery, they had to buy it from the West—those imports were racking up enormous debts to the outside world. But because capitalists had been more or less resistant to signals to develop the right kinds of new industries, they insisted on making investments in the same industries which got them very quick and very high profits, the exports that these developing countries were selling to the rest of the world, didn't change all that much and didn't develop fast enough.

So Import Substitution Industrialization set up barriers that protected domestic producers from having to compete with imports coming from more industrially advanced countries—and so these domestic producers really didn't have to innovate and had a monopoly on the different industries that they dominated. Subsequently, the economy itself did not develop at the rate that planners had expected. And, in fact, it wasn't just a subsidy for infant industries, but an overall subsidy for all industries at different levels of development.

VC: Yes, that's exactly what happened. What import substitution ended up doing was it protected local markets from foreign goods and then planners, in doing so, basically told local capitalists, "Look now you have a monopoly over the local markets." The capitalists said, "Great, we love that, give us that." Then planners turned around and said, "All right, now, we've given you monopoly over the local market. What we want you to do in exchange is make sure you're using the best up-to-date technology so that you can be competitive with producers anywhere in the world, and within five or ten years, once you've got the technology in place, you can start exporting to the rest of the world and we'll slowly start opening up our economy." What capitalists did was said, "Well, now that we've got monopolies, why should we worry about using the best technologies? Instead, what we'll do is take the money you're giving us and we'll start up new industries, new factories in other lines that we think are also profitable."

So what happened over time was the initial vision which had been to protect local industry temporarily, build it up, and then start competing with the rest of the world—that vision was pushed back by capitalists who wanted their state to keep the tariff barriers and subsidies in place and didn't give the planners any kind of real capacity to be able to plan the economy. Every time planners tried to do something, capitalists would launch some kind of political campaign against it.

So over time you just had this massive subsidization process where basically the state took public monies and handed them over to capitalists. Capitalists really didn't develop local industry at anywhere near the pace that was originally envisioned and the consequence was what you saw in the 1980s—which neoliberal economists constantly point to—which was these states were just running this huge debt. But the main reason behind the debt was that capitalists were just like pigs feeding at a trough. They were just sucking up public revenues without doing very much in return. And the basis for all of this was that states never were able to build up the capacity to really push through any kind of discipline on capitalists; they weren't able to force capitalists to concede any kind of control over investment decisions.

This is where East Asia was different. The neoliberal economists have for years pointed to Korea and Taiwan as successors of free-market policies. But in fact these are the most heavily planned state-run capitalist economies in the world. So clearly they were doing something in the planning process, in the way they managed their economies, that Latin American and South Asian countries were not. And what they were doing different wasn't that they were just letting their markets go free. They were actually planning them. They were actually able to extract from their capitalists concessions, which the other countries just simply were not.

Neoliberal pundits have argued that an inherently inefficient public sector and system of state planning led to the failure of these developmentalist states in 1970s, when they were hemorrhaging public money to subsidize private companies. Would you say that the real culprit was the balance of power between private capital and the state?

VC: Yes, it was the weakness of the state relative to local capitalists. The reason we say planning itself wasn't a problem is that there's been a huge literature now going back about twenty years which shows that Taiwan and South Korea both planned, if anything, more heavily than India or Brazil or any of these countries which are pointed to as examples of the pitfalls of planning. So the issue isn't whether or not any particular country planned; the issue is what the quality of it was, what was the quality of your state intervention. And the basic thing that differentiates the quality of state intervention is the extent to which states and planners had enough institutional capacity, enough administrative wherewithal, to extract from capitalists some kind of control over what they did with the monies that they were getting. So in Korea, when planners gave the *chaebol,* their local capitalists, cheap loans, subsidized credits, technology, they also got from them guarantees that they would use this money in ways that were consistent with the economic plan. So when planners said, "Okay, we're going to give you this money, we want you to invest it in heavy industry, or in this chemical plant, or in this kind of auto plant," they actually had the wherewithal to make sure a capitalist followed these directions and capitalists actually did it.

So over the years in Korea, you had a very different outcome than you did in India or in Argentina, for example. The outcome was that this money being funneled to capitalists actually changed the industrial structure phenomenally, which brought about much faster rates of industrial growth. And that kept revenues coming into the state, so you didn't have this, as you said, hemorrhaging by the 1980s. All the subsidies that were going to capitalists were being paid back in the form of tax revenue. And you had a drastic change in the exports that the country was sending to the rest of the world, which moved from very labor-intensive, low-revenue exports to highly capital-intensive, very profitable exports. And through this they were able to pay the bill on all the machinery that they were buying from the rest of the world. So you had planning on both sides of the world, in East Asia and in South America; the difference was that planning in East Asia was able to bring about very different results because the state had much more power over its local entrepreneurial class.

That leads us to the question of the state itself and whether Korea, for other reasons, had leverage in a way that, say, India or Brazil didn't and maybe couldn't.

VC: Yes, it very much did have the leverage—and the question is: what was the source of that leverage? Now the interesting thing here is that during the 1950s most American advisors and the World Bank and the United Nations had basically written off South Korea. They thought it would be a basket case forever and ever because the government was so corrupt and so weak against local entrepreneurs. So it doesn't seem that it was a pure kind of a historical legacy or something that they just inherited, because if it had been you would have to conclude that through accident of history some countries get better states than others and there isn't much you can do about it. What happened, though, is something quite different, which is a state that would seem to be really weak, completely incapable of doing anything, in 1960–61, was really transformed by the new military junta that came to power and turned into a really very effective powerful planning device.

Whereas in India you had a government in 1947, when India became independent, which everybody thought was ideally suited to overseeing a national capitalist development program. It had a very good bureaucracy, it was relatively free of corruption, had a deeply committed political leadership and by the late 1950s, as early as that, it was clear that the government just was not able to do much with its local capitalist class. So it doesn't seem to have been some kind of gift of history, whether a country was endowed with the right kind of state. It seems to be in the everyday politics and negotiations that go on within government, between government and local classes, where the secret to effective state lies.

What about the difference between democracy in India and dictatorship in Korea?

VC: Well, it's a very popular notion that because Korea was a dictatorship it was able to plan better. I actually don't think that's true. Minimally, we can say that it might have been a necessary condition, but certainly not a sufficient one. And we know that because in South America from the mid-1960s onward there were a number of military dictatorships that tried to put into place a planning regime—Peru, very famously, but also Argentina and Brazil. Nasser in Egypt wasn't exactly a dictator, but his was a military regime with very strong authoritarian powers. In all these cases, they just weren't able to transform their local state structures. Capitalists just were able to resist pretty effectively when planners tried to put more effective states in place.

Clearly having military dictatorship doesn't get you what you need to transform the state. I don't actually even think it's a necessary condition. And I meet with some raised eyebrows when I tell people this, but the fact is that two of the more successful capitalist planning efforts in the postwar world were in democracies, in Japan and in France. And in France, it didn't last much more than two decades and in Japan it apparently unraveled in the early 1990s. But that's a long time and these weren't dictatorships.

So I am inclined to think the secret doesn't lie there; it really lies in whether or not governments can change their internal state structures when capitalists might not be happy about their doing that. And in all these countries where planning failed and where states remained weak what they have in common is that in all of them, when politicians and bureaucrats tried to make their planning apparatuses better, give them more power, make them more able to regulate capital flows, more able to monitor what capitalists are doing—in all those cases, capitalists organized politically against them. They lobbied against it, they engaged in capital strikes, they did a lot of arm twisting, whether they were dictatorships or whether they were democracies. And in all these cases, capitalists succeeded.

What does this say about how we understand the position of the state managers within these planning regimes? I think one could assume from listening to your description of the struggles between the capitalist class and state managers in these countries that the state and its agents are a benign force that don't embody any interests and have the best interests of the nation at heart. How true is that in fact?

VC: Well, they certainly thought so. Probably an accurate characterization of all these political elites was that they thought they were acting above any kind of sectional interest for the national good and such things. But what it actually shows is that even though these politicians and bureaucrats might think that they're hovering above sectional interests, they have to deal with social groups who have different degrees of political power. And I think the lesson you take away from this is that any state under capitalism, if it breaks its links with other social groups and just negotiates with capitalists, a state in that kind of situation is more often than not going to come out on the losing end if capitalists decide that they have a different agenda. And the reason for that is simple: most politicians rely on capitalists to get elected into office. Politicians are usually from the same social circle as capitalists. But most importantly, all politicians require that their economy is relatively healthy. They want to keep jobs locally, they want to keep revenues flowing in and for that they've got to make sure that capitalists keep investing. And if they undertake policies that capitalists don't like, capitalists have the ultimate weapon in their hands which is they can just hold back on investment and send the economy into a tailspin.

This is exactly what happened in India in 1947. The Indian National Congress was very committed to having an effective planning regime, and when you look at the kind of legislation it passed to give the state powers over local entrepreneurs, it's very much like the kind of legislation and powers that Korean planners took for themselves. The difference was that Indian capitalists not only lobbied against it, they actually vocally, openly—they said it while they were doing it—they said, we're just going to stop investing until you come to your senses, because we don't want to invest in an economy where you're going to tell us what to do with our money.

So for about a two-and-a-half-year period there was a real what's called "capital strike." Just like labor can go on strike, capitalists went on strike. And by 1950 the Indian Prime Minister Nehru admitted defeat. He said, well, we had our own vision but the fact is, our capitalists won't let us do what we want— we're going to have to reach some kind of accommodation with them. And in fact the famous American economist Simon Kuznets went to India and he asked Nehru, you had all this rhetoric about planning—what are you doing? You seem to be giving these people whatever they want. And Nehru told him, if we actually tried to follow through on our planning objective today, the country would simply break apart. You can't do it.

The lesson, I think, is this: in a capitalist economy, not surprisingly, capitalists call the shots. And if you want to put measures in place which they're not exactly happy with, you need your own leverage. That is, if the government wants to put measures in place that capitalists oppose, it's going to have to step out of the closed room in which the only negotiating parties are entrepreneurs on the one hand and government agents on the other. And it's going to need leverage of its own—and that leverage has to come from other social groups.

Clearly when you speak of other social forces that could be involved in these processes of development you mean labor. But what are the consequences for labor and for the left of jumping on the bandwagon of such national capitalist development projects?

VC: Well, we can talk about this in two ways. One is what *were* the consequences? Because consequences don't come down automatically; they were partly conditioned by the choices that labor made. And the second thing that we can talk about is what *could be* the consequences if labor had made different choices?

It should be clear by now that as far as in my thinking, this term "state-led development" is actually a bit of a misnomer. You had heavy state intervention during this half century or so of developmentalism, but it wasn't led by the state in any way. It was actually led by local capitalists. States remained deeply constrained and in many cases prisoners of the initiatives of local businessman, local industrialists. So keeping that in mind, the consequence for labor of this regime was, in most countries for the most part, a progressive weakening of labor.

And this is important because when the crises of import substitution and developmentalism came into play in the late 1970s to early-to-mid-1980s, one of the reasons that neoliberalism was put into place so easily and so consistently across the board was that in almost all of these countries labor over time had become too weak to resist it. When governments adopted these neoliberal policies in the 1980s, which everyone knew would be harmful to labor, labor for the most part had found its organizational capabilities had atrophied and it had weakened so much because it had become completely dependent on the state for the condition and the welfare of the rank and file.

So the immediate consequence was that neoliberalism was pretty easily put into place and labor took it on the chin for two decades. I think it need not have been this way. In India, in Argentina, even in Brazil, you had labor movements that were actually very powerful in the 1940s. In some cases those labor movements were politically defeated. So they fought but lost and they ended up settling for whatever crumbs the government threw their way. But it's also true that big chunks of the labor movement willingly and readily subordinated themselves to this development project, partly because they identified planning with socialism, and partly because they just thought that they were too weak to really take on the government. Now hindsight is always twenty-twenty. You can say that, well, they made a mistake, they should have fought for more draconian measures against local entrepreneurs, they should have fought for more power for themselves within the state, et cetera, and they were trying something that was historically unprecedented. That's fine.

But labor today, in my view, can't make that same mistake. The basic lesson of the past half-century is that if countries adopt national capitalist development models, if they try to have some kind of interventionist state-led development model in which the government tries to impose conditions on capitalists, the basic lesson is two-fold. One is that capitalists aren't going to like it and they'll fight like hell against it. And the second is, given that capitalists aren't going to like it, the only social force that's got an interest in pushing through the measures which will give the government power over capitalists—which will allow the state to regulate where investments are going—the only real social force is labor. And this time around, the advice then goes to two agents; one is to governments saying, look, if you really want to serve the public good this time, don't sideline labor the way you did the last time because they're going to give you the leverage and the muscle to extract concessions from your local industrialists. And the second is to labor, which is to say, this time, don't sit down when you ought to be standing.

Most of us know about the case of the president of Brazil, Lula, a former metal worker who headed the Workers' Party and came to power in Brazil in 2002, and who formed an alliance with Brazilian big business. The experience there was a real disappointment for many on the left and raises the question of how does labor, once it has some sort of power, keep its autonomy.

VC: Well, keeping your autonomy is not all that hard. What's hard is knowing what to do with it. So if it comes to keeping your autonomy, it's pretty simple, which is whatever coalition you're in, you maintain organizational independence, you put into bylaws the right to strike, the right to engage in collective action, things like that. The harder thing is when you have your autonomy, when do you know when to mobilize and when do you know to accept tactical retreats and such things. And politics, unfortunately, is an art, not a science.

In the case of Brazil, I hesitate to say very much because you have to respect local actors and their judgments. So, it's hard to say whether what labor is experiencing in Brazil is just the result of an incredible array of forces, national and international, lined up against them, or whether it's in some cases the product of bad judgment.

What we do see is that since Lula came to power there has been a fair amount of conflict within the Workers' Party itself and some have actually broken away and established a new socialist party. That seems to be the result of a certain amount of frustration with Lula and a feeling that the policies that he's putting into place don't just reflect the balances of forces by the kind of rightward lurch on his part that goes beyond what the balances for forces ought to be dictating.

And there's an interesting contrast there with what's happening in Venezuela. If you looked at Chávez and Lula, who would you predict would be the one who would be building his local base, who would be energizing it, who would be giving it more autonomy and who would be taking on local industrialists?

Most certainly Lula.
VC: Yeah, you would have thought it would be Lula, but here's Chávez and he seems to be going much further in that direction than Lula. But Lula seems to be fairly concertedly demobilizing his base and I think the reason for that is simple. Chávez has found that the only way he can survive is by mobilizing the poor. He seems to have no choice and that's ironically radicalizing him to a certain degree. But much more importantly, it's creating a mass of highly political and highly organized local neighborhood-based actors who, if we're lucky, will manage to keep their autonomy, their independents from Chávez. In fact, what little news I've seen coming out of there, they seem to be fighting for this. Chávez is trying to assert some kind of control over local neighborhood political organizations that he's established, but they seem to be fighting against it.

What would you say, given the constraints of the present political and economic situation globally, can and should the left demand in terms of development?
VC: That's a tough one. You know, I think that for people in the U.S., first thing you have to demand is that the United States leave these countries alone and that it not react to any measures, any initiative for national independent economic development and some kind of redistributive measures and national economic policy, it should not react the way it historically has, which is in an extremely hostile fashion.

As I said earlier, because national capitalisms take on the complexion and their peculiarities from the local conditions, local balances of power, I seriously doubt that any one set of recommendations can be applied across the board especially from on high, from sitting over here—the devil is in the details in all of these cases—when you just don't know what's happening in these countries outside of what you get from the press.

So, I think in the U.S., our first responsibility is towards something that we can control, which is what the American government does. And that's where the demand has to be two-fold. Minimally, it has to be like what you say to doctors: the U.S. should first do no harm. That, in itself, would be a massive achievement. I mean that would be of world historic proportions if the United States just left some countries alone and let the political evolution of these countries take their own shape.

Secondly—if you can do that kind of heavy lifting, which would take a lot—I think the second demand one could make is that the United States actually spend a big chunk of the hundreds of billions of dollars that it spends on its weapons, just spend it on the basic welfare base provisions for the poor in these countries. It wouldn't take much. It just takes a few tens of billions of dollars to create clean water supply, to give vaccinations to everyone who needs them, for basic education. These are all things which can be done.

As for the rest of the world, that's a question for the poor and for the working people and for concerned citizens and the rest of the world to decide. And if and when they want the help of their sympathizers over here, people like us, organizers, political people, we should be willing to give it. But the proper thing to do, I think, is to let them take the lead while we do whatever work we can over here.

CHAPTER ELEVEN

Mike Davis: Isaac Deutscher
and the Old Left

It would appear that Isaac Deutscher is virtually unknown on the left in the United States. Why do you find that troubling?

MD: Deutscher is and was in many ways the moral and intellectual bridge between the generation of 1917, of classical revolutionary socialism, and the New Left of the 1960s. He also represents a deepening and continuation of the critical project undertaken by people like Victor Serge, trying to understand the tragedy of the Soviet Union under Stalin—but also trying to understand, which is the particular mission of Isaac Deutscher, the contradictions and possibilities of the Soviet Union, particularly after the death of Stalin in 1953. He gave people in the 1960s, at least to those of us who were willing to listen, an interpretive standpoint, an analytic context that was different from any of the received orthodoxies on the American left.

Why do you think that there weren't celebrations of Deutscher in this country on the centenary of his birth?

MD: First of all, these are craven times. A whole heroic generation of the American left has passed with little commemoration. But I think also in Deutscher's case it was precisely because he was a heretic. He had the distinction of being simultaneously denounced by leading Cold Warriors, Social Democrats, supporters of the Soviet Union, and orthodox Trotskyists. There was never a Deutscherite party or a Deutscherite faction. And I think the sheer independence of this thought and the critical sharpness of his mind did not predispose people to be his followers. All the more important, of course, to rediscover his work and to rediscover his analysis.

Of course in London, Deutscher's spirit and work is very much alive in the Isaac and Tamara Deutscher Memorial Prize; so many people who worked with him and knew him and continue on in his memory. Whereas in United States, unfortunately, he's a more forgotten figure.

What were Isaac Deutscher's origins and the milieu that he came out of?

MD: He was born in Galicia, not too far from Auschwitz. He studied in Krakow, which was the former capital of Austrian Poland and one of the greatest centers of Jewish culture. His father hoped that he would become a great rabbi.

As a teenager he was a stunning poet with a large audience. And then he went to study in Warsaw and quickly joined the underground Communist Party. Poland in the late 1920s was under the dictatorship of Marshal Piłsudski and the Communists were deep underground. He became the major editor of the underground publications of the Polish Communist Party and then went to Moscow in 1931, where he was offered several academic positions in the Soviet Union.

Not long after that time—in 1933—he was expelled from the Polish Communist Party. In what broad political context did his expulsion take place?
MD: First of all, the Polish Communist Party itself is a direct descendent of the Social Democratic Party led by Rosa Luxemburg and it inherited some of her independence of thought and critical tradition. It was a small party, but it was a smart party with a stellar group of intellectual and thinkers.

In the late 1920s, as I say, it was deep underground combating a very dictatorial regime sounding almost like Pinochet in Poland. But the Communist leadership at the time considered the regime fascist and Deutscher thought this was a huge mistake. Deutscher and others in the party who banded together as an opposition were opposed to the so-called Third Period line of the Communist International that denounced Socialists as "Social Fascists" that made no distinction between them and real Fascists like the Italian, and above all the German Nazi, dictatorships.

Deutscher's crime, for which he was eventually expelled from the party with others in 1932, was his insistence on the urgency of creating unity in the workers' movement amongst Communists and Socialists against the peril of the Nazi Party in Germany—and this was well before he was in contact with Trotsky or in any sense thought himself a Trotskyist. He was part of a larger current in European Communism that was horrified by the sectarian line of the Comintern and, with like-minded socialists, was desperately struggling to put up a United Front against the menace of Hitler.

What struggles took place in the 1920s over the fate of the Soviet Union, as Stalin solidified his control?
MD: So much of Deutscher's life—his great work in the 1950s—was the reconstruction of the struggle that occurred in the 1920s in the Soviet Union. Lenin at his death in the last year of his life waged a desperate struggle to prevent the succession of Stalin as the secretary of the party from taking over the party. By the middle 1920s, virtually the entire old guard of the Bolshevik Party had come together in a series of oppositions, but most importantly something

called the Left Opposition, against Stalin. These were the all the people—Zinoviev, Kamenev, Rykov, Tomsky, Bukharin, and so on—who were later shot by Stalin in 1937 and 1938. In the early 1920s and up through Lenin's death and even for a few years after that, great dissent and public discussion was still possible in the Soviet Union. But by 1927–28 that began to become impossible. And Trotsky, of course, was first put into external exile and then in the beginning of the 1930s kicked out of the Soviet Union. And Stalin began to increasingly consolidate his control over the party, culminating in the year 1937 when he executed literally tens of thousands of Communists.

Deutscher himself wrote about the Moscow Trials, where Stalin put his former colleagues on the stand for treason and for fomenting counterrevolution.

MD: These were nightmarish trials because people were forced to confess. It was not enough simply to arrest and kill people. People were induced to confess by being told that the future of socialism in the Soviet Union depended on their false confession and, out of misguided loyalty, great revolutionaries confessed to monstrous caricatures.

Trotsky in a way was absolutely suited to the role of what Deutscher called the "prophet outcast," fighting to defend the truth of the revolution against the falsifications and lies of Stalin. But what's so interesting about Deutscher as a historian, and Deutscher as a partisan of Trotsky, is that his magnificent trilogy about Trotsky is in no sense a hagiographic biography. He can be very critical of Trotsky and he fundamentally disagreed with Trotsky's decision to try and create a new Communist International, the so-called Fourth International.

Deutscher's argument was what—that the times were too bleak to embark on such a project?

MD: Yes and that the Communist International and the Communist parties still had such a huge hold on advanced sectors of the working class. One of the things that is most important about Deutscher as a historian is his exacting attention to social forces, the social forces that underlay the personalities.

He thought that Trotsky had made a grievous mistake by attempting to create a new International when, in fact, it was a period of defeat, of defensive struggle, and when advanced workers everywhere still believed in the mythology of Stalin's Russia and the Five-Year Plan. And this was typical of the opinions that so often separated Deutscher from the sectarian left in Europe and in the United States.

How did Deutscher draw on the parallel between the fates of the French and Russian Revolutions—with Stalin ushering in Thermidorian reaction—to understand how the latter had turned into something so horrific?

MD: In both cases, the great French Revolution of 1789 and the 1917 Revolution, the process of defending the revolution—in the first case against the crowned might of Europe and the second case against intervention by almost a dozen foreign powers—the very process of defense of the revolution, disbursed, disorganized, destroyed much of the social base of the revolution, particularly in the Russian case. By the end of the Russian Civil War in 1921, industrial production was a small fraction of what it had been in 1912; workers were either in party positions, unemployed, or had died in battle. The Soviet working class of the early 1920s was sociologically very different; it was a peasant working class. Much the same thing had happened in the course of the French Revolution. Deutscher even extends the analogy back to the Cromwellian Revolution, the English Revolution of 1640.

But at the same time Deutscher argued, more than Trotsky was prepared to, that even in its most degenerated and despotic form, even Napoleon as Emperor or Stalin virtually as new Tsar, although many of the ideals and most important democratic process as the revolution had been destroyed, the revolution still preserved a certain progressive dynamic, certainly in the case of Napoleonic era with its reforms of laws and its overthrown monarchy. But Deutscher also believed that Stalinism would not outlive Stalin and that there were other forces stemming from Stalinist modernizations, stemming from the Five-Year Plan and its huge enlargement of the working class and literacy, that would eventually transform the Soviet Union.

He was of the opinion that capitalism couldn't be restored in the Soviet Union, the revolution was unfinished, and he believed the new forces would emerge from the labor movement and above all from youth that would reinvigorate socialist opposition in the Soviet Union. And of course, tragically, that didn't turn out to be the case.

What is your assessment of Deutscher's biography of Stalin?

MD: Deutscher's book was his first big book and made quite a splash when it was published in 1949. In retrospect, I don't think you could say it was as successful, in any way, as the biography of Trotsky. The problem is not only the question of affinity.

Stalin is simply perhaps the most enigmatic figure of the twentieth century and an enormously difficult figure to understand: on one hand, his monstrous crimes and huge defeats; on the other hand, he's probably unquestionably the shrewdest and smartest of the Allied wartime leaders. What Deutscher was actually doing was writing a triptych. When he died, in the spring of 1967, he was in the midst of working on a huge biography of Lenin, which he actually thought would be his greatest work. So his real life's work were these huge mirror-like portraits of the three most important characters in Russian Revolution and the Soviet Union.

As a historian, how do you estimate the importance of Deutscher's trilogy on Trotsky?

MD: It's difficult to think of another twentieth-century biography that combines such classic elements of great tragedy. Tamara Deutscher used to talk about how when Isaac was writing the Trotsky trilogy in the 1950s, he always kept Shakespeare and Shakespeare's tragedies by his bed stand. At the same time, such almost breathtaking political and intellectual landscapes, his reconstruction of the debates amongst the Bolsheviks against the social background of a country that almost was destroyed by the First World War and the Civil War, and to understand the moral and historic stakes and, above all, the uncompleted nature, the unfinished nature of the process—Deutscher was, above all, trying to convey to his readers that not only were these struggles and debates as immense importance to humanity, but they were ongoing.

Which is why he titled the incredible book he wrote in 1967, his last book, *The Unfinished Revolution,* which was a prospectus for the possibility of profound social change in the Soviet Union. So it's not biographer as mortician. This is biographer as combatant, but a biographer capable of the kind of detachment and critical standpoint, that he could when needed separate himself from the subject, even when the subject was as overwhelming as Leon Trotsky.

Given that, given that he was a partisan, what was his relationship to organized Trotskyism?

MD: It was a conflictual relationship, almost without exception, for two reasons. One is because he did not endorse the formation of the Fourth International and, quite frankly, he saw it as a dead end. This is not because he didn't believe in small socialist groups or because he had ceased to believe in socialist organizing. On the contrary, when he came to the United States, in 1965 and then for longer visits in 1966, he hammered away at the importance of the student movement and intellectuals forging ties with rank and file labor in the United States and rebuilding socialist politics.

But he did not accept this kind of version of the apostolic succession from Lenin to Trotsky or from the Third International to the Fourth International. He also fell out with other dissident groups, including Tony Cliff and Hal Draper and the people around the Independent Socialist Clubs. He had a kind of dialectical view that what was happening in the Soviet Union in the 1960s was a culmination of halting but important reformists attempts at the top and rebellion from the bottom of society and he thought these reformist attempts at the top opened vital spaces for workers, students, and intellectuals to reassert themselves. Whereas many traditional Trotskyists and dissidents Marxists had come to believe in a kind of big bang theory where Stalinism would have to be overthrown by something like a 1917 revolution.

So for all these reasons and more, Deutscher was both a great influence on the New Left individually, but he was often the butt of ruthless criticism and often very unfair attacks. He was labeled on one hand by Cold Warriors as a supporter of Stalinism, and by loyal pro-Moscow Communists as a CIA agent, and by sections of the Trotskyist Left as an apologist for the new bureaucracy.

We've been talking about Deutscher's relationship to the movements and people he wrote about, but I want to just back up briefly and pick up the thread of Deutscher's personal chronology. He fled Poland in 1939 just before the German invasion of Poland.
MD: Yes, about six months before it and of course his entire family was consumed in the Holocaust in Poland.

Let's turn to Deutscher's life in Britain. He had to make ends meet yet had quite a difficult time breaking into academia. My father, who taught for many years at the University of Sussex, told me that Isaac Deutscher was to be offered a chair in political science at the university, but it was spiked by the liberal political philosopher Isaiah Berlin, whom Deutscher had reviewed unfavorably.
MD: Indeed, I think that's absolutely true. Deutscher was essentially blacklisted during the 1950s when he was working on the Trotsky trilogy and it imposed very great hardships on the family—Tamara Deutscher, his wife, was not only a superlative journalist but a principal collaborator on this project.

Deutscher came in 1939. He actually had been in the Polish Army in the late 1920s, doing very dangerous work doing communist agitation inside of the Polish Army. He came to England and he joined up with the Polish Army, which was based in Scotland, but was almost immediately figured out to be a dangerous subversive, so he was put on a labor detail or something like that.

When he came to England, he had mastered Russian and French, but didn't know a word of English. By 1942 he had become a regular contributor to— of all things—*The Economist*. Between '42 and I forget when—the Cold War finally ended his relationship *The Economist*—maybe 1949, he wrote something like well over six hundred articles for the economists. He contributed regularly to *The Observer* and became one of the most well known political journalists and experts, not just on the Soviet Union, but particularly during the war on European life under the Nazi occupation. And he returned to political journalism whenever he needed to earn an income, but academia remained a will-o'-the-wisp because of the blacklist. Even though Cold Warriors like George Kennan, virtually the father of the Cold War, called Isaac Deutscher a great biographer, a great writer, it didn't mean that Deutscher could put bread on the table or get an academic job anywhere.

Deutscher in adulthood became a master of English prose—often likened to fellow Pole Joseph Conrad. What can you say about Deutscher's prose style and his use of language?

MD: His prose style was absolutely classical and like Conrad and others who came as adults to English, they began to learn English not by simply reading the newspaper or comic books, but began with the classics and they began with Shakespeare. They began with Trevelyan, and the other great political biographers of the nineteenth century.

So there's a very classical quality to his writing and it's infused of course by a sense of the moral magnitude of the dimensions of the events he's writing about, by these kind of Shakespearean qualities. And this is not just something he imitated. It's something that he thought about very deeply. He read dozens and dozens of books on the philosophy of history and on tragedy as a genre, searching for the right forms in which to portray these momentous struggles inside the Soviet Union and inside the workers' movement in the 1920s and '30s.

He was also an essayist who wrote on a wide range of subjects from George Orwell's *1984* to Freud to being a non-Jewish Jew. Do you have any impressions about him as an essayist or any of the essays that you think were particularly important?

MD: First of all remember he started off as kind of avant-garde poet. He had a very strong esthetic sensibility, attuned to modernism and he unfailingly kept up-to-date with this and it informed his work. I suppose of his books of essays my favorite is *Heretics and Renegades*, which was a response to *The God that Failed* and confessions of famous ex-Communists, where he stakes out the position of a heretic, of someone who is defending Marxism against its usurpers and betrayers.

He was absolutely scrupulous, perhaps far more scrupulous than some of the German Frankfurt School exiles. For the particularly arduous process of applying for a visa to the U.S. to go to the Trotsky Archives at Harvard, he refused to engage in any of the semantic games the State Department expected him to do to deny his Communist past.

His anthology *The Non-Jewish Jew* is a wonderful book and it recalls not simply the world and contributions of Jewish intellectuals, but it reminds us how absolutely important Central Jewish secularism, Jewish radical culture, was in the constitution of modern European culture. And of course, it's written with a great sense of nostalgia because the whole world he wrote about, the world of his student days in Krakow, its underground agitation amongst the Jewish working class in Warsaw, this is the world completely gone, as you pointed out, within months of his fortunate immigration to London.

Deutscher came to the United States in 1965 and spoke at a teach-in against the Vietnam War on the campus of the University of California at Berkeley. How did you happen to hear him?
MD: Well, I was an itinerant rabble-rouser—not a student, but just an SDS kid. At the time, I considered myself to be a radical populist and never heard or really met a communist before. The teach-in was quite extraordinary. Deutscher spoke after midnight. He was preceded by Paul Krassner of *The Realist* and Norman Mailer, who gave these incredible stream of consciousness—quite brilliant—but insane rants. And then suddenly, sometime after midnight, this figure appears with a goatee. I was so naïve at the time, I turned to a friend of mine and I said, "Trotsky's dead, isn't he? I mean, he's really dead, that's not Trotsky is it?" Deutscher was almost like an apparition. His speech was short, but it's something I've never forgotten, and I think anybody who was there that night would remember the drama and the magic at that talk.

He ended that talk by saying, "We must restore meaning to the great ideas—the ideas of liberalism, democracy, and communism, yes, communism." Wow, I was stunned and I think most of the audience was. It was like a séance with dead revolutionaries and betrayed revolutions with all the hopes and dreams of the early twentieth century, except there he was standing before us. And the tragedy, of course, that he died in 1967—he was barely sixty years old and in the midst of what he considered to be his greatest work, the biography of Lenin—and before Brezhnev buried the hopes of social reform in Eastern Europe with his invasion of Prague in 1968, events that Deutscher would have, of course, been one of the keenest and most important critics and analysts of.

You mentioned Prague Spring, that attempt to create "socialism with a human face" that was crushed by the Soviet Union in 1968 after Deutscher died. It seems in hindsight, Deutscher was overly optimistic about the loos-

ening of control in the Brezhnev era and the potential for real reform. How do you think he would have viewed Prague Spring?

MD: He would have viewed it with, I think, the uttermost voracity because I think Deutscher more than almost anyone would understand that what was at stake in Prague Spring was not only the legitimacy of socialism in Czechoslovakia in Eastern Europe, but the larger struggle for the restoration of socialist democracy and the revolutionary tradition in the Soviet Union.

In his last year, in late 1966 and the beginning of 1967, there was already greater pessimism coming into Deutscher's work. A lot of the reform spirit in the early '60s in the Khrushchev period had been buried. It would be easy enough to say that he was completely wrong with his belief that there could be a restoration of democracy in the Soviet Union. But the thing about Deutscher which was so outstanding was his detailed current attention to social forces, particularly to the working class and youth and students in the Soviet Union, and he gave a huge importance to the enlargement and the kind of modernization of those social forces and the belief that their voices would be heard. And of course, from our perspective now, we can see how absolutely catastrophic Brezhnevism and the events in 1968 in Czechoslovakia had been for the future of the left.

After the Cold War and the disintegration of the Soviet Union, why is Deutscher relevant any more? Didn't he speak to an era that is now behind us?

MD: On the contrary, Deutscher's work is the key to understanding 1989. The recovery of the traditions that he represented and continued and was the tribune of, I think are essential to our future. I mean, socialism might seem dead as a doornail to some people, but consider what the alternatives were. Unfortunately, we inherited the world that Trotsky predicted in the late 1930s, but the real alternatives were a choice between some form of socialist democracy, on one hand, and barbarism. Of course, in the last instance, it's not merely a matter of reading Deutscher, Trotsky, or Rosa Luxemburg, it's a question of making ideals come to life in practice and in action.

Tamara Deutscher was both Isaac Deutscher's close collaborator and a scholar in her own right, as well as a friend of yours. What is her legacy?

MD: She was a friend of all of us at the *New Left Review* and very much our hero. When I arrived in London in the 1980, she was collaborating with Edward Hallett Carr—E. H. Carr—and Robert Davies on their extraordinary many, many-volume history of Soviet Russia. So the Deutscher project of which she was the collaborator and in some sense probably should have had her name listed as coauthor, had very strong alliance with the Carr and Davies project, which went on through the 1980s. Carr died in 1982, but Davies continued it.

Her work is inseparable from his. I mean, the writing may be his, but the research is in every sense equally hers, research that she continued in association with Carr and Davies through the 1980s. She was an extraordinary person. She could be caustic and funny and ironic and she was a person of just enormous wit. Most of all, I remember when she came back from visiting Poland at which she had left forty years before she was covering Solidarność and she visited Krakow, she visited where Isaac had lived as a teenager, and I asked her about it. She said, "You know, it's quite incredible." She said every synagogue and Jewish building has been restored, but the people are all gone. She said, "The spirit is gone, it's nothing but a country of ghosts." It was almost heartbreaking.

But she kept her pen sharp until the very end of her life, writing under her own name more frequently than she had in the 1950s and '60s. So she needs recognition as the full collaborator in Deutscher's biographies.

CHAPTER TWELVE

Tariq Ali: Anti-imperialism and the New Left, Revolt and Retrenchment

Decades after the end of the Vietnam War, do you think the symbolism of the Vietnamese victory against the U.S. has any power today?

TA: I think it resonated powerfully for a long time, but once the Communist system had collapsed and capitalism had conquered that world too, including China and Vietnam, the victory did not resonate so much.

What made it resonate was the fact that millions of people all over the globe believed that one reason for the victory, and they were not so wrong about this, was because a superior social system was confronting the United States. That victory created what came to be known in this country as the Vietnam Syndrome, which meant that the United States became reluctant for a long time to intervene directly in a country. They would organize military coups as they did in Chile and Argentina and other parts of Latin America and Asia, but they were very reluctant to intervene directly. One of its reasons for the war in Iraq, a very trivial and minor reason, was to try and end the Vietnam Syndrome forever. "Here we are, back again. We can go and take more countries." It hasn't quite worked out like that. So the echoes of the Vietnam War have not gone away. They remain.

You were active since your university days in opposing the war in Vietnam, including debating Henry Kissinger when you were at Oxford, at a time when many in the UK were apathetic about the Wilson government's involvement in supporting the U.S. in Vietnam. What did the struggle in Vietnam mean for you when you arrived in Britain in 1963 from Pakistan?

TA: When I arrived at Oxford, there was not much interest in what was going on in Vietnam, largely because people didn't know its history, what had happened there. Whereas those of us who were growing up in Asia in the 1950s— for us 1954 was the year of the Battle of Điện Biên Phủ when the Vietnamese had inflicted a stunning defeat on French imperialism. And the effects of that victory resonated throughout the continent. I remember an uncle of mine who wasn't even that political naming his son Hồ Chí Minh, just to commemorate that victory. So that was a postcolonial phase when hatred of the colonial empires was very strong and so large numbers of people throughout Asia, especially in countries which had once been colonized, felt that the Vietnamese victory was a victory for all of us.

When I got to Oxford in 1963, I was already well informed about Vietnam and its history and was following very closely the growing U.S. involvement in the region. And a year before I left for Oxford in 1962 we had read of the battle of Ap Bac in South Vietnam, where United States advisors had suffered heavy losses, and the United States had admitted that they had lots of "advisors," as they used to call them then. So Oxford in that sense was not so well informed. But then we began to organize meetings, began to organize teach-ins, to inform people of what was going on and by 1965–66 big events were beginning to take place.

I remember we had a teach-in on Vietnam where the British Foreign Secretary came and spoke, as did Henry Cabot Lodge, and our side won the debate. It was after that that I debated Henry Kissinger on satellite television, which was broadcast by CBS on coast-to-coast networks in the United States. That's when the movement really got going.

The Vietnam Solidarity Campaign was one effort that started moving some away from apathy. How did the campaign managed to raise awareness about the UK's complicity in the Vietnam War?
TA: Well, there were a number of campaigns, to be fair. There was the Vietnam Peace Campaign, there was the Vietnam Solidarity Campaign, there was the Campaign for Nuclear Disarmament. The Vietnam Solidarity Campaign was the most militant of these because they said, we want the Vietnamese to win—their country has been taken, they've been invaded; it would be tremendous if they won. We were in solidarity with the Vietnamese struggle. As a result of that, large numbers of young people joined us and came to our ranks. And when we started having demonstrations their numbers began to grow. Compared to the anti-Iraq war demonstrations they were quite small, but for those days of street protests they were incredibly significant. We used to have demonstrations—the first one was ten thousand, the second one was twenty-five thousand, the third one was a hundred thousand plus. So they began to grow and gradually an awareness gripped the nation that this was a wrong war.

Interestingly enough, the British Prime Minister at the time, a Labour prime minister called Harold Wilson, did not feel he could respond to U.S. requests to send troops to Vietnam. He was under very heavy pressure, but he refused to do it because he knew it would split his party and possibly his government and that would be the end. So he supported the war, for which we denounced him ferociously, but he did not send troops to Vietnam. It's important to remember that in the light of Blair happily sending troops into Iraq.

In 1967 you traveled to Vietnam. What impact did that trip have on your political development?

TA: It was a very formative trip. We were going on behalf of the Bertrand Russell–Jean-Paul Sartre War Crimes Tribunal as investigators to see exactly what was going on and what crimes were being committed. What we saw was horrific—massive use of defoliants, napalm, of antipersonnel weapons whose only task was to maim civilians. We saw children with their arms amputated because of these antipersonnel weapons. It was very really distressing on that level.

At the same time, it was incredibly inspirational to be in a country where the entire people were fighting back. No one was compelling them to fight back, but the mode was one of total solidarity with each other. And in large numbers of places we visited, because the men were fighting in the south, whole farms, many cities were run by women. Vietnamese women played an incredible role in that struggle and in *Street Fighting Years* I've printed some photographs I took in Vietnam at that time to show this.

I was there for six or seven weeks and the bombing was so heavy during the day that we had to travel at night; that was the only time we could travel. And so during the day we would be in camouflage villages, hearing the bombers come. I remember once we had to go into a town to see victims in a hospital at about noon and as we were going to move out—it's the town of Thanh Hó in the south of North Vietnam—and they said, we've just had a warning that American bombers are on the way, our radars detected a whole range of bombers. We said we still wanted to go and they said no, we won't let you go. And then we heard the bombs. When we went later that afternoon, the entire hospital had been destroyed. So if we had been there at that time, we would have been killed, there's no doubt about it at all.

So you saw the suffering of the Vietnamese and also their courage. And that is something which I will never forget as long as I live. It had a big impact on me.

In the late 1960s, anti–Vietnam War sentiment intersected with emergent radicalism on the left. In 1967, you and some other comrades in arms started a newspaper called *The Black Dwarf*, which took its name from a nineteenth-century publication started by an internationalist radical printer who was jailed for advocating universal voting rights in Britain. What was the significance of the latter-day *Black Dwarf* for the British left?

TA: We took the name, as you rightly point out, from an early-nineteenth-century radical magazine. It was called *The Black Dwarf* because it was a magazine designed to be read by everyone, but largely directed at miners who worked underneath the ground. When these miners came out with their blackened faces from the soot and the filth and the dirt with their backs hunched, they looked like black dwarfs, and that's why Tom Wooler decided to call his magazine *The Black Dwarf*. And he was a very interesting guy, actually, because he was prosecuted and accused of writing seditious material. His argument in court was, "I didn't write it, I typeset it." And he got off. As a result they had to change the law in Britain. So printers were subsequently held responsible for everything. You have him to thank for that.

Our *Black Dwarf,* established in 1968, was a very radical paper politically and culturally. We had lots of people writing for us—playwrights, novelists of a generation much older than ours, we got a lot of support from people like that. Later John Lennon decided to write for us. Mick Jagger used to send his songs. So it was a magazine of the radical left but it was also the voice of the cultural left. It didn't last too long. I think it finished in 1971.

You were unable to travel out of the UK for much of 1968 because of restrictions on your residency status. Why was that year so pivotal for the left—not just in Western Europe but around the world?

TA: 1968 became a pivotal year for the following reasons: you had within the space of eight months the following three big events. You had a general strike in France, involving ten million workers, which was the largest general strike in the history of capitalism. You had French workers occupying their factories and saying they wanted to run the factories. You had other French workers and their student allies saying they wanted to run France in the interest of the majority of the people. At that point, for about a week, it looked as if though the French system might collapse. It didn't collapse but nonetheless the May events of France shook Europe to its core. Everywhere frightened rulers of European countries would whisper and ask each other, "Will the disease spread? Is it going to come our way too?" And it did more or less. It traveled the whole continent.

Now May came on the heels of a massive offensive unleashed by the Vietnamese in March of that year, what became known as the Tet Offensive. And prior to that offensive, General Westmoreland the U.S. Military Commander in Vietnam had said, "we're going to win this war; the boys will be back home this Christmas," creating the impression that nothing serious was happening, that they were winning. The Tet Offensive totally destroyed that myth. Because what happened was the Vietnamese launched a series of lightning offensives in every major city in South Vietnam, culminating in the capture of the U.S. embassy in Saigon and the raising of the National Liberation Front flag on that embassy. Of course, the American troops came and took it back. It was a symbolic gesture, but it's a gesture that totally destroyed the mythologies of that war. And it's after that event that the antiwar movement in the United

States registered a very sharp rise because people said, this war is unwinnable and our leaders have been lying to us.

So you have the Tet Offensive in March, the French events of May, and then in August you have the Russian intervention into Czechoslovakia against a movement in Czechoslovakia which wanted to create both socialism and democracy, the "socialism with a human face" movement, which had also begun in the spring of 1968 and which showed that you could have a freer press within a socialist framework than ever you could within a capitalist framework. Some of the most exciting debates took place in the Czech press from March–April to August 1968.

The Russian bureaucrats—wretched, old, isolated from their own people, isolated from the Czech experience—felt threatened and felt that if it allowed such a new system to exist in Prague sooner or later people in the Soviet Union would say, "If Prague, why not Moscow?" or "If Prague, why not Budapest?" or "If Prague, why not East Berlin?" And so they decided to crush it. And they went in, removed Alexander Dubček, the Communist leader who had decided to go a different route. That event in my opinion was absolutely decisive. Even Aleksandr Solzhenitsyn, who is now regarded as a sort of great right-wing figure, he wrote that what finally finished him off with the Soviet system was the invasion of Czechoslovakia. And it had a very devastating impact on the Soviet intelligentsia. They didn't like it. There were even small demonstrations in Moscow against it. So in a curious way then we can say that these three events actually began to shape the future of that century and were very decisive events for us.

1968 was the peak of many of these movements in Europe. You write in your memoir that a former Conservative prime minister, Harold McMillan, made a statement at the height of all of this turmoil that the pendulum would soon swing the other way—and he was right. Do you think that such a reversal was inevitable? And should we then conclude that history tends to move cyclically, so to speak?

TA: Basically what happens is that when you have a rise of revolutionary movements—uprising, upsurges—either the tide totally overwhelms what exists or it begins to recede. And in the case of most of Europe, it began to recede. It didn't recede in Vietnam: that was the end of the American presence. They took another seven years to get out, but '68 finished them off. And it was the end of the Soviet bureaucracy, although it took them another twenty years.

So these were decisive events. But capitalism and the capitalist system certainly did not fall. It recuperated itself. It recovered, made concessions, permitted genuine reforms. But the effects of the French May were then felt again eight years later in Portugal, where the big uprising of students and workers and soldiers and officers toppled the fifty-year-old Portuguese dictatorship. For a while it looked as if what we were wanting to happen in France might actually happen in Portugal. But for a variety of reasons it didn't happen there either. And then after the stabilization of the Portuguese Revolution, or the way it was recuperated by the right, you then began to see the pendulum swinging the other way—Reagan's victory here in the United States, Thatcher's victory in Britain. And then you had a massive backlash in rightwing counteroffensive, which is still not over.

How much of the defeat of these movements would you attribute to failures on the left? While it might be difficult to compare different historical conjunctures with each other, what are the lessons to be learned from those days?

TA: Well, let's put it like this: one of the reasons for the defeat in Portugal was that the far left and the Portuguese Communist Party didn't fully understand the importance of democracy in a country which had been a dictatorship for fifty years. And the Portuguese Socialist Party understood that full well and that is why they basically won. Secondly, the defeat of the Czechoslovak Spring was pretty decisive for ending experiments which were a combination of socialism and democracy. Many of us argued at the time that under capitalism, which is inherently a system which promotes inequality, you cannot ever have proper democracy, but under a socialist system where property is held in common, you can create the conditions for a thriving democracy and more diversity than you could ever get under capitalism. This incidentally is something you can see in its most classic manifestation in the United States today where the bulk of the mainstream media promotes one line endlessly. It's almost as if the collapse of the Soviet Union has meant that its methods of media control have now been taken over by capitalism and you have the U.S. equivalents of *Pravda* and *Izvestia* on television each single day. And I'm not simply talking about Fox TV, which is exceptional even today.

So I think the left made big mistakes in that period which we have to learn from. Today the situation is very different. One mustn't think it's the same situation. If the twentieth century was an epoch of wars and revolutions, the twenty-first century looks like a century of wars and counter-revolutions. It's not a century where revolution has been on the agenda anywhere, with the partial exception of Venezuela in Latin America. And that is an important exception and if that Bolivarian process in Venezuela proceeds well, that could begin to change the face of Latin America. It's the first time since the collapse of the Sandinistas in Nicaragua that the isolation of the Cubans has been broken by not any old country, but the richest country in Latin America because of the oil. This is why the Venezuelan events are of extreme importance and are an oasis in a world which is otherwise a desert. So it's not that everything is over, but we fight in very difficult conditions, since the whole world has gone capitalist and that is something which has to be understood.

As the pendulum swung back to the right, many left fellow-travelers of the 1960s and '70s ended up renouncing their radicalism and echoing the "God that failed" sentiments of former Communist members in the 1950s. What do you make of this phenomenon?

TA: It's a phenomenon which is as old as the hills. You can go back to the English revolution of the seventeenth century, when for the first time in history a monarch was executed for defying the will of the people. The English Revolution, though it was garbed in religious rhetoric, was nonetheless a very radical revolution. But then a counterrevolutionary movement began. And once it was successful, and you had a restoration of the monarchy in the 1660s, then what you also saw was some of the most radical supporters of the English Revolution who had criticized Cromwell from the left—some Diggers, some Levellers—actually supported the Restoration. So you can have this development historically in periods of defeat, that many radicals cross over. And it is the experience of defeat which does that.

You have similar groups of people today. I personally know members of governments all over Western Europe who were with us in the 1960s and '70s and now today are serving extremely reactionary governments. You have similar developments inside the intelligentsia. Quite a few of the old SDS people in the United States are now pretty rightwing, supporting military interventions, constantly attacking the antiwar movement. I think one has to sort of see it as something which happens. It's not these people as individuals taking that decision—it is that, of course—but they take the decision in bad times. And from that point of view, it's the bad times which are really a test, because it's the bad times that try people. And if you decide to capitulate, completely cave in to the dominant culture, then one has to ask, how deep was what you believed in in the first place?

You were in the International Marxist Group in the UK until 1980. You've written that you didn't have the stomach for sectarian politics and all the internal battles. Did your experience on the left over decades lead you to conclude that the radical left needs to organize itself in a different way than these traditional left parties?

TA: Very much so. In fact, the reason why I joined the Fourth International and the International Marxist Group, was that it was at a time when there was a big rise in the revolutionary movements, at a time when the movements was so large outside that in order to relate to them, especially in our organization, that you had to be very open and broad-minded.

It's when these movements were on the decline that people turned in on themselves. There was a crazy business going on inside the Fourth International. The white-collar workers, especially teachers and social workers, were being told they weren't good enough unless they went and worked in a factory. I mean, this was akin to me to a sort of religion. This is what religious cults do, to try and break the back of people who are in their organizations, wanting total obedience. It wrecked many a life and it wrecked a great deal of the political work that people had done. So I was very angry about that and I remember when I criticized it quite strongly—this whole so-called turn to industry, you know, the cult of the proletariat which was already on the decline—I remember being told, "But why are you so angry? No one is going to ask you to do that," which I thought was so cynical. I was disgusted. That was the key event. That and the endless factional disputes, which I just decided I was not going to spend what was left of my life doing. So in 1980 I left and have been an independent leftist since. I've been associated with the *New Left Review*, Verso, and New Left Books, so that has been my base of operations, if you like.

When you went to Vietnam in the 1960s, you were impressed not only by the formidable resistance of the Vietnamese, but also the socialist project that they were trying to see through, the socialist nature of their struggle. In Iraq that doesn't exist obviously. Do you think that the fact that there is no radical left agenda within the Iraqi resistance makes it hard for people to organize against the war in the U.S., Europe, and elsewhere?
TA: Well, it does and it doesn't. In the first place, we have to ask ourselves, where is there a strong left today outside Latin America? So the whole picture is very different.

However, it is absolutely the case that in Iraq there is no leftwing group inside the resistance. The largest group which used to be on the left, the Iraqi Communist Party, is collaborating with the occupation in the United States and served in the very first occupation government, which discredited it. And the religious parties have become incredibly dominant in the known armed resistance. But the rest of the Iraqis who are fighting include many former soldiers of the army who just didn't want that country to be occupied.

I think that we are now in a pre-1917 situation. There's no socialist bloc. There's no socialist country. There's been no socialist revolution. And so people fight as they see fit. It's like people in the Sudan who fought the British and they were led by religious leaders like the Madhi, who defeated General Gordon in

Khartoum. And I remember reading what the socialist writer William Morris wrote in a letter to his daughter, saying, "Khartoum and the Sudan is back in the hands of the people it belongs to and that in itself is a cause for celebration." And that's my attitude to Iraq—that there's no progressive force fighting inside the resistance, but the United States and the West have no right to be there. And so anyone who manages to push them out, it will mark a step forward and then hopefully things will develop.

You've spoken about the late-nineteenth-century organization in the U.S. the Anti-Imperialist League, founded by Mark Twain and with members like Henry and William James. Why do you think people in the U.S. should read the history of the League now?

TA: Well, it was a response to the U.S. occupation of the Philippines. The United States was involved in rivalries with Spain, both in Latin America, in Cuba in particular, and elsewhere. And they decided to go and get the Spaniards out of the Philippines and occupy it themselves, which they did. They weren't prepared for the resistance that followed, it was quite a staunch resistance, but they occupied it. And lots of American intellectuals and writers were shocked by the brutalities and the fact that their country had gone so far out to occupy another country, because illusions were very strong about the United States being a different sort of power. Even though it expanded internally people for whatever reasons did not see that as necessarily wrong. Some did, not many. But when they went thousands of miles away to conquer the Philippine Islands, that did anger lots of people and that is when the call was put out by Mark Twain, the James brothers, and many, many other luminaries of the period to create an Anti-Imperialist League. It was founded in Chicago and within five years it had tens of thousands of members and chapters all over the country and it played a big part in radicalizing American public opinion against what was going on. Some of Mark Twain's most radical stuff was written in the last years of his life because he devoted a great deal of time to founding the League and playing a part in it.

When I come to the States, I always remind people of that. That we have writers like Gore Vidal and Thomas Pynchon and, possibly, Norman Mailer who should do the same thing today. There would be support for it and there probably would be broad support for it. But so far, no one has taken up my call.

The way the left has conceptualized this war by and large has been that it's been a war for oil. Why do you think that's misguided?

TA: I think it's too instrumentalist. Of course, nothing that happens in the Middle East is unconnected to oil. I mean, that's the reason that is such a strong area. But the United States has got big military bases dotted all over. No one is going to stop the flow of oil to the United States. They were even buying it from Saddam Hussein illegally during the sanctions. So it's, I think, not simply about oil, but it's also about a global overall geopolitical strategy to assert U.S. hegemony in a largely capitalist world, to control this region so securely that it's a shot across the bows of their largest rivals in the Far East, and says to these rivals, "Of course, there will never be any problems. You're getting the oil, but we are the ones watching over it." That will be enough. That's what they wanted to do, hence the pressure on the occupation of Iraq and hence the pressure on Iran. But it's not going well for them, so we will see what happens.

CHAPTER THIRTEEN

John Sanbonmatsu: Postmodernism and the Politics of Expression

Can you give us a working definition of postmodernism, that enormously influential set of theories that have dominated the left and academia over the past three decades?

JS: "Postmodernism" is a notoriously difficult term to define. However, the way I use it in my book, *The Postmodern Prince*, is to describe a particular current in critical theory. Postmodernism, in this sense, is a shorthand for post-structuralist-inflected philosophy. Essentially, poststructuralism originated with a group of thinkers in France—in the theoretical ruminations especially of Michel Foucault, Louis Althusser, Jacques Lacan, Julia Kristeva, Jacques Derrida, and some others—who came after what was called the structuralist movement in France. The so-called structuralists were academics like the anthropologist Claude Lévi-Strauss, the Marxist Louis Althusser, and also the historian Foucault, who for a time was identified by some with the structuralist movement. Lévi-Strauss tried to identify universal structures in human culture and experience, while Althusser, who identified himself with the French Communist left (and was in essence a Stalinist), defended what he called a "scientific," objective Marxism that would be free of the messiness of culture and subjective human experience and interpretation. Finally, Foucault looked to what he called the *episteme*—an almost subterranean structure of knowledge that he argued had undergirded much of what we call science and positive knowledge since the Enlightenment. Like Althusser, Foucault looked askance at the Enlightenment myth of a rational, self-identical subject (i.e. human being), emphasizing instead the structures of society that make us who we are, chiefly at the level of discourse and bodily practices.

Post-structuralism, the broad intellectual movement that followed structuralism, had some key things in common with the structuralist vision, above all the notion that the human being is best seen as an effect of power, as something almost wholly produced by power and discourse. At the same time, unlike the structuralists, poststructuralists were skeptical about, or simply uninterested in, identifying specific material structures and institutions in society where power might be concentrated—institutions or systems, say, which define or limit human life chances. You might say that poststructuralism is structuralism imploded, collapsed in on itself. On the one hand, we see a similar skepticism toward humanism and universal subjects; on the other hand, we see a far greater emphasis on discourse and language in defining social reality and individual identity. The movement in fact converged with the deconstruction-ist movement of the 1970s, which originated in the work of the literary theo-rist Paul De Man and the philosopher Jacques Derrida. Hence the shorthand for the poststructuralist movement as a whole—the "linguistic turn."

This is only a very rough sketch of what is in fact a quite complicated and diverse movement. Nonetheless, one can identify a core set of assumptions that all poststructuralists seem to share, and these are worth looking at. From the point of view of the needs of praxis, I would emphasize four assumptions in particular that have been damaging.

First, the proper relation of the intellectual to knowledge is one in which she deconstructs so-called positive knowledges—that is, reveals the historical and discursive determinants of what society happens to call "truth," without herself laying claim to empirical facts (even provisional ones). Second, the inde-terminacy or overdetermination of positive knowledge requires the theorist to avoid making arguments for particular moral and social norms or univer-sal ideals. Third, theoretical knowledge can be, perhaps even must be, devel-oped independently of the demands of practical knowledge and material social need. Fourth, the fundamental or primordial nature of social reality is always already one of "difference" and "dissensus"—i.e., no two perspectives or iden-tities can coincide with one another, except by doing violence to both. What are the consequences of such assumptions for our praxis?

The first assumption, the deconstructive element, prohibits us from the outset from engaging from the outset the dialectical analysis or description of our socioeconomic totality. How then are we to know what strategies and tactics to use, or where to search out fissures or points of weakness in the system? The second assumption, the aversion to laying claim to moral truth, or even affirming the ideal of universal liberation, has the effect of ceding the terms of moral and social order to the political Right. What kind of life, what mix of social arrangements and institutions do we want to see realized some day? We are prohibited from dwelling on the question. In the third assump-tion, the disarticulation of theory from praxis, social movements are denied access to theoretical knowledge while theorists are given license to develop their theories without giving a thought either to the demands of practice or to social need. How hasn't just this rupture between theory and practice led to the grotesque "playfulness," self-ironizing, and uselessness we find in so much critical theory today? Finally and fourthly, the postmodernist obsession with the metaphysics of difference and dissensus has obscured every possible basis for developing solidarity, mutual aid, and common ground among our many movements. Haven't we seen a politics of dispersion take the place of a politics of unity? Has critical theory not contributed to this tendency, directly or indirectly?

What I try to do in *The Postmodern Prince*, therefore, is to show how the various elements of the new poststructuralist orthodoxy became wedded to a certain vision of politics, one which I and many others find unhelpful for the left today.

When did poststructuralist and postmodernist thought gain ground and what was the context in which they appeared?

JS: Well, postmodernist and poststructuralist thought rose to some prominence in France in the 1970s. It didn't come to the United States until somewhat later, in the late 1970s and early '80s, where it took off in the humanities in the United States.

Postmodernism didn't have any impact or influence on the New Left, because it mostly came after it, chronologically speaking. But the reverse is not true. That is to say that the New Left very much *did* have an impact on postmodernism. In the streets of Paris in 1968, in the Free Speech Movement in the early 1960s in Berkeley, and many other kind of cultural and political uprisings around the world, theorists and philosophers generally on the left thought they were seeing a new kind of political practice being born, one that was decentralized, one that was passionate about the aesthetic dimensions and possibilities of daily life, one that was not given over to the traditional forms of movement organization. For example, they weren't union-based; they weren't working class-based movements. And in fact the communist parties and socialists around the world in many cases in the 1960s and earlier were opposed to these kinds of "cultural" protests because they saw them as spontaneous, they saw them as not sufficiently grounded in the working class, and so on. So for theorists like Foucault, these movements seemed to auger or to portend a new way of expressing previously marginalized perspectives.

You write in *The Postmodern Prince* about how the New Left engaged in a type of political practice that you term "the politics of expression." Why was it problematic, in your view?

JS: The New Left developed in the early 1960s and was inspired in large part by the civil rights movement struggles in the South and in the Northern states— by the Southern Christian Leadership Council (SCLC) and later the Student Nonviolent Coordinating Committee (SNCC). SDS, Students for a Democratic Society, for example, sought to build on the experiences of the civil rights movement. The early civil rights movement was what I would call *strategic*, especially during its incarnation under the direction of the SCLC. That is, this was a very conscious effort to smash segregation in the South. There were material targets. Ralph Abernathy and King and so forth were able to work with the masses through the churches to define strategic targets and to devise campaigns that would continue to apply pressure on segregation until it was smashed.

In my book I describe—perhaps in somewhat simplistic terms, but I think I have a point to make—a kind of tension in the praxis of the New Left between *strategicism,* on the one hand, which is grounded in a reasoned approach to thinking about social change, and *expressivism,* on the other, in which the need or even compulsion to express one's rebellion against established values was seen to trump longer-term planning and the careful articulation of tactics to strategy. What I argue is that with the New Left we can see a key transition from a more strategic politics to a more expressivist one, i.e. a politics in which concrete thinking about how to achieve a desired objective was not considered as important as that primordial moment of giving expression to speech—"letting speech run wild in the streets." While there were intimations of this shift as early as the early 1960s, for example, in the Free Speech Movement in Berkeley, the expressivist impulse only came to full flower in the streets of Paris in 1968. In a famous interview with the French philosopher Jean-Paul Sartre at that time, Daniel Cohn-Bendit—or Danny the Red, one of the leaders of May '68—said, to paraphrase, people say right now that speech is running wild in the streets and, you know, people say crazy things, but that's necessary. What I argue in my book is that while this was a very important moment in our political practice, there's no reason to fetishize expression today. And in fact, perhaps it's gotten in the way of an efficacious politics.

So you see a divide between articulating what ends one wants to achieve, and the strategies that will lead to them, and simply going out there and doing, say, political theater and things that may be aesthetically innovative and appealing but don't necessarily convert anyone except those who already agree with you in the first place.

JS: Yes, I couldn't have said it better. I mean, I've protested many, many times, but if you think about the word *protest* if you think about what that actually means, it's not clear how protest, per se, is to translate into social change. I've marched around many abandoned financial centers on weekends against war and for women's rights and so forth, over the years, and I've often done so with a sense of futility because the only people who are aware that this is going on are the protestors. The media generally don't cover it or they give it very short shrift. Then we get on the buses and we go home. And what has all that achieved?

I'm not saying that, in the right circumstances, protest cannot be powerful and useful. However, there's protest and then, as you say, there's the privileging of an aesthetic element in protest, a focus on theatricality. Even theatricality can be of course wonderfully effective, for example if it's Bread and Puppet Theater in Vermont, which subordinates its aesthetic expression to a pedagogy of politicization and enlightenment. Bread and Puppet tries to educate people about actual issues, using Brechtian drama and handcrafted puppetry. Their actions rarely seem designed to preach only to the choir: they direct their art not towards the movement itself, but to anyone with a heart and a brain. By contrast, there are many theatrical elements to our protest today that are simply about giving voice to certain cultural identities and so on, that are about self-display, and which therefore in themselves do not change or challenge consciousness.

Let's turn to one of the most influential French theorists of poststructuralism, Michel Foucault. He wrote on many issues ranging from madness to discipline and punishment and the human body. What was Foucault's approach to politics and his influence on radical activism?

JS: Foucault came late to politics. He was out of the country during the protests of 1968, and when he returned to France, he found a country transformed politically and culturally. He developed some sympathies with the Maoists, at the time—i.e. with the more militant sectors of the French left who had broken with the standard Communist Party in France (which Sartre had rightly described as "sclerotic" at the time—it had calcified and became a conservative element in many ways). Foucault was rising as a scholar. He was a brilliant intellectual and his writings continue to inform us on a number of different subjects. However, initially Foucault was not a particularly political person and it was only over time that he became kind of swept up in the milieu that he found in France. Eventually, though, he became a champion of prisoners' rights and also came out as a gay man, a rare public figure at the time who very courageously spoke around the world in the 1970s on the rights of gays. While I find Foucault's politics very admirable, in the sense that he was an engaged intellectual, I find there are some really problematic elements with his political writings.

What were the essential dimensions of Foucault's thinking as it relates to action?

JS: A lot of his intellectual and scholarly work had to do with the critique of modernity and to some extent the Enlightenment (although one of his late essays, "What is Enlightenment?," is kind of a defense of a certain aspect of

Enlightenment thinking). But Foucault was very skeptical of what we would call liberalism and liberal regimes of power, whether they be juridical, political, or social. And he spent a lot of time researching the ways that disciplinary and carceral institutions end up controlling the human body and regulating behavior and so forth. He was also especially critical of modern liberal notions of the subject as self-defining, as essentially free, as being rational.

And when you say the subject, do you mean human beings?
JS: Yes, I am sorry, I'm talking about people. In theory we say "subjects"—one of the problems, I think, is that we talk about subjects and not persons (including, I would add, nonhuman persons, i.e. animals). Foucault saw the problem of the subject from the perspective of what he called power-knowledge. There are regimes of control—not so much domination, as control, but control without a "controller," i.e. without a determinate class or social group *in* control—and the way to overcome them is to allow what he called "subjugated knowledges," forms of experience that are suppressed or at least hidden, to come to the surface of society. Not, however, through political organizing per se—certainly not through a strategic kind of approach. Rather, intellectuals would deconstruct the myths of society and so forth, thus enabling these subjugated knowledges to percolate up spontaneously.

My problem with Foucault is that he was very outspoken against a kind of language that I feel was helpful in earlier struggles for social change, a language, for example, of *freedom*. He was very skeptical that we could talk meaningfully about one system versus another as being more free than another. He was uncomfortable with any language of strategy and how to get from point A to point B. He repeatedly attacked any notion of strategy in his interviews.

If I understand what you're saying correctly, Foucault and other poststructural theorists believed that the arena of struggle was not the traditional arena of struggle of the left, whether at the point of production or out in the streets. Rather they believe that it's at the level of language, at the level of discourse, and so were highly critical of those earlier strategies and shunted them to the side.
JS: Yes, that's right. Foucault at one point says that the problem is not what's inside people's heads, their consciousness. And that I think was a very important break that he made both with Marxism and with humanism. You have to understand that Foucault and the other French structuralists and poststructuralists really turned their backs not only against any language of socialism and Marxism, but also against humanism per se. Now in turning against consciousness, that means that you're not interested in thinking about the world

in terms of antagonists, people who have power and people who don't have power. If you're an Althusserian, for example, your focus shifts away from analyzing the relationship of the state to civil society, or looking at the strategic objectives of the neocons and how they are trying to destroy the labor movement through fiscal disciplinization and monetary policy, to abstract, anonymous, and essentially "authorless" processes of "interpellation" by which subjects are called or summoned into being by particular discourses. And if you're a Foucauldian, similarly, you aren't interested in the division of labor, or who controls the wealth, or how racism might be the ideological expression of the bad faith of whites. You're not interested per se in material institutions.

Nor are you interested in trying to *educate* people—e.g. to teach them the sociology of power. First of all, because you're skeptical that power is primarily a problem of who controls the resources of society. Second, because you conceive your own role, as an intellectual, not as that of an educator trying to enlighten the masses (still less to serve as a *leader*), but as a "specialist" whose role must be limited to conducting genealogical research into the origins of particular disciplinary practices. In short, you're interested in changing language, changing the way we comport our bodies. This got to a point towards the end of Foucault's life when he spoke of changing the way we comport our bodies and, as he said, stylizing our existence—a kind of aestheticization of politics, or rather an overcoming of politics by aesthetics.

Now, I myself have a problem with certain aspects of the Marxist and socialist tradition. Yet the language of solidarity, to take one example of a concept socialists take for granted, is utterly lacking in Foucault. While Foucault himself engaged in political actions, in his actual theories there's no good way to get traction on collective action using his framework. That's one of the things I find problematic.

Would you then say that action devolves to the individual and how a person chooses to live her or his life?
JS: Well, unfortunately, there is that tendency within Foucault's thought. Now as I've said, he himself was politically active. As far as I can discern he didn't have much of an impact on the prison system in France, but he did take a courageous position there and in some other instances. But one nowhere gets the sense reading Foucault that one can sit down and actually figure out how to change existing structures in society. His prescription is simply to act, and to act in ways that disrupt particular discourses. Yet the left does that to this day, or tries to, but we can see that action for the sake of action does not lead to material transformation, at least not automatically. So there is something missing in Foucault's account.

Clearly that ties back to what you have been saying about the New Left and the politics of expression. In *The Postmodern Prince*, you contrast the work of Foucault to that of Antonio Gramsci, the Italian Marxist who died in a Fascist jail in 1937. What was Gramsci's approach and how is it at variance with Foucault's?

JS: Foucault and Gramsci are both very popular theorists these days and a lot of people use both of them, but what I argue in my book is that they represent almost antithetical or antipodal approaches to thinking about social change. Gramsci, as you say, was an Italian Marxist. He was actually one of the founders of the Italian Communist Party and although he described himself as a Leninist, in many ways he was very critical of that kind of authoritarian and bureaucratic organization of the Communist Party. One can see this throughout his prison writings.

Gramsci believed that the only way to change society was to lead it in a new direction. That is, to establish a new set of norms more in keeping with a truly egalitarian, socialist ethos. Such a normative framework could not be expected simply to just "happen" on its own, spontaneously. It had to be organized. And the way to organize that kind of a movement, he thought, was to create what he called the *hegemonic bloc*. Theorists today tend to reduce the meaning of the hegemonic bloc to a kind of "coalition." But really, what Gramsci had in mind was something with a much more organic unity and longevity than is implied in the term *coalition*, with its opportunistic and ephemeral connotations. This organic unity would take form or shape in order to lead society in a new direction.

Foucault, on the other hand, was very skeptical of any leadership on the left or elsewhere. He felt that intellectuals had gotten in the way of ordinary people and that they should step aside and let the people kind of rise up on their own.

Now, one look at our own polity today would indicate that people are misled a lot of the time, that they have what the Marxists used to call "false consciousness." But that's just not something Foucault was willing to acknowledge—that the people could in fact misconstrue the nature of society, their "real conditions of existence," even their own interests. I think Foucault's almost naïve optimism regarding popular consciousness stemmed from the fact that at the time that he was most productive in his political writings there was a lot going on politically. He clearly felt that things were "moving" politically, and that events would continue to unfold in ways that were progressive. This helps to account for Foucault's initial infatuation with the Ayatollah Khomeini. As Janet Afary and Kevin Anderson show in *Foucault and the Iranian Revolution*, Foucault ignored evidence that the Islamists were systematically repressing leftists, feminists, and liberals in the immediate aftermath of the Revolution. From his basically Maoist perspective, there was no daylight between Khomeini and the Iranian people—they were one.

Foucault thus had a faith in spontaneous uprisings that Gramsci didn't have. Gramsci, of course, was as you say imprisoned by Mussolini and he saw the tragedy of the Italian left, which was fragmented, had dissolved into factions, and did not understand how to speak in a language that could unite the different elements of Italian society. So Gramsci, unlike Foucault, felt that the unity of the oppositional elements of society was possible, necessary—it was the only way to lead society. Foucault by contrast placed his hope and faith in what is now called "difference" or dispersion—in essence, decentralized, uncoordinated activity. And as I've been arguing, I don't think that approach is getting us anywhere.

This is a key dimension of the argument that you make in *The Postmodern Prince*, where you elucidate Gramsci and Foucault's two very distinct modes of thinking about politics and struggle. Foucault wrote about micro-political struggles and it is striking how his legacy can be found today in the global justice movement, where local struggles are emphasized while the ability and desirability of formulating struggle on a large scale tend to be dismissed. How does this the Foucauldian approach contrast with Gramsci's?

JS: As you say, Foucault believed in micro-politics at the level even of the individual human body. He said we shouldn't be thinking about grand strategy, we shouldn't be thinking about unity. Instead we should be thinking about difference, we should be thinking about local action and so forth. Gramsci, certainly, did not turn his nose up at local actions but he felt that unless the activity in question was somehow subordinate to and integrated with a larger vision, a strategy that could be coordinated at a national or even international level, that the different parts of the movement would tend to work at cross purposes to one another. He really believed that our differences did not have to get in the way of our understanding one other as human beings, and he felt that we could work together for common cause. That's obviously a socialist vision. What made Gramsci unique among Marxist thinkers was the way that he understood the dynamics of advanced capitalist culture. And he felt that in advanced capitalist contexts it was possible to ground a movement that wouldn't simply be based in, say, an abstract or deracinated proletarian consciousness, but rather in different social groups' *life experiences* and cultural identifications. Hence he sought a language of politics that could unite the workers in the north of Italy, say, with the peasants in the south with islanders and mainlanders, and so forth. So, it's a completely different way of viewing the world.

The key thing, just to bring it back to your original question, is that it's not a question of local versus global. It's a question of how to integrate the local into the global, and that's what Gramsci offers us.

I'd like to step back and talk about the larger social, political, and economic forces at work that allowed for the ascendancy of theories like those of Foucault to become so prominent and widespread. You link this emergence to a shift in the organization of production under capitalism.

JS: What I argue is that postmodernism came to ascendancy in the United States not on its own intrinsic merits (which is how the postmodernists account for their hegemonic control over the humanities as a field of knowledge), but because there were particular changes occurring in the Western university system in capitalist society, a reorganization of knowledge that favored the rise of this school of thought. In fact, unless we look at the social origins of postmodernism, we're not really going to understand why it has this hold on critical theory that it does to this day.

The Western university system expanded exponentially after World War II, when it became clear that the postwar American economy would need a highly skilled and highly educated work force. Millions of returning soldiers entered a newly modernized workforce, and many took advantage of the GI Bill and went to college. That was the beginning of a massive expansion in the system of higher education. By the 1960s, there was a felt need on the part of university administrators to corporatize the university, to streamline it, and so forth. The Free Speech Movement in Berkeley, which developed to challenge the University of California's prohibition against distributing political literature on campus, is one example of resistance to this new way of organizing knowledge, basically to turn the university into a factory of education (which of course is what we have ended up with today, in the twenty-first century).

Postmodernism or post-structuralism, meanwhile, began to be taken seriously in the United States and UK by the late 1970s, and by the 1980s had achieved certain vanguard status within the humanities (and later, by the 1990s, even in sectors of the social sciences). Now, what was going on at this time in the organization of knowledge? Within the university, partly out of resentment of the student protests of the New Left period, but mostly because of neoliberalization and the need to rationalize knowledge production, universities as a whole began to privatize and commodify knowledge in the sciences. At the same time, there was a decrease in state or public funding for education. Eventually, the humanities and social sciences began to feel the pinch.

New pressures began being placed on scholars in the humanities to produce more. There was a drive for innovation in critical theory that mirrored the Reagan era's new emphasis on entrepreneurial "innovation" in the economy. But at the same time, academic disciplines tend naturally toward conservativism and bureaucracy.

So a paradoxical dynamic sprang up in sectors of the humanities in which scholars were under contradictory pressures to, on the one hand, distinguish their intellectual "products" from the rest of the field (amid terrible professional pressures and dwindling jobs), and, on the other hand, to stay within the narrow boundaries of what was becoming received theoretical orthodoxy— the poststructuralist canon. This pushing and pulling on critical theory led to a certain standardization of thought. It also generated incentives for increasingly "sexy" forms of theorizing as a way for "sympathetic" or left intellectuals to maintain or advance their position in a crowded academic field.

It also provided some psychological consolation to intellectuals who were more and more marginal to state and society alike—a way to compensate for the decline of the left and the consequent marginalization of left intellectuals. Many young left intellectuals, after all, migrated from the 1960s street movements into the university system. How else are we to explain the fact that at precisely the same moment when the global left recedes into the historical background, loses all this power, we see postmodernism and all the various offshoots flourish to the wild extent that it has? It's surely paradoxical, that at this very moment of decline we see a huge boom in theory. You can buy a hundred thousand books on critical theory. But guess who is actually in charge, politically, socially? My point is that without this reorganization of knowledge in the university and, as I say, the commodification of knowledge, I don't think that postmodernism could have gotten the leg up that it did in academic thought and so come to mesmerize activists as well as academic intellectuals. Why does this matter? Because from about the mid-1970s to the present, left ideas and left thinking have yielded more and more diminished returns.

What I argue in my book is that the faddish quality of postmodernism, what I call *baroque theory*, after baroque architecture and art—i.e. a very elaborate and sophisticated-looking work that nonetheless has no real functional value—stems directly from the increasing commodification of knowledge that one sees from the 1980s onward. Whereas in the past a particular critical idea or concept—the state, say, or patriarchy or the division of labor—was used to illuminate empirical reality, and so had a direct "use value" for praxis, the concepts and ideas associated with the postmodern turn these past twenty-five years—the argot of cyborgs, border crossings, bodies, *différance*, the lack, abjection, et cetera—have not maintained a direct relation to the empirical world, let alone a connection with actual social movements trying to change concrete institutions. No sooner does one postmodernist scholar spin off one new concept—"Empire," say, or "the multitude"—than another one comes along and introduces yet another new theory-commodity, like "the state of exception" or "memes." We might say that the increasing pace of technological artifacts and commodities is being mirrored in the increased rate of the forced obsolescence of knowledge commodities—a faster and faster turnover rate of ideas.

You suggest that the ascendancy of poststructuralism was emblematic of a break between theory and practice that had not occurred on the left until then. Perry Anderson in *In the Tracks of Historical Materialism* argues that the theorists of the left traditionally were active leaders of mass movements as well. So someone like Rosa Luxemburg or Antonio Gramsci was connected to the movements that she or he were writing for and writing about. Would it be fair to say that after the defeats of the left, and the Stalinist ossification of the communist movement as well, the leaders of the left went into—or came out of—the universities, where they produced for the market rather than for activism?

JS: Yes. One of my central arguments is that the use-value of theory, as I call it, has been eclipsed by the exchange-value of academic theory. Which is a fancy way to say just what you've said, namely that with the growing gap between people who are getting paid to generate ideas and people who are active on the ground, actually struggling to change things in their communities, theory naturally becomes more elitist, certainly more distanced and abstract and complicated. Now, I have nothing against abstraction and complication. But I think the growing disjuncture between theory and practice has impoverished both practice and theory alike by making theory abstract and complicated in ways that tend to obscure social reality, rather than to illuminate it. Theory has become very highfalutin, head-in-the-clouds, and actually very strange in many ways (try reading Homi Bhabha sometime!).

Meanwhile, at the same time, we as activists and socialists became stuck in a kind of a rote script of protests and militancy, i.e. in activity disengaged from a general strategy of social change. We react to whatever is happening, whether it's the invasion of Iraq or the mining of the harbors of Nicaragua. We react and march around and then dissolve and then we just come together at the next crisis. And this would have been completely anathema to these earlier leaders who you mentioned, leaders like Rosa Luxemburg or Gramsci, who rightly understood that you have to be thinking long-term: you have to be thinking in terms of the totality of action, the balance of forces, where you want to go, articulating means to ends, and so forth.

I'm not just romanticizing the Old Left or socialism, either, because in the early stages of the second-wave feminist movement too, in the 1970s, there was not this rift, this great chasm between theory and practice. The feminists who were writing were also the ones making the social change.

Poststructuralist and postmodernist accounts of globalization tend to celebrate fragmentation, flows of capital and flows of culture and networks, and the erasure of place. It is striking how much they parallel in myriad ways the neoliberal celebration of the information society, information technology, and so on.

JS: Oh, absolutely. I'm glad you mentioned that, because in Hardt and Negri's book *Empire*, for example, they continually talk about border crossings and flows and so on as being liberatory and transgressive. There is a definite parallel between what's going on in terms of global capital and the way capital is organizing itself. Now Hardt and Negri are not dumb about this, they understand that. But what's odd is that they seem to be cheerleading capitalism itself. They seem to think that this is going to be capitalism's undoing. Somehow, this new mobility and the transfer of culture and information and technologies across continents, the mass movements of human beings and what they call bodies and bio-power, is going to lead to world transformation along the lines of a preferred leftist vision. But frankly, if you're a war refugee or an economic refugee or migrant worker, it just doesn't look that great on the ground.

Also, we know that with cultural instability can come fascism. Rootlessness doesn't mean that people will become more enlightened. Prospects for world socialism are not going to improve simply because there's a lot of activity and a lot of border crossings.

On the contrary, we human beings are threatened by change, we're all threatened by change to some extent, and that's one reason you're seeing a resurgence of neo-fascism and fundamentalism of all stripes, whether it's Christian or Muslim or Hindu or Judaic. The return of fundamentalist ideologies is directly related to all of this upset and to what Marx said, famously, in *The Communist Manifesto*, about the constant revolutionizing of the forces of production. All that is solid melts into air. And our reaction to that, as human beings, is often reactive and reactionary. So I don't think that simply cheerleading the forces of transitoriness, flux, dispersion and so forth is going to get us anywhere. It seems, if anything, as though this chaotic mess we're in is going to have the effect of further fragmenting our already fragmented movements, movements which are simply struggling to hang on in the face of enormous odds.

The global justice movement on the whole took the lack of a unifying vision as a positive. One would frequently hear that the strength of the movement was that it was made up of a multiplicity of movements and affinity groups and there was no leader and no one vision. Do you think they made a virtue out of weakness or was this the advent of a new flexible left?
JS: I think it's a kind of collective psychosis, I really do. Because, my God, look at the state of the world. Look at the acceleration of global warming, the destruction of the great coral reefs throughout the world. Look at the growth of Mormonism in Latin America, look at the explosive growth of evangelical and fundamentalist movements. You've got to ask yourself, if this diversity is our strength, how come it's not translating into actual political or social gains? I just find it almost, as I say, a psychosis, and I'm not even kidding. I do think that there is a kind of collective delusion on the left that we can just continue doing what we're doing and somehow everything will work out. And on the contrary, nothing is working out, really.

We need unity. We need the coherent hegemonic bloc Gramsci outlined in his *Notebooks*.

That isn't to say that diversity isn't essential. It is. Diversity is a part of our strength, because different movements reveal different aspects of the totality. I'm not suggesting that we go back to the Old Left. The "new" social movements of the last forty years together represent a crucial evolution in our understanding of oppression and society. The older Marxist-Leninist movements, for example, would probably never have recognized the need for gay rights. They would have seen it as maybe even reactionary and bourgeois. So, it's not a question of going back to a blinkered or monocausal view of the social order. On the other hand, we have to refuse the reification of the new movements themselves. This can be done by showing the relations and interconnections between and among different movements. Thus, to say that the gay rights movement or ecology movement is unrelated to or disconnected from the movement for class justice would be a misapprehension of the nature of injustice, which is of whole cloth, and of the nature of power, which also functions as a totality. What I'm saying is that the surface diversity and fragmentation masks an underlying commonality of interests and, therefore, the potential for unity in action and vision.

Yet couldn't the problem with the left being unified or not being unified stem from something deeper than the way we've gone about organizing ourselves? Could it be that the left is made up of a kind of a hodgepodge of working and middle class organization? The vision of a future society is not a bone of contention while we're languishing in opposition. But if

there were ever a chance to take power, would, say, groups like the Sierra Club find common ground with the Biotic Baking Brigade, HERE, or the Workers Solidarity Alliance?

JS: That's a great question. What I think you're getting at is the fact that there are contradictions and conflicts between and among our movements, which is of course true. There's no getting around it. But I'm not suggesting that we should unify ourselves by pretending that we don't have these conflicts and differences. What I'm saying is that if the Sierra Club really wants to change the way that nature is being systematically dismantled around the world, then it needs to adopt an anticapitalist view of things. If people in the women's rights movement want to create a feminist world, they will have to take seriously the oppression of animals and the way that our destruction and torture of animals is related to the domination of women historically and ideologically—and so forth.

It's not that we're going to agree on what the vision is overnight. What I'm saying is that right now we have a kind of theoretical bias in favor of fragmentation, a view of movement dispersion as though that's an end in itself and a self-evident virtue. It isn't. Certainly it's possible that dispersion could be a good tactic in some specific social circumstance; but in the present context, fragmentation is almost legislated by global capitalism. But if the nature of capitalism today is batch production, and fragmentation, or what the Hungarian Marxist Georg Lukács called reification, then we need to think very carefully before we intentionally mimic the spatiotemporal dynamics of capitalism at its strongest hour. Maybe we need to say, since fragmentation seems to be the order of the day, let's *not* fragment. That to me would be thinking counter-intuitively and creatively.

Having said that, it will not be easy to overcome fragmentation because there are different interests and conflicts within our movements. However, the task before us as I see it is to begin laying down the material and ideological or philosophical basis for achieving unity. That's going to be a long, arduous task. But I think we need to begin working on it.

What I've argued in *The Postmodern Prince* is simply that the left needs to think strategically and to take strategy seriously, which it does not right now. I also argue that the left needs leadership and that we need to develop a new generation of leaders who can think about these questions, coherently and at a global level. Just making that shift in our own movement culture, that change in the way we operate—thinking of ourselves in almost spiritual terms and seeing ourselves as cultivating leaders and developing strategy—that alone would constitute a revolutionary transformation in our movements.

Many activists see these fragmented, often nonhierarchical forms of organizing as an alternative to the deep-seated legacies of Stalinism, sectarianism, and authoritarian hierarchical traditions within the left. Is there a way to have leadership and yet avoid the problems of the past?

JS: I was asked that question. The woman who asked it was an activist—I won't say with which organization, but it's a national, very grassroots, radical organization. And she said that this question of leadership was coming to the fore in her own organization because the rank and file wanted to embrace radical, democratic politics and therefore didn't want leadership. And yet everybody knew that they were leaders in their own organization. They were just unwilling to establish some formal mechanism of accountability for them.

So I'd say, first of all, and this is something Gramsci said, that even in the most "spontaneous" organizations there are always leaders. There are people who are either more capable, who persevere more, who just show up at the meetings and de facto they become leaders. And I think having leaders who are not accountable is a big problem. Secondly, Stalinism does not necessarily simply mean a top down, hierarchical organization (although we have that with, say, International ANSWER and some of the sects who have been controlling the peace movement in recent years). Stalinism can be a kind of ethos, it can be political correctness of a certain kind, it can be silencing, it can be orthodoxy, and one sees this all the time on the left. And not just on the left of course—it pervades our dysfunctional society, in civil society, in nonprofits, in the corporate world. So there's no guarantee that "Stalinism" does not permeate even the most radical anarchist group. I mean, I know some very intolerant and closed-minded anarchists. Of course, I know some wonderful anarchists too—but what I'm saying is that I know people who I would not want in positions of power because they silence people and so forth, even though they are not formally acknowledged as leaders.

In short, I don't think that embracing disorganization and fragmentation is any kind of inoculation against authoritarianism or abuse of power within a particular movement. You can have authoritarianism in scattered movements. In fact, you might just get stuck with fifty different tinplate dictators, instead of one.

What opportunities are posed for the left by the financial meltdown of capitalism?

JS: Certainly the world economic crisis offers the best strategic opening the left has had since the early 1930s. Here's an opportunity to organize the unemployed, educate the public about the way banks really work, and hasten the legitimation crisis of the whole system. An antiglobalization movement in today's context, when the financial system is being held together with wax and baling wire, would look very different than it did in 1994, at the apogee of finance capital. Yet where is there any sign of the left organizing a response? Where are the mutual aid societies at the community level, to shelter the homeless, feed the poor, politicize the under- and unemployed? Where is the coordinated international response? Nothing is happening. On the contrary, it is the extreme right that is rallying the grassroots in the U.S. and Europe.

I believe that so long as the left clings to its familiar rituals and its fragmented view of itself, it will be unable to respond to this crisis, or to convince the rest of humankind that a more just and egalitarian world order is possible. Unfortunately, to return to my obstinate theme in this interview, postmodernist theory has so dulled the left's senses that few people are giving sustained thought to how we might go about things differently.

CHAPTER FOURTEEN

Noam Chomsky: Anarchism, Council Communism, and Life After Capitalism

You've identified from a young age as an anarchist, and during your lifetime the popularity of anarchism has fallen and risen. Has your core philosophy, your anarchism, evolved or changed during the course of your life?
NC: It's not what it was when I was ten years old. Fundamentally, it has not changed. That's because the core philosophy just seems like common sense I don't see how anybody cannot accept it. The core principles as far as I understand it—anarchism covers a wide range, you can't encapsulate it in formulas—but there seems to be a thread that runs all the way through it. It's basically a skepticism about any form of authority, or domination, or submission. The basic idea is that domination and hierarchy are not self-justifying. They have to justify themselves and the burden of proof is theirs to bear. And if they can't justify themselves, then they should be dismantled. And that covers everything from personal relations to international affairs. Then out of that comes various varieties of anarchism depending on what you're looking for in the future, what are the alternatives to authority, and so on. But almost everything decent in human life seems to fall under that. So no, that hasn't changed.

The tendency of anarchism that you subscribe to—anarcho-syndicalism—overlaps fairly closely with council communism, with the notion of worker councils. For the public at large, the assumption is that an anarchist society is one where people run amuck, where chaos reigns.
NC: That's the propaganda that people are exposed to. Actually anarchist views were mostly of highly organized societies.

What would that society look like—a society of worker councils?
NC: Worker councils I think should be one component of it. So it means in any institution, say a university, a factory, whatever it is, the participants would run it; would run it through councils in which people participated, where they could make decisions. Actually, It's not unlike a faculty, which is about as close to the model as we get in our world. There are outside controls, but the faculty pretty much makes decisions of what happens to the faculty internally. Actually, one of the things that makes university life appealing, much more so than higher paid professions, is that you're running your own life to a large

extent. I mean, there are duties but technically they are supposed to be shared and shared by common agreement. You may decide to work eighty hours a week, but it's the eighty hours you pick and it's the topics that you choose to work on, and it comes out as a inner need rather than external compulsion. And I think that's the kind of model everything should turn towards.

Worker councils would be one component of a freely organized society, but they'd have to interact with others. So an institution, say a factory, whatever it is, is in a community and the community should have a comparable form of self-organization and self-management, and then they have to interact. And those are complex interactions, because many people are part of a lot of them.

As an anarchist society would develop, of the kind that I think is desirable, it would have to deal with quite concrete problems about the nature of self-government, the nature of administration. Do you want to distribute jobs so that they are fixed or do you want circulations of responsibilities and of actions? And there's no simple answer to that. Like you want people to be trained as surgeons and on the other hand you don't want all the dirty work to be done by a special category of people. So that has to be worked out, the distribution of job functions, interactions between different forms of what should be voluntary association. And there are many other problems like what if somebody doesn't want to be part of it and take on the responsibilities of a community? Those are problems that would exist in any society. And they would exist in a different form in a more free society. And at this point you have lots of different ideas, so there are people, basically anarchists, who think that pay, payment, what you earn from your work, should be proportional to effort. There are others who think that's not an appropriate model, that it should be independent of effort. I tend toward the latter, but most of my friends tend toward the former. But these are real questions and there are innumerable ones.

Thinking about the road to a stateless society, you have written that radicals should defend those gains that have been fought for and won and are embodied in the state, such as Social Security and progressive taxation. Other anarchists might argue that this holds people within the paternalistic grip of the state. Why do you come down where you do?
NC: You have to ask what the alternatives are. Many anarchists just consider the state as the fundamental form of oppression. I think that's a mistake. I mean of the various kinds of oppressive institutions that exist, the state is among the least of them.

The state at least to the extent that society is democratic with various degrees and types—but to the extent that it's democratic you have some influence on what happens in the state. You have no influence on what happens in a corporation. They're really tyrannies and as long as society is largely dominated by private tyrannies, which is the worst form of oppression, people just need some form of self-defense. And the state provides some form of self-defense. And to say, let's dismantle Social Security, means concretely let's decide that that disabled widow across town will starve to death. I don't agree with that.

In recent years there's been a fair amount of debate about what the fundamental transformation of society might require. There are those who argue that radicals need to change the world without taking power, while others believe that a revolution of some kind would be necessary. Do you see one side or the other as correct? And do you see the role of preexisting state formations—say nationalized industries—as playing a part in such a transformation?

NC: I don't there's a general answer. It depends a lot on circumstances. So, say right now, with the bailout of the banks, a dedicated anarchist might say, "Look, I don't even want to talk about this. There shouldn't be any banks." That's like saying, "I'm not going to talk about getting rid of nuclear weapons because everyone should live in peace." I mean, these things are kind of like a chess game. There's no point in coming in and saying, "Well, I just want to mate the king." No, you've got to say, "What are you going to do about that pawn over there?" You have to get places in stages. It's just a gift to the forces of oppression to say, "I'm not going to talk about anything except the final state." Okay, then fine, we'll keep things as they are.

So sometimes things like nationalization might be a positive step. For the government to have, say, bought Citigroup, I think it would have made more sense than to have bailed it out at a far greater expense. Once it's bought, then the question comes up: how's it run? Is it run by the community, by its participants? Is it sold off to some other corporation? I just don't see how there can be a general answer. You have to ask about the particular circumstances. Like I say, if you're playing chess you have to ask about whatever happens to be in front of you.

One of the currents within anarchism in the U.S. does not view class as a central axis for understanding society and conceiving a future society. Why do you think that this tendency has gotten traction—and why don't you agree with it?

NC: It's gotten some traction because of the class struggle which exists has become one-sided. I mean, there is one group of people who are basically vulgar Marxists and who are dedicated to class struggle, constantly: that's the business class. It's a highly class-conscious business class. They are fighting a bitter class struggle all the time. If everyone else had said, "Hey, we're going to worry about something else," they win. And it's become an attractive position, for one thing, because it allows you to focus your attention on things that are quite important, but aren't going to change the class struggle. Take gay rights. It's a good cause; you can be working on gay rights. But if gays had hundred-percent rights, the institutional structure of oppression, the core of it, would remain unchanged. You can see that.

Take South Africa. Overthrowing apartheid was a major achievement, but for the majority of the population it didn't mean a lot. Now there are black faces in the limousines, but the townships are as awful or worse as they ever were. The class structure remained. Just one aspect of it softened, so now its not strict white-black.

There's less resistance from power centers when you are trying to right cultural and social wrongs, than there is trying to modify the fundamental core properties of oppression and domination, so its easy to drift into those. And it's not wrong. It's right. We should deal with these things. But the class struggle is not going to go away—unless you abandon it and say, "Okay, they win."

Switching gears slightly, I wanted to ask you about science—and of course this interview is being conducted in your office at MIT. How do you understand science? Do you think it's socially or politically neutral?
NC: To a degree. I mean, of course it's influenced by outside forces. Science goes where the money is. It has to. It doesn't much in my field—we work with pencil and paper. But say if you're in the chemistry lab, you just have to get money. Otherwise you can't do anything. And money comes from one of several sources: it could come from the government or it could come from a private corporation. That's about it. Those are the basic sources of money. Of which you pick, and what you do, does affect the work you do. Also what you do is affected by general cultural attitudes. It's been argued with some plausibility I think that the way evolution is interpreted has been influenced by the kind of society in which evolutionary theory was developed. It's been argued with some degree of plausibility, I don't know how much, that the competitive, nature red-in-tooth-and-claw Social Darwinian approach to evolution is affected by the fact that it developed within a competitive state capitalist society.

One very well known biologist has argued—this is Lynn Margulis, whose work was on symbiogenesis—that species change takes place not by competition and the defeat of some genes by others, but by incorporating some genomes into other organisms, say bacteria. It's kind of a cooperative mode of evolution, if you like. It's possible those things are influenced by general social cultural values. The fact, say, that nuclear physics developed is not unrelated to that fact that the military wanted nuclear weapons.

But by and large, I think, science develops from its own internal needs. You can only work on the problems that are at the borders of understanding. It's one of the reasons why when the Pentagon supported science—like MIT, like me, say—it tended to be the most free. MIT, say, in the 1960s was about 100 percent Pentagon funded. I was working in a lab that was 100 percent funded by the three armed services. It was also one of the country's centers of anti-war resistance. There was no real conflict over that. In the Pentagon's view, I presume, they were funding the development of the next stage of the economy. And from our view we were working on things that looked interesting. So the two more or less mesh; there's some influence from one on the other.

Since the 1970s, postmodernism has had a great deal of influence on at least part of the left in this country. It has been characterized, among other things, as quite critical of science and the Enlightenment tradition. I wonder if you could talk about your view of postmodernism and whether you think its influence is waning?

NC: I have to say that a lot of postmodern work I just don't understand, so I can't comment on it. It seems to me to be some exercise by intellectuals who are talking to each other in very obscure ways and I can't follow it and I don't know if anyone else can. Postmodern views of science, by and large, have been pretty embarrassing. There is some interesting work on this. There's a book by two physicists, Jean Bricmont and Alan Sokal, both of them happen to be political radicals, just running through, mostly Paris postmodernists, but what postmodern commentators have said about science—and it's really embarrassing, to the extent that you can understand it.

On the other hand, there is a point, insofar as they say that everything people do is some kind of social construction that depends on the historical context, on the cultural context; that part is true. I don't know if you need the whole postmodern baggage to say those things. My feeling is not. At least personally I haven't seen anything that seems to me can't be said in monosyllables (to exaggerate for effect); insofar as I understand it, it's pretty straightforward. There is a drive among intellectuals to make things look difficult. It's a kind of self-protection. "If what I'm doing can be done by the guy who's repairing my furnace, then who am I? Then there's those physicists over there who talk in complicated things and have to, and I don't understand them, so I'd like to be like them." That drive is clearly there and I think should be resisted. We should say things simply so people can understand them.

Postmodernism has also been characterized by a fairly fierce attack on the legacy of the Enlightenment.

NC: It has. I have no idea what that means. I'm happy to be part of the legacy of the Enlightenment.

That's what I want to ask you about. In some circles, it's actually a quite an unpopular stance to take. What does that mean to you to continue in some way the legacy of the Enlightenment?

NC: Well, the Enlightenment, like any major movement in human life, was pretty complicated, but among its major features were its commitment to ideas that I feel were basically anarchist. So take say ideas about, say, the division of labor and let's take a typical Enlightenment figure like Adam Smith. What did he have to say about the division of labor? Here it's worth reading. I mean, everyone has read the first paragraph of *The Wealth of Nations*, where the butcher does his thing and everybody else does their own thing and everything comes out fine and the division of labor is marvelous. On the other hand if you read into it a few hundred pages he comes out as a figure of the Enlightenment. He says the division of labor will turn human beings into creatures as stupid and ignorant as a person can possibly be. It will drive them into repeating rote work on command. And therefore in any civilized society the government will have to move in and stop it. Well, that's a version of a standard Enlightenment idea: that your own intelligence and creative abilities derive from what you do freely, out of inner impulse, not on command.

Wilhelm von Humboldt, one of the founders of what we call classical liberalism, a figure of the Enlightenment, he encapsulated it by saying that if a craftsperson does—he said "craftsman" of course—if a craftsman produces a beautiful object on command, we'll admire what he does but we'll despise what he is. He is a tool under somebody else's control, like a machine that's producing that beautiful object. If we want that person to be a real human being, they should be doing things under their own internal impulses and then even if he doesn't create that beautiful object, we'll still admire that person who he is. And that's an Enlightenment idea that grows out of a conception of human intelligence, human creativity, and it's a very good ideal. The same with say values like freedom of speech. I think we should preserve that. Even the questioning of authority and dominance, that's a core Enlightenment value. So I don't see what's wrong with them.

I'd like to ask you about another set of ideas, perhaps as labyrinthine as postmodern ones: conspiracy theories, which have become quite popular

amongst those people who identify as progressive. I know you've been fairly critical of those ideas. Why do you think that they are popular now?
NC: First of all, there are conspiracies. No question about it. In fact, sometimes they have big effects. Take the suburbanization of America. It's the result of huge government, corporate-state engineering projects, which were largely dedicated to maximizing the inefficient use of fossil fuels, with everything that goes along with it. It may destroy the species, so it's not insignificant. But it did start as a literal conspiracy of General Motors, Standard Oil of California, and Firestone Rubber to buy up and destroy the fairly efficient electric transport system in Los Angeles and other cities and turn it into the monstrosity we have. That was a conspiracy. In fact, they were taken to court and fined a couple thousand dollars.

But looking for something hidden that's beneath the surface and that's really running things—I think that sometimes it's true—but usually in my view it turns out to be a pathology. I think it comes from a sense that "I don't like the way things are so there must be some hidden hand somewhere that's manipulating and controlling it." Whereas when you look closely I think you just see the normal workings of institutional structures. That makes you, of course, raise questions about the nature of the society, who we are, how we tolerate it, and so on.

So, for example, its appealing to believe that say John F. Kennedy, one of the main figures in what are called conspiracy theories, it would be nice to believe he was just a fantastically nice guy, who was going to do all kinds of great things, and they just shot him down because he was so wonderful and the world has gone off to hell in a handbasket since then. Well, it's a comforting feeling. It's less comforting to realize what I think the documentary record demonstrates, and the historical record, that he was kind of a hawk, a politician who was trying to gain power by the usual techniques. He was kind of affable and friendly and smiled and knew how to butter people up. But if you take a look at what he was doing, he was pretty horrible. He was one of the worst, most dangerous creatures of the twentieth century and fortunately didn't blow up the world, but came pretty close. That's a less comforting position. I happen to think it's largely true.

The same with Barack Obama. There's a widespread feeling on the left, with Middle Eastern commentators, and so on that he's really dedicated to doing wonderful things, it's just that dark forces are preventing him. So we just have to hope that he's going to be able to overcome the dark forces, like the hero in a fairytale and somehow he'll get rid of the witches and dragons, and everything will be nice. I don't think there's any truth to that. I think he's exactly what he seems to be, and nobody's going to ride in on horseback and get rid of the dragons and the witches. We've got to do it ourselves. That's harder.

Right. So would you say that conspiracy theories in general are not particularly helpful for radical politics and radical action?

NC: If they are inaccurate. I mean, if they are accurate, as they sometimes are, then, sure, they help explain the world. But most of what happens . . . In a sense, it's a conspiracy if the board of directors of General Motors get together and decide, okay, here are our plans for next year. It's kind of a conspiracy, but we don't call that a conspiracy theory because it's the normal working of institutions. And similarly when during the Second World War, the highest State Department planners and comparable figures from the private sector, like the Council on Foreign Relations, did meet and extensively discussed the nature of the postwar world and laid plans which were pretty well executed; well, this happened to be public. But was this a conspiracy when they got together, they worked up plans, they later implemented them? Small groups of people; they have special interests, not the interests of the population. Exposing that makes perfect sense. But it's not what is called a conspiracy theory, because that's the way institutions operate. That makes sense.

What you have to ask is whether the theories of the conspiracy are accurate. So let's take, say, the idea that the Bush administration plotted to blow up the World Trade Center. That attracts huge support. Maybe a third of the population believes it, and there are very dedicated groups of people, many of them on the left, who are just committed to that. Is it plausible? Suppose somebody conspired to blow up the World Trade Center. We know what they did. They blamed it on the Saudis. Would the Bush administration blame it on the Saudis thereby shooting themselves in the feet, if they wanted to invade Iraq? So if they organized it, they would have blamed it on Iraqis, then they'd have no problem at all getting Congressional authorization, a UN resolution, NATO would join in, and everybody saying let's invade Iraq. Instead whoever did it blamed it on Saudis. That absolves the Bush administration, short of outright insanity. Why harm your relations with a valued ally instead of blaming it on the people you want to invade? So it's already a barrier to even entertaining the possibility. The elaborate work that goes into—I mean, there's a lot of work that goes into questions like "is there nano-thermite in Building 7" or whatever it is—it's kind of beside the point. Maybe there was, maybe there wasn't. Unless you have a pretty sophisticated knowledge of civil engineering and structural architecture, you can't even make a judgment about whether it means anything. But there are obvious, clear phenomena that the theory has to deal with somehow and doesn't. And if it doesn't, then I don't see any reason to take it seriously.

So yes, then it becomes one of these kinds of conspiracy theories that just mislead and misdirect energy. In fact, it wouldn't surprise me that, say, forty years from now that we get some declassified documents that show that the Bush administration was very sympathetic to these theories; they were diverting energy from real crimes into things that were basically a wild goose chase. Actually, we have documents like that about the Kennedy assassination, so there are Pentagon advisory documents which advise the government to periodically leak information about the Kennedy assassination basically so as to keep people out of their hair. You know, let them follow those nonexistent leads, instead of asking us questions that we really don't want to answer.

So it's a real conspiracy theory then?
NC: And there we had the actual documents. It wouldn't shock me if there are similar things about 9/11 conspiracies. I mean, they do have an immediate effect. They drew a lot of energy and effort away from major crimes, the crimes which are a lot worse than blowing up the World Trade Center. So that's convenient for the powerful. You know, the theories seem to have just major logical problems that I don't see how they can confront, like what I mentioned. It does seem to me to be the kind of theory which misleads and misdirects and it's not hard to see why it's popular. I mean, there are some terrible things going on, there should be some dark hand behind it. "We hate Bush and Rumsfeld for good reasons. So maybe they're behind it."

It seems indisputable that we're facing an ecological crisis. And obviously different currents within the radical left view it in different ways. One current within anarchism—anarcho-primitivism associated with John Zerzan and Derrick Jensen—postulates that the only way for the planet to survive is if we go back to pre-industrial society or even pre-agrarian societies. What do you think of that kind of argument?
NC: That's a factual claim. I mean, if they happen to be right, then we have to be in favor of mass genocide on a scale that's never even been contemplated. Okay, what happens to the six billion people around the world? They can't live in a stone-age society or an agricultural society. So if that factual claim happens to be correct, we're lost.

It's not a prescription for action. Nobody's proposing a course of action seriously that will lead us to a pre-industrial society. I mean, you couldn't get ten people to even listen to you if you suggested that. For good reason: it means mass genocide. So it's not a prescription; it's a factual claim. Which I doubt is correct. But if it happens to be correct, then we're lost.

CHAPTER FIFTEEN

Andrej Grubačić: Libertarian Socialism for the Twenty-First Century

David Graeber and you wrote a very influential essay titled "Anarchism, or the Revolutionary Movement of the 21st Century." How did you characterize this new anarchism and how it differed from the anarchism of old?

AG: That essay was originally written for *Le Monde Diplomatique*, but they ended up rejecting it. The idea was very simple: we felt that there was a new orientation within the global justice movement, and that this orientation resembles those characteristics that anarchists traditionally celebrated. At the same time, we observed that, in conjunction with the new global movement, a new anarchist movement was emerging. What was a decisive quality of this new configuration, and principal reason why we emphasized its novelty, was the global orientation of this emerging anarchism.

In anarchist history, the term *new anarchism* was usually used as a reference to a few British and American thinkers: Herbert Read, Alex Comfort, Colin Ward, Murray Bookchin, and Paul Goodman. The more recent type of anarchism, however, resembled those glorious days of the early twentieth century, when anarchism was the heart and soul of the global revolutionary movement, when Italian Errico Malatesta was organizing in Buenos Aires, and Cuban Tarrida del Mármol was giving passionate talks about "anarchism without adjectives" in Barcelona. The new anarchism David and I were describing was anarchism without adjectives, or "small-'a' anarchism," as we called it, existing largely outside of the historical anarchist organizations, and without much interest, or patience, for sectarian and dogmatic conversations about how many anarchist martyrs can dance on the head of a pin.

As a revolutionary tradition that was historically the least Eurocentric, anarchism was ideally placed to become a new inspiration for the new, global movement. This was an exciting development. There were networks, decentralized and experimental models of directly democratic organization, global days of actions, celebration of new forms of democracy.

As a fellow traveler of Peoples' Global Action yourself, how formally close was the relationship between the antiglobalization movement and this new strain of anarchism, as you saw it?

AG: I would actually paraphrase Faulkner and I would say that the movement was not anarchist-centered, but it was and is definitely anarchist-haunted, in the sense that I would be very hesitant to call the courageous people in Argentina or *campesinos* in Bolivia or other places, or Zapatistas even—to call them anarchists. But they are definitely always what anarchists have purported to defend.

They are practicing the principles of prefigurative direct action, of creating a new society based on egalitarian practices without any coercive institutions, without states or private coercive institutions. And in that sense I think that anarchists were right in one particular thing, which is that the most interesting leaps to postcapitalist society do come from people who are still in some kind of touch and communication with their precapitalist, prestatist, prehierarchical life ways—so indigenous people in the Global South.

The relationship between the antiglobalization movement and anarchism was an exciting one, of mutual recognition, and mutual discovery. There would be no new anarchism without the new global movement, and without new anarchism the global movement would have probably looked quite different. Peoples' Global Action, it is important to note, was never an anarchist organization. PGA was formed around five simple hallmarks including rejection of capitalism and imperialism, all systems of domination and discrimination; a call to direct action and civil disobedience; and an organizational philosophy based on decentralization and autonomy.

There were never spokespersons, founders, experts, or members. This was a truly global network, inspired by the Zapatista uprising, and co-created by Global South farmers and European activists. But, reading these hallmarks, it is impossible to miss the anarchistic sensibility that underlines it. Insistence on horizontality, autonomy, decentralization, and direct action, is part and parcel of anarchist tradition. However, networks such as PGA stayed very clear from traditional anarchist institutions, soaked in history, like the CNT or the IWA.

Although the movement claimed to have none, anyone who was close to it knows that there were de facto leaders. Do you think the organizational structure of the alter-globalization movement was a weakness in any way—the presence or absence of leaders, the fragmented and heterogeneous nature of the movement—given how quickly it fell apart following the invasions of Afghanistan and Iraq?
AG: After 9/11 in the United States, and Genoa in Europe, the networks and connections that were built during the cycle of struggles in the 1990s were still in place. But there was not a coherent response to imperial globality and neoliberal violence, owing partially to some profound mistakes made by the movement. The World Social Forum was in a serious crisis, and Peoples' Global Action had more or less disappeared from the revolutionary horizon. Groups

I used to work with, like Direct Action Network in New York, were nowhere to be found, and the global movement was in a process of a search for a new orientation. The whole context that David Graeber and myself had described as a coalescing "new anarchism" was in a state of confusion.

Ezequiel Adamovsky wrote an important essay on the need for new institutions. I agreed with him, which led to a political disagreement with many comrades from the antiglobalization movement. It became clear to me that, at least in the long term, we should not anchor our efforts in the hope for encounters and summits. The lifestyle of activists who "summit hop" from one brief-lived action to the next is, in the long-run, unsustainable. Not because counter-summits are useless—we used them as schools and laboratories of direct democracy and new internationalism—but because they were not enough. There was a need for a new emancipatory program. It was my feeling that in running away from traditional models of organizing we ended up running too far, and far too quick.

In *Wobblies and Zapatistas*, which you coauthored with Staughton Lynd, you argue that the way out of the impasse that radicals have found themselves is to be found in a fusion of anarchism and Marxism. Why do you think a synthesis with Marxism is desirable?

AG: The way that people are defining anarchism—in the new anarchism—is an effort to create what we like to call prefigurative or anticipatory institutions in the here and now and try to live these institutions, to live these experiences, to experience as much as we can. And to create viable experiments that might eventually replace the dominant structure of society and dominant distribution of power. Marxism, on the other hand, works to delineate the idea of and effort of understanding the structure of the society that we live in, so we can act with more efficiency, with more intelligence, with more courage, and with more strategy. And I think that we need both.

I think it would be extremely irresponsible to say that we don't need both theory and action at the same time—what in Yugoslavia we called praxis, following Marx. And in that sense, and in that particular context, libertarian socialism—the red and black, as you like to call it—the unity of red and black, or the movement of red and black, is a very appropriate way of thinking about a revolutionary synthesis that would animate a truly popular movement today here in the United States.

We need both orientations to accomplish the needed task of transformation, and formulation of a new program. Staughton and I have argued that in North America there is a tradition we termed the "Haymarket synthesis," the tradition of the so-called "Chicago school" of anarchism, represented by Albert

Parsons, August Spies, and the other Haymarket martyrs, who all described themselves as anarchists, socialists, and Marxists.

Today there is a serious resurgence and revival of anarchism, but I would also say left libertarianism more generally—a meeting of leftwing Marxism, like council communism and ideas courageously expressed by Rosa Luxemburg and many others, of spontaneity, democratic socialism, that come very close to anarchism. And they are rooted in what many people today would criticize as old-fashioned workerist ideas of councils and council communism and the industrial structure of the society.

Anarchism has always had very many strands. And I always thought—and this I guess is what makes me an anarchist—that anarchism is a theory and philosophy of freedom and the very essence of freedom, and thereby the very essence of anarchism, is diversity. I mentioned earlier a particular strand of anarchism called anarchism without adjectives, which actually comes from the Global South—comes from the Cuban anarchists back in the nineteenth century—and it goes to the idea that anarchism needs to embrace diversity of different strands. But the way that I like to think about anarchism is that it is a profoundly beautiful tradition, not an ideology—certainly not an identity—but a tradition that is by its very definition not just nonsectarian, but very aggressively—or should be—antisectarian. And in a way that's what it should be.

That is the kind of anarchism or libertarian socialism that I am advocating. And in that sense, a synthesis with Marxism is a very natural thing. We are not trying to reinvent the wheel. Libertarian socialism is something that many serious revolutionaries have been involved in: Rudolf Rocker comes to mind and the whole revolutionary syndicalist tradition. The United States is a particularly interesting country and North America is a really interesting continent for thinking about different historical examples of this meeting. But it's absolutely desirable.

Let's turn to the origins of the split between anarchists and socialists. In 1864, the International Working Men's Association was founded as an umbrella of radicals, trade unionists, socialists, and anarchists—all opponents of capital. But the anarchists, led by Mikhail Bakunin, and the socialists, led by Karl Marx, rancorously parted ways in 1872 over means rather than ends. Since then, anarchists and socialists have been uneasy allies, and often outright antagonists. What were the stakes for socialists and anarchists at the time of the split?

AG: The First International, and the internationalists in general, were sort of a motley crew, where all sorts of socialists of the time were meeting and encountering each other. There were different traditions—and we have to remember always the situation, the relationships between what became known as the anarchists, and people who followed and read closely and were close with Karl Marx, was not always a hostile one. The thing is that, for me as a historian, that really beautiful and challenging century—the nineteenth century— discloses so much of an amazing revolutionary potential that has been mobilized through the internationals.

One way of thinking about the split is as a conflict between two powerful personalities: Mikhail Bakunin and Karl Marx. But I think it goes beyond that. There were strategic differences that I think are very important to talk about. The internationals also not only combined different political temperaments, but they combined people coming from different regional traditions. So, for example, people who were artisans, people who were coming from the Mediterranean—especially people coming from the Mediterranean—and who used to look very suspiciously at the new industrial order and to new ideas being promoted by what they recognized as authoritarian revolutionaries. And the very word authoritarian does come from this period. And later on to be recognized by Bakunin as people who were promoting the red bureaucracy, which Bakunin called "the vilest lie of our century." And I think that he was right, he was amazingly perceptive that if we instituted that kind of bureaucracy, what we were going to end up having would be somebody worse than the Tsar, worse than the emperor himself in Russia.

So the basic differences between what we should call the anarchist-inspired current, that was to become an anarchist movement in the nineteenth century, and what was to become a Marxist political movement, in its two incarnations— one being revolutionary Marxism, and the other being social democracy, which was especially strong as you know in Germany—the main differences were the ways in which we go about creating the new society and creating a new revolutionary movement. Engels argued in 1882, that the anarchists understood the thing from the wrong side—they had it upside down is the famous quote from Engels. Anarchists disagreed.

As you just mentioned, Marxists and anarchists, despite their moments of overt conflict and animosity, from the nineteenth century to the present, believe in similar ends: establishing a communist society. In some ways, the fact that the ends were agreed upon is fairly remarkable. Yet the difference, particularly as it was framed in the nineteenth century, was about the means to get there—and particularly the question of the state. Marxists argued that there needed to be a transitional process where the state was used to by the working class to keep the capitalists from coming back to

power and to transition into a state of communism. Whereas for anarchists, the state was seen as intrinsically problematic, even in transition.

AG: Absolutely. May I mention an intimate way of thinking about this that goes back to my family and the way that I was brought up? I was raised in Communist Yugoslavia and my whole family was actually involved in bringing about a Communist revolution in 1945. There was a huge eruption, a huge social transformation, because the guerrilla warfare was led by the Communist partisans. So my family was very intimately involved in this process of revolutionary transformation. They were all Marxist Leninists.

The thing that is interesting about this story is that because of how bureaucratic socialist countries worked, some of them ended up in a little bit of trouble. My grandmother had a particularly problematic experience, yet remained a communist until her very last days. She was a great inspiration for me. I remember I was twelve years old and she gave me all kinds of books to read and I remember she gave me Feuerbach and all kinds of things that usually twelve-year-olds can't really understand. So I was really confused, but then again I was really enthusiastic and I was reading this and trying to understand what the hell this was all about. And she said, "It's time for you to become a materialist—please don't become an idealist." And this was where she was coming from. And I remember specifically this conversation when I was about twelve years old, when she told me, "You know, I'm still a communist."

Yugoslavia was truly independent of the Soviet Union and very much antagonistic to both the capitalist West and the Soviet Union. In 1948, under Marshal Tito they discovered something, in an interesting way, they stumbled upon guild socialist writings. Although this was never made public, the main theorist of Yugoslav self-management Edvard Kardelj immersed himself in books by G. D. H. Cole about guild socialism and books by Rudolf Rocker about anarcho-syndicalism. The guild socialists were also trying to find a synthesis between libertarian and some other currents within the socialist tradition. So the architects of Yugoslav self-management, this different conception of socialism, discovered something that was called the Yugoslav path to socialism, in opposition to Stalin. And it definitely contained, within this rigid, authoritarian framework, some libertarian elements. When I say libertarian, I mean it in the European sense—left libertarian, meaning libertarian socialist, meaning emancipatory.

But, going back to my grandmother, the thing that she told me was, "I will always be a communist, even in this situation where Yugoslavia, this beautiful dream that I gave my life to, is falling apart. We were profoundly mistaken about the path we took to discover and institute communism. So the role of your generation is to find a different path to communism." I was twelve and

I was transformed by her words. And I went on reading and that's how I discovered anarchism and later on libertarian socialism as a component of anarchism, where anarchism meets the left wing of the Marxist tradition. I thought back then, and I still think today—especially in the framework of global capitalist crisis that we are living through today—this is a path that I would choose to walk toward what my grandmother used to see as the communist ideal.

When I became an anarchist, of course, I became very critical of the socialist heritage of my grandparents and of socialist Yugoslavia. Today I am much less critical, because it's a serious dilemma. And it cuts to the heart of the disagreement between Marxists and anarchists, and even Marx and Bakunin. Because the idea was very simple: people like my grandfather and my grandmother said that people are too injured by capitalism, they're too injured by the systems of domination and hierarchy—they used a slightly different language but that was the basic point—that we simply cannot expect them to be able to create a new society within the shell of the old. What we need to do is to seize state power and then—and that was a famous socialist phrase—create a new socialist humanity and create a new man. After meeting many people who call themselves anarchists and Marxists, I am much less harsh on my grandparents for thinking that taking state power and then creating something new is most viable thing.

However, I do think—and I still believe—that we have enough strength in ourselves, in the way that we organize, that there are enough seeds beneath the snow of the centralized authoritarian possessive institutions, that there is enough in this humanity that we have here today with us within this present structure that we can use to build a new society without the necessity—which is the great disagreement between anarchists and Marxists—of taking state power.

What moments of synthesis between anarchism and socialism would you point to in the late twentieth century?
AG: I'm going to surprise you with the answer and not say 1968. I'm going to a few years before and say the Hungarian Revolution of 1956. After the 20th Congress of the Russian Communist Party after Khrushchev decided to apologize for the misdeeds of Stalin, there was a huge upsurge in Hungarian civil society, as it would be called today. Students and activist intelligentsia came and started something that was called the Petőfi Circle and they started creating new institutions. They started organizing what I call self-activity or self-governance. It just spread all over the country in a few days, maybe even in a matter of hours. It was absolutely fascinating. And then a few months after that, the workers joined. So it was a meeting of workers, creating their own institutions, and what we might call students and activists, intelligentsia, cre-

ating their own institutions, creating self-acting committees all over the place, all over Hungary. It was just an amazing experience. There were extremely interesting debates and some of this is preserved in the archives, some of this has been published, but most of this was destroyed by the Soviet intervention that happened very soon afterwards and crushed it.

Out of practice, these ideas of anarchists and Marxists, of anarchism and socialism—this Haymarket synthesis—it just keeps being reinvented in each country with every new historical and social context. Hungary is my favorite example, because it also gives us an idea of a useful role for people who have a specific anarchist, or specific socialist, affiliation or identity. Whenever I travel and whenever I speak I hear people say, "I have this enormous privilege—I'm white, I'm a student, et cetera, and I don't know what to do with this"—it becomes a source of paralysis. And actually thinking about these situations, both in Hungary in 1956, but also in Russia in 1905, and especially in 1968 in the United States, you have a situation where students—middle class elements, activist intelligentsia—came first, breaking what Gramsci called the hegemony of bourgeois ideas and creating a space for workers to think and act for themselves. This space for emancipation that was opened by a specific political intervention of the students—many of them were anarchists, many of them were leftwing Marxists—was extremely useful.

So I'm very distressed to see today that people, instead of reading history and seeing that actually so-called middle class revolutionaries can play a very useful role, can be paralyzed. There is a very important role for all of us to play in the emancipatory project, and there is a new sense of urgency that was have to face today.

What happened in Hungary in 1956 brings to mind the Marxist notion of dual power, which you evoke in *Wobblies and Zapatistas*. It is a somewhat different concept than the notion of creating the new society in the shell of the old, because it takes place during a moment of upheaval, when power resides both in the existing state structure and elsewhere on a mass scale—such as in workers' councils. Yet it seems that this notion is a place where anarchist and leftwing Marxist ideas can and do cross over.

AG: I'm glad that you brought up dual power strategies, because there is a lot of intelligent discussion about this taking place in both Marxist and anarchist circles. And dual power is a fascinating concept in that sense. And I still haven't met a single anarchist who would dispute dual power as a potential revolutionary strategy.

The very idea—the practice, although the term was not used—but the practice of dual power, the practice again of creating new institutions that are eventually going to replace the old ones through the process of social revolution, revolutionary transformation, is something that anarchists were talking about from the beginning of the nineteenth century, since the formulation of anarchism as a political movement without using the word. And, yes, definitely it could be a possible bridge—one of the many bridges—of bringing those two traditions, those two colors, together.

The centrality of class is fundamental to the Marxist perspective. Do you think that that Marxism would enrich anarchism in practice by reorienting its focus, at least in North America, back towards class?
AG: I think that anarchists need to—and I stress, really need to—rediscover the importance of the concept of class. Of course, we need to be generous with present-day anarchists because they have reacted to something that was extremely problematic—a certain reductionism that came with the most bureaucratic and the most dull interpretations of socialism in the United States in the 1960s and '70s, through different Maoist groups and others, through a somewhat less interesting socialist heritage. The reaction to that is normal. But in reaction to it, I think the anarchists took it too far. And there are many ways of thinking about this. Some people are keen on the term *identity politics*. Identity politics are not always bad. But if it's interpreted in a vulgar way, as I fear many anarchists interpret it today, well, then we have problems.

One of the most gifted theorists of anarchism in the United States was Murray Bookchin. And Murray Bookchin helped us. As I mentioned earlier, he was involved in a tendency that was roughly called the new anarchism, back in the 1970s with people like Colin Ward, together with many people in Great Britain. The thing is that all these people were not talking so much about capitalism. They were focusing, maybe as a reaction to this class reductionism, on other elements of domination and exploitation, so not only class. I think this was very valuable. But I think that today, because class is so neglected in anarchist circles, we need to start reading Marx again, but also the anarchist classics. We need to rediscover the tendency in anarchism, from the very inception of anarchism as a political movement, of thinking about anarchism as being socialism, among other things.

So I think you are completely right. And my recent encounters with many people on the anarchist left—or they would say post-left, and some don't even consider themselves leftists, introducing a significant semantic confusion about all of these things—is that they don't like to think of things in terms of class. Which is detrimental. It's detrimental to building a movement. Because what I think both anarchists and leftwing Marxists agree is that we need a truly popular movement that's going to be based on wide strata of society against both state and private coercive institutions and which is going to take its inspiration, not from a handful of theorists, students, professors, Marxist and anarchist intellectuals, but from popular creative energies.

In the last few years we've seen the rise of an insurrectionist tendency amongst parts of the radical movements in North America and Europe, from those who reject the politics of process and consensus in favor of revolutionary transformation in the here and now. What do you make of this current? Do you see it as a reaction in any way to the new anarchism of the antiglobalization movement?

AG: I understand the insurrectionists' impatience. I admire it. But I do not understand their claim of novelty. For much of my life as a revolutionary I was haunted by what I called "Michelet's problem." It is enough to remind ourselves of the history of revolutions. No revolution has ever taken place without ad hoc popular institutions improvised from below simply beginning to administer power in place of the institutions previously recognized as legitimate. On the other hand, every single one of the ventures or experiments in government from below existed for only a few months or years. In many societies they were drowned in blood. In others, they were drowned in bureaucracy. The same could also be said about Russia, Spain, Hungary, France, or Oaxaca.

Why do I call this Michelet's problem? Michelet was a famous French historian, who wrote the following words about the French Revolution: "that day everything was possible, the future was the present, and time but a glimmer of eternity." But, as Cornelius Castoriadis used to say, if all that we create is just a glimmer of hope, the bureaucrats will inevitably show up and turn off the light. The history of revolutions is, on one hand, a history of a tension between brief moments of revolutionary creativity and the making of long lasting institutions. On the other hand, the history of revolutions often reads like a history of revolutionary alienation, when the revolutionary was, more than anything else, ultimately and almost inevitably alienated from his or her own creations. Michelet's problem is really about resolving this tension between brief epiphanies of revolutionary hope and the hope for long-term institutionalization of revolutionary change.

The crucial question then is how to create such lasting institutions, or better yet, an ongoing culture of constructive struggle. This is the challenge that we have to face, with an original, revolutionary answer.

In the contemporary anarchist movement there is a lot of talk about "the insurrection" and considerable fascination with "the event." The French accent and sophisticated jargon are perhaps new and in fashion, but these are not new topics. They appear to crop up, with disturbing regularity, with every next generation of revolutionaries. The old refrain that organizing is just another word for going slow is being rediscovered by this new tendency. But, just like with the Haymarket synthesis, there is nothing really new here.

I think that we can say that there are, risking some oversimplification, two ways of thinking about revolution. There is the negative idea of revolution, very much present in insurrectionist movement literature. Remember the words of "Solidarity Forever," when the song affirms: "We can bring to birth a new world from the ashes of the old." This is the negative, apocalyptic perspective. Contemporary insurrectionism had not invented it, all references to "unprecedented novelty" and "biopolitics" aside.

A second view of revolution is positive: a new society, new anarchist society, can develop from what was already in being, and from below. Free socialist society must grow from existing strengths. As Edward Thompson used to say "No one . . . can impose a socialist humanity from above." This is an image of a constructive, not apocalyptic, revolution—built on the positives, of a socialist commonwealth emerging from existing creations improvised from below, as a result of patient organizing, prefigurative organizing, building the structures of new society in the shell of the old, in a manner that connects local and global. Upon these positives, and not upon the debris of a smashed society, the free socialist community must be built.

The insurrectionist refusal of the prefigurative dimension of revolutionary work, a dimension which is, to my mind, the signature quality of the anarchist tradition, and their almost nihilistic impatience, fails to provide a serious libertarian answer to Michelet's problem.

What should be the priorities of radicals, whether anarchists or others, during this period of crisis?
AG: The movement, at least in the United States, is far from having achieved any strategic clarity. I believe that the future of emancipatory politics rests on our ability to "balkanize" politics, in other words to experiment, fuse and synthesize different elements of anarchism and Marxism, always paying close attention to the local conditions.

I was very impressed by the politics of the indigenous from the pan-Andean federation. They talk, just like the Zapatistas, about the need for antiauthoritarian politics without and beyond states, organized along the lines of direct democracy, decolonization, and decommodification. We already discussed the importance of the "Haymarket synthesis" in the revolutionary history of North America. Revolutionary socialism will inevitably mean different things in different parts of the world. This is not a bad thing. What we need to do is to find ways of connecting these local ideas, experiences, and practices, in a global conversation. Institutions like the World Social Forum can be helpful here. This should be our radical priority.

What do you think is the relationship between the movements that have emerged in opposition to austerity—in Greece, France, the UK, Ireland, and elsewhere—and the anarchist movements of the past decade? Do you think they can lead to a renewed left?

AG: This is an interesting question. Some of the networks, and some of the radical infrastructure that were established during the antiglobalization cycle of struggles merged with new developments and new configurations of militancy. It would be impossible to imagine the climate justice movement without the background of the new anarchist and radical global movement.

However, I think that what David Graeber and I dubbed "new anarchism" does not exist anymore, at least not in the form that we described in our essay. Some of the movements, especially those in California, have emerged almost in opposition to prefigurative efforts that were at the heart of new anarchism.

There is a new generation of student radicals around, with insurrectionist, left-communist, or "ultra-leftist" politics. Other movements appear to be based on the immediate needs and reaction to the politics of austerity. Others still, like the one in Greece, cannot be properly understood outside of their specific historical, and sociocultural context.

My concern is to avoid having the austerity of politics become an answer to the politics of austerity. We are going through a time that offers many opportunities. We need to use them wisely.

Acknowledgments

MOST OF THESE CONVERSATIONS, WITH A FEW EXCEPTIONS, ORIGINATED AS INTERviews for the program *Against the Grain* on KPFA—the mother of public radio in the United States—and were later expanded in print. I would like to thank the sixteen contributors to this volume for bringing these important ideas to light, as well as their work in fleshing the original interviews out in response to more questions. I am grateful to KPFA Radio for granting me permission to publish these interviews and I would particularly like to thank my colleague C. S. Soong, who allowed me to use the original interview with Ellen Meiksins Wood, which he hosted and I produced on the program *Living Room*. Wholehearted thanks go to my comrades past and present at the benighted KPFA—Amelia Gonzalez, Brian Edwards-Tiekert, Mitch Jeserich, Esther Manilla, Laura Prives, John Hamilton, Vanessa Tait, Aileen Alfandary, Rose Ketabchi, Eric Klein, Lemlem Rijio, and many others—who have managed to keep doing vital work in spite of a parent organization and governance system as byzantine, destructive, and antiworker, on its small scale, as any neoliberal regime.

This book started its life at Monthly Review Press and I would like to acknowledge with gratitude the work that the Press and editor Michael Yates invested in it. At PM Press, I am indebted to the masterful John Yates for his ingenious designs for the Spectre series, including the cover of this book, Shael Love for his crowd-sourcing transcription skills, and intrepid camerawoman Jai Jai Noire for her grace under pressure. Thanks also to the meticulous Brian Layng for the book's handsome interior, Gregory Nipper for his ever-skillful copyediting, the indefatigable Dan Fedorenko and the adept Stephanie Pasvankias for their vital support, along with PM grandee Craig O'Hara for his enthusiasm about the book. My gimlet-eyed editor at PM Press, Ramsey Kanaan, deftly improved the text. It goes without saying, hence, that culpability for any and all errors, omissions, and faulty ideas should be firmly laid at his feet.

I owe a large debt to Iain Boal, Gillian Cartwright Boal, Summer Brenner, Cal Winslow, Faith Simon, Dick Walker, Jane White, Jim Davis, Juliana Fredman, Laura Fantone, Ignacio Chapela, Lisa Thompson, Eddie Yuen, Joseph Matthews, T. J. Clark, Ann Wagner, Andrej Grubačić, and the comrades at Retort, for creating a vibrant community of antinomians, where the radical flame burns bright without the acrid whiff of sectarianism. I am particularly grateful to Iain, Cal, Eddie, and Jim for their valuable critical feedback on this book. Sally Phillips and Bonnie Simmons have provided hilarity at every opportunity, for which I am singularly appreciative. I am especially indebted to Kay Trimberger and Barbara Epstein for their ongoing intellectual support, kindness, and friendship over many years.

For his sage advice, I would like to thank my brother Jake Lilley. I am grateful to Ann Kanaan and Andrew Parkin for their generosity and hospitality, providing refuge in Sydney during the writing of this book. Likewise, I am in the debt of Marcia Fisch, for her generosity of spirit and domicile. My father, Ted Lilley, exposed me to radical politics at an early age and has encouraged me to think analytically ever since—with perhaps unforeseen consequences. He has been an enthusiastic supporter of this volume, my intellectual ventures, and the edifying virtues of writing every day, for which I am abundantly thankful. Similarly, I am enormously grateful to my husband, Ramsey Kanaan. For his patience, both connubial and literary, I am forever in his debt. Our marriage is a daily reminder that utopian aspirations, and the unity of the red and the black, are eminently possible.

Above all, I would like to thank my mother, Kathleen Lilley, both for her steadfast and wholehearted support for my radical labors, and for her own. From her groundbreaking feminism in Lewes, her opposition on both sides of the Atlantic to militarism and war, and her tireless work against the perversions of the media system, corporate and alternative, she has been a force of nature. She is an unceasing inspiration to me. This book is dedicated to her.

Contributors

Greg Albo teaches political economy at the Department of Political Science at York University in Toronto. He is coeditor of the *Socialist Register* and the coauthor of *In and Out of Crisis: The Global Financial Meltdown and Left Alternatives*, published by PM Press/Spectre.

Tariq Ali is a writer and filmmaker. He has written more than a dozen books, including *Street Fighting Years, Bush in Babylon, The Clash of Fundamentalisms*, and *The Obama Syndrome*, published by Verso. He is an editor of the *New Left Review*.

Vivek Chibber is professor of sociology at New York University and the author of *Locked in Place: State-Building and Late Industrialization in India*, published by Princeton University Press. He is coeditor of the *Socialist Register.*

Noam Chomsky is professor emeritus of linguistics at the Massachusetts Institute of Technology and the author of more than 150 books, including *Chomsky on Anarchism*. His most recent DVD, "Theory and Practice: Conversations with Noam Chomsky and Howard Zinn," includes the full interview from which his contribution to this book is excerpted.

Mike Davis is a radical scholar, political activist, and urban theorist. He is the author of many books, including *City of Quartz, Ecology of Fear, Late Victorian Holocausts*, and *Planet of Slums*, published by Verso.

John Bellamy Foster teaches sociology at the University of Oregon. He is the editor of *Monthly Review*. His many books include *Marx's Ecology: Materialism and Nature* and *The Ecological Revolution: Making Peace with the Planet*, published by Monthly Review Press.

Sam Gindin is former research director of the Canadian Autoworkers Union and is the Visiting Packer Chair in Social Justice at York University. He is a member of the Socialist Project and the Greater Toronto Workers' Assembly and is coauthor of *In and Out of Crisis: The Global Financial Meltdown and Left Alternatives*, published by PM Press/Spectre.

Andrej Grubačić is an anarchist dissident and historian from the Balkans. He has been active as an organizer in networks such as the post-Yugoslav coalition of antiauthoritarian collectives DSM!, Peoples Global Action, and the World Social Forum. He is coauthor with Staughton Lynd of *Wobblies and Zapatistas: Conversations on Anarchism, Marxism, and Radical History* and author of *Don't Mourn, Balkanize! Essays After Yugoslavia*, both published by PM Press.

Gillian Hart is professor of geography at the University of California–Berkeley and serves as an honorary professor at the University of KwaZulu-Natal. She is the author of *Disabling Globalization: Places of Power in Post-Apartheid South Africa* and the forthcoming book *The Anger of the Poor: Unfolding Challenges in South Africa and Beyond.*

David Harvey is Distinguished Professor of Anthropology at the Graduate Center of the City University of New York. Amongst his many works are *Limits to Capital* and *A Brief History of Neoliberalism.* His most recent book is *The Enigma of Capital: And the Crises of Capitalism*, published by Oxford.

Doug Henwood is editor and publisher of *Left Business Observer.* His books include *Wall Street* and *After the New Economy.* He is a contributing editor at *The Nation* and hosts *Behind the News*, a weekly program on KPFA Radio.

Ursula Huws is director of the research consultancy Analytica and the editor of the journal *Work Organisation, Labour and Globalisation.* She is the author of *The Making of a Cybertariat: Virtual Work in a Real World*, published by Monthly Review Press.

Sasha Lilley is a writer and radio broadcaster. She is the cofounder and host of the critically acclaimed program of radical ideas *Against the Grain* and the series editor of PM Press's political economy imprint, Spectre.

Jason W. Moore is assistant professor of environmental history in the Department of Historical, Philosophical, and Religious Studies at Umeå University in Sweden and coordinator of the World-Ecology Research Network. He is the author of "Ecology and the Accumulation of Capital."

David McNally teaches political science at York University in Toronto. He has authored numerous books, including *Another World Is Possible: Globalization and Anti-Capitalism* and most recently *Global Slump: The Economics and Politics of Crisis and Resistance,* published by PM Press/Spectre.

Leo Panitch is the Senior Canada Research Chair in Comparative Political Economy and Distinguished Research Professor of Political Science at York University, Toronto, and is coeditor of *The Socialist Register.* His many books include *American Empire and the Political Economy of Global Finance, In and Out Crisis: The Global Financial Meltdown and Left Alternatives,* and *The Making of Global Capitalism,* with Sam Gindin.

John Sanbonmatsu is associate professor of philosophy at Worcester Polytechnic Institute. He is the author of *The Postmodern Prince: Critical Theory, Left Strategy, and the Making of a New Political Subject,* published by Monthly Review Press.

Ellen Meiksins Wood is the author of many works including *The Origin of Capitalism* and *Empire of Capital.* Her latest book is *Citizens to Lords: A Social History of Western Political Thought from Antiquity to the Middle Ages,* published by Verso.

Notes

1 The leader of the German Communist Party, Ernst Thälmann, illustrated the perverse politics that come from such catastrophism when he declared, "After Hitler, our turn!" In 1944, he was shot in Buchenwald, on orders from Hitler.

2 See chapter 5, "Sam Gindin, Greg Albo, and Leo Panitch: Capitalist Crisis and Radical Renewal."

3 Fredric Jameson, "Future City," *New Left Review* 21, May–June 2003, 76. See Iain Boal, "Climate, Globe, Capital: The Science and Politics of the Abyss," *SUM Magazine,* December 2009, for a reminder of the pitfalls of catastrophism.

4 I'm unfashionably choosing to use the term "left" to describe everything from anarcho-communism to traditional social democracy.

5 The vantage point of this book is centered in the United States, at the heart of empire, and is intended for radicals in the Global North. This perspective necessarily colors the ideas within it—for example, the prospects for radicals in the U.S. are clearly different than in South Korea or even France.

6 *Against the Grain* is a program of radical ideas originating from KPFA Radio in the San Francisco Bay Area, cofounded by C. S. Soong and Sasha Lilley.

7 Walden Bello, "Keynes: A Man for This Season?" *Huffington Post,* July 9, 2009, http://www.huffingtonpost.com/walden-bello/keynes-a-man-for-this-sea_b_228934.html; Interview with John Bellamy Foster for *Página/12,* "Can the Financial Crisis Be Reversed?" *MR Zine,* October 10, 2008, http://mrzine.monthlyreview.org/2008/foster101008.html.

8 Polanyi argued that capitalism alternates between the unfettered market and some form of a social safety net. The latter comes about when elites, worrying that the poor are being stretched to their breaking point, step in to limit the market's impact. Polanyi, *The Great Transformation: The Political and Economic Origins of Our Time* (1944; repr., Boston: Beacon Press, 2002).

9 Aaron Brenner, Robert Brenner, and Cal Winslow, eds., *Rebel Rank and File: Labor Militancy and Revolt from Below During the Long 1970s* (New York: Verso, 2010), 3.

10 Robert Brenner, *The Boom and the Bubble: The U.S. in the World Economy* (New York: Verso, 2002), 12.

11 See chapter 10, "Vivek Chibber: National Capitalism in the Third World."

12 See chapter 2, "David Harvey: The Rise of Neoliberalism and the Riddle of Capital." Also David Harvey, *A Brief History of Neoliberalism* (Oxford: Oxford University Press, 2005).

13 Steven Rattner, "Volcker Asserts U.S. Must Trim Living Standards," *New York Times,* October 18, 1979.

14 David Stuckler, Lawrence King, and Martin McKee, "Mass Privatisation and the Post-Communist Mortality Crisis: A Cross-National Analysis," *The Lancet* 373, no. 9661, (January 31, 2009): 360–62. "The transition from communism to capitalism in Europe and central Asia during the early to mid-1990s has had devastating consequences for health: UNICEF attributes more than 3 million premature deaths to transition; the UN Development Programme estimates over 10 million missing men because of system change; and more than 15 years after these transitions began, only a little over half of the ex-communist countries have regained their pretransition life-expectancy levels."

15 See chapter 10, "Vivek Chibber: National Capitalism in the Third World."

16 McNally, *Global Slump: The Economics and Politics of Crisis and Resistance* (Oakland: PM Press, 2011), 51.

17 "We Did It! The Rich World's Quiet Revolution," *The Economist* December 31, 2009. According to the International Labour Organization, "the number of employed women grew by almost 200 million over the last decade, to reach 1.2 billion in 2007 compared to 1.8 billion men": ILO, "Global Employment Trends for Women 2008: More Women Enter the Workforce,

But More than Half of All Working Women are in Vulnerable Jobs," March 6, 2008, http://www.ilo.org/global/about-the-ilo/press-and-media-centre/press-releases/WCMS_091102/lang--en/index.htm#1

18   Land-grabbing has always been a part of the capitalist *modus operandi*, as Wood reminds us, under the guise of "improvement." Following the 2008 spiking of global food prices, governments and corporations have laid claim to huge swaths of land in Africa and elsewhere, displacing populations whose livelihoods are dependent on agriculture. See Neil MacFarquhar, "African Farmers Displaced as Investors Move In," *New York Times*, December 22, 2010, 1.

19   The U.S. state during much of the twentieth century actively exported American grains to the Global South as food aid, which undercut domestic agriculture in those countries and provided a means of keeping food prices—and hence wages—low, further incorporating these countries into the capitalist world economy and inoculating them from communism. That system unraveled in the early 1970s. But neoliberalism has reordered the world agricultural system to keep labor costs low through different means, restructuring food production in the Global South and reorienting it towards export.

20   Amongst scholars on the Marxist left, debates rage about the origins of the present crisis: was it caused by long term stagnation of the economies of the Global North, as some have argued, which originated in the 1970s? Or has neoliberal capitalism been dynamic on its own terms, driving up the level of exploitation through the restructuring of industry, the harsh disciplining of labor, the phenomenal growth of Chinese capitalism, and the increased expansion of capital on a global scale, leading to genuine increases in productivity and profitability? Has debt been a means to keep capitalism going over the past three decades while wages fell and capitalism stagnated? Or were those repressed wages part of the reason for capitalism's dynamism in recent years, coming up short in the past decade? And most importantly, perhaps, what does this crisis mean for neoliberalism and capitalism? These arguments are touched upon in this volume, although admittedly with some partisanship.

21   See chapter 4 "David McNally: The Global Economic Meltdown."

22   "Conservative Advocate," *Morning Edition*, NPR, May 25, 2001.

23   Similarly, the notion that nation-states and their sovereignty have been eviscerated by neoliberalism is equally misguided. Ellen Meiksins Wood points out that rather than eclipsing the nation-state, neoliberalism is constituted through such states, providing the political, legal, and administrative infrastructure that capital needs to operate globally. Gillian Hart makes a related point, in her critique of the narrative of the impact of the "global" from above on the passive "local," as if the global were not made up of capitalist social relations, in all their complexity, based in specific places around the world.

24   See chapter 5. See also Greg Albo, Sam Gindin, and Leo Panitch, *In and Out of Crisis: The Global Financial Meltdown and Left Alternatives* (Oakland: PM Press, 2010).

25   It remains to be seen whether this social-ecological crisis, as Jason Moore frames it, is simply developmental, meaning it can lead to new forms of dynamic accumulation, or terminal, spelling the end of capitalism and necessitating the emergence of a new mode of production.

26   Ursula Huws, *The Making of a Cybertariat: Virtual Work in a Real World* (New York: Monthly Review Press, 2003). Unlike those who would presuppose that we live in a postindustrial society, now dominated by services, Huws insists that services have been with us throughout capitalism and we just seem unable to take their measure consistently, while forgetting domestic servants in assessing the working class of an earlier era. Such myopia about service industries has led generations of leftists to undervalue (often female) proletarians working not in factories, and left them woefully unprepared for an era when service organization is paramount.

27   John Sanbonmatsu provocatively suggests that the process of commodification is at work in the faddishness of postmodernism: "Whereas in the past a particular critical idea or concept—the state, say, or patriarchy or the division of labor—was used to illuminate empirical reality, and so had a direct 'use-value' for praxis, the concepts and ideas associated with the postmodern turn these past twenty-five years—the argot of cyborgs, border crossings,

bodies, *différance*, the lack, abjection, et cetera—have not maintained a direct relation to the empirical world, let alone a connection with actual social movements trying to change concrete institutions. No sooner does one postmodernist scholar spin off one new concept—'Empire,' say, or 'the multitude'—than another one comes along and introduces yet another new theory-commodity, like 'the state of exception' or 'memes.' We might say that the increasing pace of technological artifacts and commodities is being mirrored in the increased rate of the forced obsolescence of knowledge commodities—a faster and faster turn-over rate of ideas." Chapter 13, "John Sanbonmatsu: Postmodernism and the Politics of Expression."

28   Chapter 9, "Ursula Huws: Labor and Capital, Gender and Commodification."

29   "Profits, But No Jobs," *The Economist,* August 5, 2010.

30   See chapter 8, "Gillian Hart: The Agrarian Question and Multiple Paths of Capitalist Development in East Asia and South Africa."

31   As Hart points out, the degree to which movements resist dispossession from land, and link struggles between land and labor, may shape the strength of subsequent industrial organizing, as in South Africa.

32   Catherine Rampell, "Corporate Profits Were the Highest on Record Last Quarter," *New York Times,* November 23, 2010 http://www.nytimes.com/2010/11/24/business/economy/24econ. html?_r=1&hp

33   For an account of the U.S. occupation at Republic Windows & Doors see Kari Lydersen, *Revolt on Goose Island: The Chicago Factory Takeover, and What It Says About the Economic Crisis* (Brooklyn: Melville House, 2009).

34   French boss-nappings have taken place at Sony, Caterpillar, 3M, and Lipton factories, spawning companies specializing in boss-napping prevention.

35   In Japan, union density fell from 35 percent in the mid-1970s to 20 percent in 2002. New entrants to the European Union from the former Soviet Bloc have seen union density fall precipitously. Estonia, the most extreme case, went from 88 percent in 1992 to 14 percent in 2002.

36   Sophia Lawrence and Junko Ishikawa, "Social Dialogue Indicators: Trade Union Membership and Collective Bargaining Coverage," International Labour Organization, Working Paper 59, October 2005.

37   See chapters 4 and 5.

38   Huws also argues that homeownership often leads to increased spending on various capital goods like washing machines, which intersects with the processes of commodifying domestic unwaged labor, another impetus to accumulation. Huws, *Making of a Cybertariat*, 44.

39   Cited in Barbara Ehrenreich and Deirdre English, *For Her Own Good: Two Centuries of the Expert's Advice to Women* (New York: Anchor Books, revised edition, 2005), 163. This point is made by Ursula Huws.

40   *Ibid.*

41   The U.S. state had actively fostered homeownership in the 1920s through its Better Homes in America campaign, headed up by then–Secretary of Commerce Herbert Hoover.

42   Margaret Thatcher was asked why a family should be able to buy their council house when there were so many other families on the waiting list for public housing. She responded by saying, "Many council tenants live there for the rest of their lives. The house is already off the market, why shouldn't they have a chance to buy and hand something on to their children? Why shouldn't they have the chance to become little capitalists?" *Romford Recorder,* August 15, 1980.

43   As Clinton put it in a speech on the first National Homeownership Day in 1995, "You want to reinforce family values in America, encourage two-parent households, get people to stay home? Make it easy for people to own their own homes . . ." Alyssa Katz, *Our Lot: How Real Estate Came to Own Us* (New York: Bloomsbury, 2009), 35.

44   Katz, *Ibid,* 33. As Katz points out, members of the Clinton administration were instructed to replace the term "affordable housing" with "affordable homeownership."

45 Seth Tobocman, Eric Laursen, and Jessica Wehrle, *Understanding the Crash* (Berkeley: Soft Skull Press, 2010), 42.

46 Huws, *Making of a Cybertariat*, 46.

47 Workers increasingly spend their free time on "consumption work," unpaid labor that has been offloaded from businesses onto consumers, such as automated phone systems and online forms, where the customer now does the work previously done by paid workers. See chapter 9, "Ursula Huws: Labor and Capital, Gender and Commodification." And despite the crisis of traditional media, people in the United States watch almost thirty-seven hours of television a week, which, beyond being almost as time consuming as a full-time job, tends to be an atomized and ideologically-charged pursuit. See "The Great Survivor," *The Economist*, April 29, 2010, http://www.economist.com/node/16009155

48 E. P. Thompson, "Eighteenth-Century English Society: Class Struggle Without Class?" *Social History* 1, no. 2 (May 1978): 149.

49 Chapter 12, "Tariq Ali: Anti-imperialism and the New Left, Revolt and Retrenchment."

50 Nancy Fraser, "Feminism, Capitalism, and the Cunning of History" *New Left Review* 56, March–April 2009, 114. Fraser argues that both feminism and neoliberalism share a hostility to traditional authority. I would disagree that this is the basis for the affinity she describes, which would be better understood by looking at the class aspirations of much of the feminist movement. Like the New Left, the feminist movement, especially as it broadened, was not at its basis anticapitalist, but like the New Left embodied the contradictions that often beset movements of middle class discontent—veering at times towards radicalism and at times away from it.

51 David Harvey, *A Brief History of Neoliberalism* (Oxford: Oxford University Press, 2005), 42. Harvey contends that the material underpinnings of these contradictory elements was the makeup of the New Left itself, which brought together, on the one hand, workers, who became increasingly militant into the 1970s, and middle class students on the other. However, the desires for personal liberation and collective change don't appear to be so easily separated along class lines, as working class people embraced personal freedom from the strictures of the state, schools, and the family as much as middle class people did.

52 Consonantly, John Sanbonmatsu has argued that one of the failings of the New Left was its fixation with expressing one's outrage, rather than strategic forms of action.

53 Thomas Frank, *The Conquest of Cool: Business Culture, Counterculture, and the Rise of Hip Consumerism* (Chicago: University of Chicago Press, 1997), 9. Hip consumerism remains very much with us today.

54 *Ibid.*, 25–26.

55 Nancy Fraser, "Feminism, Capitalism, and the Cunning of History" *New Left Review* 56, March–April 2009, 97–117.

56 Of course, many working class women were already in the waged work force at the time of the feminist movement.

57 Fraser uses the example of the feminist championing of market solutions like microcredit, which has provided small loans to women in the Global South, right at the time that governments have slashed social supports and aid to the poor. Fraser, "Feminism, Capitalism, and the Cunning of History" *New Left Review* 56, March–April 2009.

58 The working class, the traditional bedrock of the left, famously allied with students in France and Italy, while in the U.S., African American workers, along with students, were at the center of the Civil Rights movement to end segregation in the South. But students and intellectuals tended to view the working class with some suspicion and that sentiment was often mutual.

59 Chapter 13 "John Sanbonmatsu: Postmodernism and the Politics of Expression."

60 See Doug Henwood, *After the New Economy* (New York; The New Press, 2003) for a detailed accounting of the hype and the reality.

61 Postmodernism, it should be noted, is now out of fashion, but its legacy lives.

62 Liza Featherstone, Doug Henwood, and Christian Parenti, "Action Will Be Taken," *Left Business Observer*, 2004, http://www.leftbusinessobserver.com/Action.html

63   Yet, as a number of critics in this volume have emphasized, that nostalgia misinterprets the demise of Keynesianism and the rise of neoliberalism. And it loses sight of the nature of the state under capitalism.

64   See for example Jerry Mander and Edward Goldsmith (eds.) *The Case Against the Global Economy: And for a Turn Toward the Local* (Berkeley: Sierra Club Books, 1997).

65   In the U.S., this already-existing tendency was only accentuated after September 11, 2001, when in a defensive mode, activists turned towards focusing on the local communities where they lived.

66   Personal conversation with the author, San Francisco, September 2010.

67   Julie Guthman illustrates this in her outstanding book *Agrarian Dreams: The Paradox of Organic Farming in California* (Berkeley: UC Press, 2004).

68   It goes without saying, however, that this is not an endorsement, therefore, of large capitalist firms and banks. See interview with Doug Henwood by Sasha Lilley on "Ask an Economist," *Morning Show*, KPFA, July 8, 2010, http://www.kpfa.org/archive/id/62417

69   Henry Bernstein, "Class Dynamics of Agrarian Change: Writing a 'Little Book on a Big Idea,'" Agrarian Studies Colloquium, Yale University, March 5, 2010, 12.

70   Russell Jacoby, *Picture Imperfect: Utopian Thought for an Anti-Utopian Age* (New York: Columbia University Press, 2005).

71   Fredric Jameson, "The Politics of Utopia," *New Left Review* 25, January–February 2004, 35.

72   The Spanish Revolution is one of the most obvious examples. Workers took control of production in a number of provinces under the banner of anarchism, but the anarchist CNT-FAI nonetheless was not able to resolve the question of how to maintain workers' control against the forces of reaction. They ended up subordinating themselves to the Spanish Popular Front government.

73   It has been argued by Jacoby and others that within utopian literature there is a strain of authoritarianism—of wanting to draw up a blueprint of a future society down to the size of the toilets. But I would argue that neither socialism nor anarchism has projected such a vision onto the future. Marx famously rejected the idea of "writing recipes for the cook-shops of the future" and wrote very little about what communism might look like. The perversions of Stalinism appear to have been created *in situ*, and were driven by a desire to stifle the revolution's utopian impulses, not an obsession with perfecting them.

74   An anticapitalist vision for this moment of crisis, however, requires navigating a path between thinking that anything is possible if one has enough revolutionary fervor and the idea that nothing is possible. Outside of a small (but influential) part of the radical left, the latter overwhelmingly dominates.

75   Arran Gare, "Soviet Environmentalism: The Path Not Taken," in *The Greening of Marxism*, ed. Ted Benton (New York: The Guildford Press, 1996) and chapter 6, "John Bellamy Foster: The Ecological Dimensions of Marx's Thought."

76   This is not to suggest that sectarianism is the only thing standing in the way of a renewed left. Unfortunately, the problems that beset radicals are much larger.

77   Raymond Williams, *Culture and Materialism* (1980; repr., New York: Verso, 2005), 116.

78   Davis claims that heating and cooling cities, along with urban production and transport, produce 70–85 percent of the world's greenhouse gas emissions. Mike Davis, "Who Will Build the Ark?" *New Left Review* 61, January–February 2010, 41.

79   Ibid., 30.

80   Rodchenko wrote in 1925, "The light from the East is not only the liberation of the workers, the light from the East is in relation to the person, to woman, to things. Our things in our hands must be equals, comrades, and not these black and mournful slaves, as they are here." Constructivist theory regarded the object as not a commodity to be passively exchanged, but an active participant in the socialist project. See Christina Kiaer, *Imagine No Possessions: The Socialist Objects of Russian Constructivism* (Cambridge, MA: MIT Press, 2005).

81   William Morris, *Useful Work Versus Useless Toil* (1888; repr., London: Penguin 2008), 14.

Index

ABOUT PM PRESS

PM Press was founded at the end of 2007 by a small collection of folks with decades of publishing, media, and organizing experience. PM Press co-conspirators have published and distributed hundreds of books, pamphlets, CDs, and DVDs. Members of PM have founded enduring book fairs, spearheaded victorious tenant organizing campaigns, and worked closely with bookstores, academic conferences, and even rock bands to deliver political and challenging ideas to all walks of life. We're old enough to know what we're doing and young enough to know what's at stake.

We seek to create radical and stimulating fiction and non-fiction books, pamphlets, t-shirts, visual and audio materials to entertain, educate and inspire you. We aim to distribute these through every available channel with every available technology—whether that means you are seeing anarchist classics at our bookfair stalls; reading our latest vegan cookbook at the café; downloading geeky fiction e-books; or digging new music and timely videos from our website.

PM Press is always on the lookout for talented and skilled volunteers, artists, activists and writers to work with. If you have a great idea for a project or can contribute in some way, please get in touch.

PM Press
PO Box 23912
Oakland, CA 94623
www.pmpress.org

FRIENDS OF PM PRESS

These are indisputably momentous times — the
financial system is melting down globally and the
Empire is stumbling. Now more than ever there is a
vital need for radical ideas.

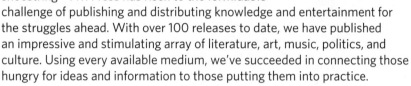

In the three years since its founding—and on a mere
shoestring—PM Press has risen to the formidable
challenge of publishing and distributing knowledge and entertainment for
the struggles ahead. With over 100 releases to date, we have published
an impressive and stimulating array of literature, art, music, politics, and
culture. Using every available medium, we've succeeded in connecting those
hungry for ideas and information to those putting them into practice.

Friends of PM allows you to directly help impact, amplify, and revitalize
the discourse and actions of radical writers, filmmakers, and artists. It
provides us with a stable foundation from which we can build upon our early
successes and provides a much-needed subsidy for the materials that can't
necessarily pay their own way. You can help make that happen—and receive
every new title automatically delivered to your door once a month—by
joining as a Friend of PM Press. And, we'll throw in a free T-Shirt when you
sign up.

Here are your options:
- **$25 a month** Get all books and pamphlets plus 50% discount on all
  webstore purchases
- **$25 a month** Get all CDs and DVDs plus 50% discount on all webstore
  purchases
- **$40 a month** Get all PM Press releases plus 50% discount on all
  webstore purchases
- **$100 a month** Superstar — Everything plus PM merchandise, free
  downloads, and 50% discount on all webstore purchases

For those who can't afford $25 or more a month, we're introducing **Sustainer
Rates** at $15, $10 and $5. Sustainers get a free PM Press t-shirt and a 50%
discount on all purchases from our website.

Your Visa or Mastercard will be billed once a month, until you tell us to
stop. Or until our efforts succeed in bringing the revolution around. Or the
financial meltdown of Capital makes plastic redundant. Whichever comes
first.

Global Slump: The Economics and Politics of Crisis and Resistance

David McNally

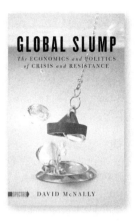

ISBN: 978-1-60486-332-1
$15.95   176 pages

Global Slump analyzes the world financial meltdown as the first systemic crisis of the neoliberal stage of capitalism. It argues that—far from having ended—the crisis has ushered in a whole period of worldwide economic and political turbulence. In developing an account of the crisis as rooted in fundamental features of capitalism, *Global Slump* challenges the view that its source lies in financial deregulation. It offers an original account of the "financialization" of the world economy and explores the connections between international financial markets and new forms of debt and dispossession, particularly in the Global South. The book shows that, while averting a complete meltdown, the massive intervention by central banks laid the basis for recurring crises for poor and working class people. It traces new patterns of social resistance for building an anticapitalist opposition to the damage that neoliberal capitalism is inflicting on the lives of millions.

"In this book, McNally confirms—once again—his standing as one of the world's leading Marxist scholars of capitalism. For a scholarly, in depth analysis of our current crisis that never loses sight of its political implications (for them and for us), expressed in a language that leaves no reader behind, there is simply no better place to go."
—Bertell Ollman, professor, Department of Politics, NYU, and author of Dance of the Dialectic: Steps in Marx's Method

"David McNally's tremendously timely book is packed with significant theoretical and practical insights, and offers actually-existing examples of what is to be done. Global Slump urgently details how changes in the capitalist space-economy over the past 25 years, especially in the forms that money takes, have expanded wide-scale vulnerabilities for all kinds of people, and how people fight back. In a word, the problem isn't neo-liberalism—it's capitalism."
—Ruth Wilson Gilmore, University of Southern California and author, Golden Gulag

In and Out of Crisis: The Global Financial Meltdown and Left Alternatives

Greg Albo, Sam Gindin, Leo Panitch

ISBN: 978-1-60486-212-6
$13.95   144 pages

While many around the globe are increasingly wondering if another world is indeed possible, few are mapping out potential avenues—and flagging wrong turns—en route to a postcapitalist future. In this groundbreaking analysis of the meltdown, renowned radical political economists Albo, Gindin, and Panitch lay bare the roots of the crisis, which they locate in the dynamic expansion of capital on a global scale over the last quarter century—and in the inner logic of capitalism itself.

With an unparalleled understanding of the inner workings of capitalism, the authors of *In and Out of Crisis* provocatively challenge the call by much of the Left for a return to a largely mythical Golden Age of economic regulation as a check on finance capital unbound. They deftly illuminate how the era of neoliberal free markets has been, in practice, undergirded by state intervention on a massive scale. In conclusion, the authors argue that it's time to start thinking about genuinely transformative alternatives to capitalism—and how to build the collective capacity to get us there. *In and Out of Crisis* stands to be the enduring critique of the crisis and an indispensable springboard for a renewed Left.

"*Once again, Panitch, Gindin, and Albo show that they have few rivals and no betters in analyzing the relations between politics and economics, between globalization and American power, between theory and quotidian reality, and between crisis and political possibility. At once sobering and inspiring, this is one of the few pieces of writing that I've seen that's essential to understanding—to paraphrase a term from accounting—the sources and uses of crisis. Splendid and essential.*"
—Doug Henwood, *Left Business Observer*, author of *After the New Economy* and *Wall Street*

"*Mired in political despair? Planning your escape to a more humane continent? Baffled by the economy? Convinced that the Left is out of ideas? Pull yourself together and read this book, in which Albo, Gindin, and Panitch, some of the world's sharpest living political economists, explain the current financial crisis—and how we might begin to make a better world.*"
—Liza Featherstone, author of *Students Against Sweatshops* and *Selling Women Short: The Landmark Battle for Worker's Rights at Wal-Mart*

SPECTRE CLASSICS **from PM Press**

William Morris: Romantic to Revolutionary

E. P. Thompson

ISBN: 978-1-60486-243-0

$32.95   880 pages

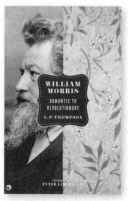

William Morris—the great 19th-century craftsman, architect, designer, poet and writer—remains a monumental figure whose influence resonates powerfully today. As an intellectual (and author of the seminal utopian *News From Nowhere*), his concern with artistic and human values led him to cross what he called the "river of fire" and become a committed socialist—committed not to some theoretical formula but to the day-by-day struggle of working women and men in Britain and to the evolution of his ideas about art, about work and about how life should be lived. Many of his ideas accorded none too well with the reforming tendencies dominant in the Labour movement, nor with those of "orthodox" Marxism, which has looked elsewhere for inspiration. Both sides have been inclined to venerate Morris rather than to pay attention to what he said. Originally written less than a decade before his groundbreaking *The Making of the English Working Class*, E. P. Thompson brought to this biography his now trademark historical mastery, passion, wit, and essential sympathy. It remains unsurpassed as the definitive work on this remarkable figure, by the major British historian of the 20th century.

"Two impressive figures, William Morris as subject and E. P. Thompson as author, are conjoined in this immense biographical-historical-critical study, and both of them have gained in stature since the first edition of the book was published... The book that was ignored in 1955 has meanwhile become something of an underground classic—almost impossible to locate in second-hand bookstores, pored over in libraries, required reading for anyone interested in Morris and, increasingly, for anyone interested in one of the most important of contemporary British historians... Thompson has the distinguishing characteristic of a great historian: he has transformed the nature of the past, it will never look the same again; and whoever works in the area of his concerns in the future must come to terms with what Thompson has written. So too with his study of William Morris."
—Peter Stansky, *The New York Times Book Review*

"An absorbing biographical study... A glittering quarry of marvelous quotes from Morris and others, many taken from heretofore inaccessible or unpublished sources."
—Walter Arnold, *Saturday Review*

A New Notion:
Two Works by C. L. R. James
"Every Cook Can Govern" and
"The Invading Socialist Society"

Edited by Noel Ignatiev

ISBN: 978-1-60486-047-4
$16.95   160 pages

C. L. R. James was a leading figure in the independence
movement in the West Indies, and the black and working-
class movements in both Britain and the United States. As
a major contributor to Marxist and revolutionary theory, his project was to discover,
document, and elaborate the aspects of working-class activity that constitute the
revolution in today's world. In this volume, Noel Ignatiev, author of *How the Irish
Became White*, provides an extensive introduction to James' life and thought, before
presenting two critical works that together illustrate the tremendous breadth
and depth of James' worldview. "The Invading Socialist Society," for James the
fundamental document of his political tendency, shows clearly the power of James's
political acumen and its relevance in today's world with a clarity of analysis that
anticipated future events to a remarkable extent. "Every Cook Can Govern," is a short
and eminently readable piece counterposing direct with representative democracy,
and getting to the heart of how we should relate to one another. Together these
two works represent the principal themes that run through James's life: implacable
hostility toward all "condescending saviors" of the working class, and undying faith in
the power of ordinary people to build a new world.

*"It would take a person with great confidence, and good judgment, to select from the
substantial writings of C. L. R. James just two items to represent the 'principal themes' in
James' life and thought. Fortunately, Noel Ignatiev is such a person. With a concise, but
thorough introduction, Ignatiev sets the stage and C. L. R. James does the rest. In these
often confusing times one way to keep one's head on straight and to chart a clear path to
the future is to engage the analytical methods and theoretical insights of C. L. R. James.
What you hold in your hands is an excellent starting point."*
—John H. Bracey Jr., professor of African-American Studies at the University of
Massachusetts–Amherst and co-editor of *Strangers & Neighbors: Relations Between
Blacks & Jews in the United States.*

*"C. L. R. James has arguably had a greater influence on the underlying thinking of
independence movements in the West Indies and Africa than any living man."*
—*Sunday Times*

Theory and Practice: Conversations with Noam Chomsky and Howard Zinn (DVD)

Noam Chomsky, Howard Zinn, Sasha Lilley

ISBN: 978-1-60486-305-5
$19.95   105 minutes

Two of the most venerable figures on the American Left—Howard Zinn and Noam Chomsky—converse with Sasha Lilley about their lives and political philosophies, looking back at eight decades of struggle and theoretical debate. Howard Zinn, interviewed shortly before his death, reflects on the genesis of his politics, from the Civil Rights and anti-Vietnam war movements to opposing empire today, as well as history, art and activism. Noam Chomsky discusses the evolution of his libertarian socialist ideals since childhood, his vision for a future postcapitalist society, and his views on the state, science, the Enlightenment, and the future of the planet.

Noam Chomsky is one of the world's leading intellectuals, the father of modern linguistics, and an outspoken media and foreign policy critic. He is Institute Professor emeritus of linguistics at MIT and the author of numerous books and DVDs including *Hegemony and Survival: America's Quest for Global Dominance*, *Chomsky on Anarchism*, *The Essential Chomsky*, and *Crisis and Hope: Theirs and Ours* published by PM Press

Howard Zinn is one of the country's most beloved and respected historians, the author of numerous books and plays including *Marx in Soho*, *You Can't Be Neutral on a Moving Train*, and the best-selling *A People's History of the United States*, and a passionate activist for radical change.

Sasha Lilley (Interviewer) is a writer and radio broadcaster. She is the co-founder and host of the critically acclaimed program of radical ideas, *Against the Grain*. As program director of KPFA Radio, the flagship station of the Pacifica Network, she headed up such award-winning national broadcasts as *Winter Soldier: Iraq and Afghanistan*. Sasha Lilley is the series editor of PM Press' political economy imprint, Spectre.

"Chomsky is a global phenomenon... perhaps the most widely read voice on foreign policy on the planet."
—*The New York Times Book Review*

"What can I say that will in any way convey the love, respect, and admiration I feel for this unassuming hero who was my teacher and mentor; this radical historian and people-loving 'troublemaker,' this man who stood with us and suffered with us? Howard Zinn was the best teacher I ever had, and the funniest."
—Alice Walker, author of *The Color Purple*